Barbara Korte
Represented Report

Barbara Korte (Prof. Dr.) teaches English Literature and Culture at the University of Freiburg.

Barbara Korte

**Represented Reporters.
Images of War Correspondents
in Memoirs and Fiction**

[transcript]

Printed with the support of the German Research Foundation (DFG).

**Bibliographic information published by
the Deutsche Nationalbibliothek**
The Deutsche Nationalbibliothek lists this publication in the Deutsche Nationalbibliografie; detailed bibliographic data are available in the Internet at http://dnb.d-nb.de

© 2009 transcript Verlag, Bielefeld

Cover layout: Kordula Röckenhaus, Bielefeld
Proofread & typeset by Sandra Schaur and Georg Zipp
Printed by Majuskel Medienproduktion GmbH, Wetzlar
ISBN 978-3-8376-1062-8

Distributed in North America by

Transaction Publishers
New Brunswick (U.S.A.) and London (U.K.)

Transaction Publishers   Tel.: (732) 445-2280
Rutgers University   Fax: (732) 445-3138
35 Berrue Circle   for orders (U.S. only):
Piscataway, NJ 08854   toll free 888-999-6778

CONTENTS

Chapter 1: War Correspondents in Action and Representation

>»To me it has always seemed that the day a
newspaper man receives his commission as a
war correspondent, he has won the Victoria
Cross of journalism; and if he has it in him his
footsteps henceforth may move amidst the
footprints of the mighty, for his work will take
him amongst great men and greater deeds«
(A.G. Hales 1901, 205).

>»It always used to irritate me to hear journalists
referring to real incidents in the lives of real
people as ›stories‹, with all the connotations
which the word brings with it: dramatic incident,
neatly rounded narrative, a satisfying ending.
Gradually, though, I came to realize that the
most important function people like me could
perform was indeed to tell stories: not in the
sense of making up comfortable lies to keep the
viewers happy, but of providing an accurate
digestible way to make sense of the confusion
and apparent chaos of everyday life«
(John Simpson 2002, 95).

War Correspondents as an Object of Cultural Interest and Cultural Studies

The epigraphs to this chapter were written by war journalists to describe their professional activity, and the texts from which they are taken were published to serve an apparent interest of the general public. At the time of writing, there is no doubt that this interest in correspondents and their practice is as intense as it was in the final decades of the 19th century, the so-called Golden Age of war corresponding. It has been at a high level since the 1990s, when the Gulf War and the civil wars in former Yugoslavia brought war reporters once more to the public's attention; the war in Iraq in 2003 involved correspondents in a manner that brought this attention to a new climax. It seems as if the omnipresence of war in today's news media has even increased their traditional significance as »essential contributors to the public understanding« of war (Tumber/ Webster 2006, 166). Some conflicts of the recent past, such as the Gulf War of 1991 and the war in Kosovo, have been characterised as ›techno‹, ›video‹ and ›virtual‹ wars fought with long-distance weapons and perceived through long-distance media,[1] but such circumstances have not rendered war correspondents obsolete. Quite on the contrary: As audiences are flooded with images of war, the mediation of these images through a correspondent, an actual human presence at the actual site of war, appears to gain particular importance. After all, only a human being involved with body and mind, with senses, intellect, memory, emotions and conscience, can fulfil what Greg McLaughlin (2002, 3f.) deems the central function of war journalism: »to make sense of war«, to make »us think about a conflict in terms of history, context and the human cost.«

This basic cultural function of presenting and explaining war(s) to a wide audience has been a constant in war reporting since its origins in the 19th century, but of course there have been significant changes as well, caused by developments both in the media and the conduct of war, and these changes have had consequences for the public perception of war correspondents. The war in Iraq, for instance, added new facets to the popular image of war reporters as ›embeds‹ accompanied troops into the battle zone and freelancers ventured into dangerous terrain without military protection – both types of correspondents were equipped with state-of-the-art communication technology that made instant transmission possible. The war reporter in ›live action‹ has thus become a familiar presence on television: in front, or even in the middle of a live war scenario, exposed to the likelihood of being injured or killed – under both enemy and friendly fire.

Even apart from the current topicality of war correspondents it is hardly surprising that they should receive widespread attention. In mediatised societies, awareness of the actors, institutions and forms that shape people's perception of the world seems a natural phenomenon and is not restricted to journalists that cover war. As soon as the press developed into a system of mass communication in the course of the 19th century, its actors and practices became the object not only of self-

---

1   It is this new technological side of warfare and its mediation which is at the core of major academic studies about recent wars, such as Baudrillard (1991) on the Gulf War and Ignatieff (2000) on the war in Kosovo.

reflection within the medium but also of broader cultural scrutiny and fascination. By the end of the century, short stories and novels about journalists and newspaper culture in general were published in great numbers in Britain and the United States, that is, the leading newspaper nations of their day. These narratives addressed an audience interested in all aspects of the profession, from ethical considerations to the intricacies of news communication.[2] In the 20th and 21st centuries, journalists have continued to appear as major and minor characters in fiction and some plays – such as the widely known *Front Page* (1928) by Ben Hecht and Charles MacArthur – and above all in film and television, including 1970s movies and series such as *All the President's Men*, *Network* and *Lou Grant*, or the more recent *Good Night, and Good Luck* (2005) and Woody Allen's *Scoop* (2006). All these representations engage with their respective time's conception of journalism and, in a wider sense, the role(s) which the media play for the (self-)understanding of modern and postmodern cultures.[3]

How the media and their protagonists are perceived by the public and represented by the culture industries thus concerns not only media theorists and practitioners, but is also of relevance to cultural studies. It is in this area that the present study situates itself, with a focus on war corresponding as a branch of journalism with a particular visibility and a distinct cultural impact. Based on the elementary premise of cultural studies that all notions of identities – images of self and images of others – are engendered by and circulated through representations,[4] this book

---

2 Rudyard Kipling, a writer with considerable journalistic experience himself and greatly popular for his short stories, published several stories with reporters as characters during the 1890s. Kipling's story »A Matter of Fact« (1892), for instance, focuses on three newspapermen from Britain, South Africa and America who find themselves confronted with marvellous sea serpents and a dilemma as to how the extraordinary encounter can be covered in a medium devoted to facts.

3 Measured against this cultural significance, the representation of journalists in literature and film has received comparatively little scholarly attention. See, however, Jacobi (1989) on journalists in German literature of the 1920s, Good (1986) on the image of journalists in American fiction between 1890 and 1930, and Engesser (2005) who compares the image of journalists in literary bestsellers (from Germany, the US and Britain) to empirical results of communication studies. Lutes (2006) investigates the image of women journalists in American fiction.

4 In British Cultural Studies, the multiple relationships between the formation of identities and representation have been configured in the influential model of the so-called »circuit of culture« by the Open University team around Paul du Gay and Stuart Hall (du Gay et al., 1997, 3).

9

investigates media products of different periods that present war correspondents and are directed at a general audience. As Martin Bell writes at
the beginning of one of his memoirs: »It is a book about journalism but
not only for journalists. It is intended to interest real people« (Bell 1995,
1). It is assumed that such and other kinds of representations for ›real
people‹ reproduce and react to prevailing notions of correspondents and,
at the same time, participate in the further construction of the war reporter's cultural image. With its specific focus on representation(s), the
book is a complement to studies of war correspondents in other academic
fields: from media and communication studies[5] to history[6] and ethnol-
ogy.[7]

War corresponding is a particularly rewarding form of journalism for
the kind of cultural analysis intended here. As we have seen, war correspondents enjoy particular cultural attention (and have thus frequently
become the object of cultural representation), not only because of the
charisma that has formed around their profession, but also because their
professional interest is of high cultural relevance per se: As a situation of
national and/or international crisis, a war may directly concern audiences
and arouse intellectual and emotional responses even where an audience's nation is not immediately involved. Wars certainly put special
demands and pressures on those who cover them: War reporters are confronted with atrocities that arouse their feelings and stir their conscience
while their professional ethos obliges them to do justice to the facts.
They have to decide how far they can go when showing crimes against

---

5   See in particular Greg McLaughlin's comprehensive study *The War Corre-
    spondent* (2002). Since the 1990s, it has become common for journalists
    and academics in media studies to exchange their opinions on reporting
    war. See, for instance, the volume edited by Allan/Zelizer (2004), which
    was occasioned by the war in Iraq but also includes general articles on war
    reporting.

6   Daniel (2006a) is a pioneering volume comprising articles on correspon-
    dents in different wars and from different countries. In the 1990s military
    historians began to re-evaluate the reporting of historical wars; see the
    series ›The War Correspondents‹ (published by Alan Sutton), with volumes
    dedicated, among others, to the Crimean War (Lambert/Badsey 1994) and
    the South African War (Sibbald 1993).

7   Pedelty (1995) presents an ethnography of the international press corps in
    El Salvador. He conducted his research on the premise that reporters are »a
    community in and of themselves. They work together, play together, and
    often, live together. They share an integrated set of myths, rituals, and be-
    havioral norms. They are, in short, a culture – as coherent as any in the
    postmodern world« (4).

humanity (a central question of media ethics in general). War reporters also stand between their audiences' need to be informed and attempts by those in power to control the information flow. Not least, they have to deal with the dilemma that, despite all atrocities, a war may be profitable for them because it is ›big‹ news and can make a correspondent famous. Furthermore, reporting a war may entail an exciting personal experience and opportunities for adventure. Of the various actors in the news media, war correspondents have thus always been perceived as a group of their own, as ›special‹ correspondents indeed whose profession is imbued with an aura more intense than that of ordinary, day-to-day journalism. In the first epigraph to this chapter, the late-Victorian correspondent A.G. Hales speaks of the Victoria Cross variety of journalism, and a more recent assessment echoes this sentiment:

»War journalists are thought to do what all journalists do, only in a more heightened, vibrantly important fashion. To cover the story will entail, more likely than not, encountering conditions of an entirely different order than anything ordinarily associated with newswork. Images of the war reporter as adventurer or risk-taker, in the optimum sense, or as dare-devil, fortune-hunter, or rogue, in the negative, help to fuel their celebration in novels, films, plays, and other fictional treatments. Similarly implicit here, however, is the notion that war reporters somehow ›do journalism‹ better, that their experiences are more authentic, engaged, and noteworthy than those of other kinds of journalists. [...] Journalists are expected to function variously during war: to be present enough to respond to what is happening, yet absent enough to stay safe; to be sufficiently authoritative so as to provide reliable information, yet open to cracks and fissures in the complicated truth-claims that unfold; to remain passionate about the undermining of human dignity that accompanies war, yet impartial and distanced enough to see the strategies that attach themselves to circumstances with always more than one side. In these and related ways, then, war reporting reveals its investment in sustaining a certain discursive authority – namely that of being an eyewitness« (Allan/Zelizer 2004, 4f.).

As an ›outstanding‹ kind of journalists, war correspondents took hold in the cultural imaginary very soon after their profession had been created in the mid-19th century.[8] Almost instantly the profession generated

---

8 Before war reporting in the modern understanding, that is, by professional journalists, the press often employed officers to report on wars: »Before the Crimea, British editors either stole war news from foreign newspapers or employed junior officers to send letters from the battlefront, a most unsatisfactory arrangement. For not only were these soldier-correspondents highly selective in what they wrote, regarding themselves first as soldiers and then as correspondents; they also understood little of the workings of news-

myths and celebrities such as William Russell of *The Times*, the alleged ›father‹ of the trade, and his later rival Archibald Forbes. The illustrious line continues, among others, with Winston Churchill, a dashing hero of the South African War. The major conflicts of the 20th century also had their iconic reporters: Philip Gibbs for the First World War, the writer-reporters and photographers of the Spanish Civil War (with Ernest Hemingway, Martha Gellhorn and Robert Capa in the frontline), Ernie Pyle and Alan Moorehead during the Second World War, or James Cameron, David Halberstam and Michael Herr in Vietnam. The televised wars of the late 20th century established the war correspondent as a visible cultural presence, and in the age of 24/7 news, war correspondents are more than ever figures of popular interest and household names, such as Peter Arnett and Christiane Amanpour of CNN, or Kate Adie and John Simpson of the BBC.

The stardom of these recent correspondents is not fully explained by visual presence alone. It is also encouraged by the tendency in today's commercially oriented news media to offer infotainment and ›human interest‹ apart from facts. As Kate Adie observes in *The Kindness of Strangers*, this is a development which pushes the correspondent him- or herself to the fore and personalises the act of reporting for the audience:

»And if economic profitability and the biggest audience are deemed to rule the roost, then perhaps the performance of the reporter needs a little ›attention‹. If the audience is interested in individuals, then the reporter's included in that game. Facts, please; but how do *you* feel, the one watching events on our behalf? A string of vivid adjectives, a catch in the voice, a shake of the head. It does not take long for the idea to catch on that reporting is bereft of authenticity if the reporter's heart fails to be in the story, preferably in view on the sleeve. Sentiment stirs the crowd.

It's a step towards the ›infotainment‹ world, where the pill of fact has to be sugared by a performance. Reporting – in particular on television – always has a narcissistic element, but now it's been encouraged to flower« (Adie 2002, 168).

---

papers or even of what constituted ›news‹« (Knightley 2004, 2). Historical accounts of war corresponding, which are usually written by journalists themselves and therefore with a certain celebratory ring, have been produced since the early 20th century. Frederick Bullard's rather anecdotal *Famous War Correspondents* dates from 1914. Phillip Knightley's more ambitious *The First Casualty* is a frequently cited source and has been updated several times; the latest edition to date (2004) extends to the war in Iraq. Roth (1997) is a comprehensive and very useful dictionary of war journalism, also in its historical dimensions.

This flowering of personalisation in war reporting is also noted critically by David Welch, who draws attention to the concomitant proliferation of war reporters' personal accounts of their experiences:

»Wars offer unique opportunities for reporters to impose themselves on a news story [...]. There can be little doubt that in recent conflicts, war correspondents have acted not simply as conduits of information, but as personalities in their own right. It has become *de rigeur* for correspondents to publish their memoirs of war. After the conflict we now anticipate the publicity fanfare of a war correspondent hawking his or her story around the media. The ›celebration of the correspondent‹, whereby the messenger becomes as important – if not more important – than the message has, according to some critics, led to a ›dumbing-down‹ of reporting news from war zones« (Connelly/Welch 2005, xiv).[9]

The citations above suggest that war correspondents in the contemporary media often function as actors in a double sense: They act in their specific professional field and, at the same time, deliver the performance *of* a war correspondent for an audience. The element of performance in the latter sense is particularly strong where correspondents report on television, as a visible, embodied presence and – via the camera – directly addressing an audience. As we shall see, however, an element of role-play marked the behaviour of war correspondents long before the advent of television, and it is in this performative dimension that cultural images of the war correspondent manifest themselves with particular clarity.

This book will not concern itself with the actual performance of war correspondents but with autobiographical and fictional representations in which the figure of the correspondent and his or her behaviour are (re-)constructed and thus (re-)configured. Representations select and highlight specific aspects of war correspondents and their behaviour, according to the perception of correspondents themselves or that of the writers and filmmakers who look at the profession from the outside. Both as inside and outside views, representations of war correspondents grant

---

9   On the tendency of correspondents to become news themselves, see also Willcox (2005, 32), who cites John Simpson as an example: »Despite his protestations, Simpson's image dominates news items that he reports, becoming synonymous with the BBC's conflict analysis. His subsequent books have emphasized this depiction of himself as both a reporter of and component of news events. He is part of a growing number of celebrity journalists, many of whom have a number of publications to their name.« A comment by Sue Arnold in *The Independent* goes in the same direction: »What really depresses me about the whole depressing situation is the unashamedly personal spin that every correspondent seems to put on his reports nowadays« (20 March 2003, 22).

access to the cultural conceptions according to which they were constructed and are therefore pertinent to an investigation of the cultural significance associated with war journalism. In sharper contours and more consciously shaped than an ethnographic account, autobiographical and fictional representations indicate which cultural images and meanings are associated with war correspondents at a given time, and they participate themselves in the ongoing negotiation of this cultural significance.

The Represented Reporter

The recent surge of war correspondents' memoirs noted by David Welch above has been accompanied by a wave of representations in other modes. In the first years of the 21st century, war reporters appear in popular television production, feature films and literary as well as popular novels. They are the subject of poetry[10] and have made their appearance on the stage: When Shakespeare's *Henry V* was produced at the National Theatre in London in May 2003 (directed by Nicholas Hytner), allusions to the war in Iraq seemed irresistible and, in addition to the play's customary personnel, the fields of France were peopled by embedded correspondents. Such contemporary representations have precursors that reach back to the 19th century, when memoirs of war correspondents first became a staple of the book market and popular writers such as Sir Arthur Conan Doyle and Rudyard Kipling chose war correspondents as subjects of their short stories and novels. In its later chapters, this book will discuss some of the aesthetically and intellectually more significant fictional representations. But it is important to note, from a cultural point of view, that war correspondents also frequently appear in popular fiction and film, just because the type per se is topical and/or has an aura of adventure and romance that is entertaining.[11] A particularly curious ex-

---

10   Ciaran Carson's poem sequence »The War Correspondent«, for instance, was published in the *Times Literary Supplement* on 29 December 2000, 8f.

11   There is, for example, a whole range of thrillers and romances in which war correspondents have appeared as major or minor characters in recent years: Barbara Taylor Bradford's *A Secret Affair* (1996), Colin Falconer's *Dangerous* (1996), Willow Tickell's *Cooling Off* (1997), Jessica Mann's *The Survivor's Revenge* (1998), Peter Temple's *In the Evil Day* (2002), or Patrick Coleridge's *Rut* (2006). For an earlier example see James Hilton's *Knight Without Armour* (1933), whose protagonist begins his adventures, most of which take place in revolutionary Russia, as a correspondent during the Russo-Japanese War. James Gant's thriller *Zero-O-One* (1957) is

ample of the latter is found in an episode of the television fantasy series *The Lost World*. This series is loosely based on Sir Arthur Conan Doyle's scientific romance of the same title and presents characters of the early 20th century stranded in a surviving prehistoric world peopled by dinosaurs and more or less aggressive human tribes. The writers managed to smuggle a correspondent even into this unlikely scenario: In the episode »Brothers in Arms« (2002), one of the regular characters, a journalist, remembers his time as a young correspondent in the First World War.

While popular representations tend to employ clichéd perceptions, for example of the war correspondent as adventurer and hero, more subtle portrayals engage with general cultural attitudes towards war, opinions about the role of the media in war, ethical implications of war journalism, and they also provide critical investigations of the profession's myths. In any case, the representations of war correspondents are part of a cultural circuit:

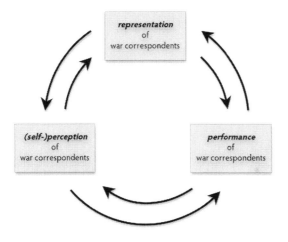

set in Japan during the Second World War. Gant was a former correspondent himself, and his book was published in the paperback series ›Untold Stories of a War Correspondent‹, which used the flair of the war correspondent as an obvious marketing strategy. Film in particular has exploited the heroism and romance around war correspondents from its early days, beginning with the early short *The War Correspondent* (USA 1913, dir. Robert G. Vignola). *War Correspondent* (USA 1932, dir. Paul Sloane) is a melodrama featuring a war correspondent in picturesque Shanghai. In *The Angry Hills* (USA 1959, dir. Robert Aldrich), a film based on a bestselling novel by Leon Uris, an American correspondent in the Second World War gets involved with the Greek underground and is pursued by the Nazis. As a minor figure, a correspondent is also among the enduring American soldiers in *Objective, Burma!* (USA 1945, dir. Raoul Walsh).

Representations of war reporters respond to existing cultural conceptions, and in turn have repercussions on the cultural understanding and perception of war correspondents. Providing cultural frames for behaviour, they also affect the actual performance of correspondents, which, in turn, may give rise to new representations. As we will see, war reporters are quite familiar with their colleagues' memoirs as well as with novels and films that feature war reporters, and they may model their behaviour on the patterns they find in these representations – or deliberately distance themselves from patterns nourished by fiction. Many journalists interviewed for a recent study of journalism ›under fire‹ »expressed a desire *not* to be classified as war correspondents« because of the public image of their profession: »They were concerned about being painted as ›war junkies‹, unsavoury obsessives who move compulsively from one conflict to another« (Tumber/Webster 2006, 63). For others, memoirs, novels and films may be important for building a sense of tradition of their trade. From what they write in their self-representations, war journalists seem particularly inclined to measure themselves against the icons of their profession, thus implicitly putting themselves into the illustrious line. John Simpson, for example, emulates William Russell,[12] and Kate Adie writes admiringly about Martha Gellhorn:

»Every conflict needs a Martha Gellhorn, with a clear eye and an unfailing grasp of what she was doing, why she was doing it, and the guts and style to do it well.
I met her just before she died. She was stunning – and still reporting: stylish and perceptive, wise and witty. It became immediately clear that the precepts and principles which she had held for decades were enduring and relevant« (Adie 2002, 401).

Sometimes correspondents will have met their idols, as in Adie's example, but more frequently, they will only have read their texts, both reportage and reminiscences, or encountered them through films and novels.

Representation and actual performance are thus closely interlinked, and in some instances, this interweaving can be quite intricate: for instance in the case of fiction films that are recognisably based on the experiences of real war correspondents but where these real reporters, though appearing under their own name, are characters played by actors. In such cases, the war correspondent's original performance is re-enacted

---

12   »He had [...] considerable toughness and determination, bags of literary talent, and a proven ability to get on with soldiers« Simpson (2002, 26f.); in all, Simpson devotes a full ten pages to Russell's career.

and, at the same time, reconfigured after certain images and myths associated with war journalism. The fictionalised Ernie Pyle in *The Story of G.I. Joe* (1945) or Sydney Schanberg in *The Killing Fields* (1984)[13] are portrayals of the biographical Pyle and Schanberg but at the same time exhibit traits associated (at the respective time they were produced) with war reporters in general so that the characters also have a significance as types.

In a number of ways, then, representations provide material for a cultural reading of war correspondents: They indicate dominant cultural conceptions of correspondents, they permit us to trace the history of such images, and they thus reveal cultural frames for the behaviour of correspondents. This book will primarily be concerned with representations, but it is necessary to remain aware of the relationships in which these representations stand to general cultural perceptions and correspondents' actual performance.

Sources

Of the many forms in which correspondents have been represented,[14] memoirs, novels and films will receive special attention. As extensive narrative forms, they can provide a large scope for the correspondent's ›(self-)fashioning‹ and show him or her as an actor with several dimensions: mental and physical, professional and personal. They have the fullest potential to present war reporters as human agents in the cultural mediation of war. However, these sources differ in their specific qualities and in what they suggest about cultural conceptions of war correspondents. It has already been mentioned that distinctly popular representations show a tendency to use clichéd images and foreground elements of entertainment. In other respects too there is notable variation in the artistic qualities of literary and cinematic texts. Correspondents' memoirs are often close to reportage and comment, but some have more obvious literary ambitions. The poet James Fenton, for instance, was an occasional war reporter in Vietnam during the late phase of the war. The reminiscences of his experiences in Vietnam, which form a part of *All the Wrong Places*, declare a literary intent that distinguishes them from other examples: »Although I had a few journalistic commissions, I was not going primarily as a journalist. I wanted time and solitude to write, and

---

13 For a discussion of *The Killing Fields*, see pp. 123-124.
14 Apart from the formats discussed here, there are also, for example, cartoons and photographs representing war correspondents.

knew that travel would tend to make me fall back on my own company«
(Fenton 1990, 4).

As a form of autobiographical writing, memoirs emerge from a correspondent's authentic experiences. They convey their authors' personal
views of these experiences, but also of their profession in general. The
term ›memoir(s)‹ is used to identify a branch of autobiographical writing
in which the public dimension of the narrated experiences is emphasised.[15] It is used here because correspondents' reminiscences do, of
course, relate many personal impressions of and reactions to what their
respective author witnessed, but they also include general opinions on
various aspects of the profession, the military, the media and war. Like
more privately oriented autobiographies, however, memoirs are also always constructions. In Jerome Bruner's words, they constitute

»a way of construing experience – and of reconstruing and reconstruing it until
our breath or our pen fails us. Construal and reconstrual are interpretive. Like
all forms of interpretation, how we construe our lives is subject to our intentions, to the interpretive conventions available to us, and to the meanings im-
posed upon us by the usages of our culture and language« (Bruner 1993, 38).

The memoirs of war correspondents present memories of incidents or reflections which their authors have selected as significant for the interpretation of their (professional) lives and which are deemed significant
for other people's views of these lives and war reporting in general. They
are important sources for an analysis of war correspondents' self-images
and the ways in which they relate to images which others have formed of
their profession.

Novels and films may, as we have seen, be based on a real correspondent's life, but by fictional contract, they are not bound to a factual
basis and free to develop the figure of the war correspondent in various
directions and dimensions, from flat stereotypes to psychologically complex portrayals that establish war correspondents as fully-fleshed, thinking and feeling human beings. While memoirs are retrospective and usually written in the limited perspective of the first person, novelists have
the option to present their narrative in the third person and thus to set up
an external view of their correspondent characters, also with a physical
dimension that is not always realised in correspondents' memoirs. They

---

15 See, for example, the definition in Abrams (1993, 15): »Autobiography is a
    biography written by the subject about himself or herself. It is to be distin-
    guished from memoir, in which the emphasis is not on the author's devel-
    oping self but on the people and events that the author has known or wit-
    nessed.«

can use the narrative voice to deliver overt comments, or they can simulate a correspondent character's immediate experience by letting readers share his or her inner life, that is, perceptions, thoughts and emotions, thus creating opportunities for empathy. Fiction films have their own narrative options, and in contrast to literary narrative, their action is presented in a truly performative mode. Thanks to this performativity of their own representation, films have a particular capacity to expose performative elements in their correspondent character's behaviour.

In the following study, emphasis will be on the conception and representation of war correspondents in *British* culture from the 19th century to the present. This restriction ensures a coherence of background and tradition (including national journalistic traditions) and pays tribute to the fact that many enduring myths about the profession originated in the British context. Here a cultural imaginary of the war correspondent found an especially fertile ground to develop, not only because of Britain's many imperial wars during the second half of the 19th century, but also because of a highly developed and competitive press system. The memoirs and novels to be analysed were all produced by British correspondents and literary writers, or such that lived in Britain for a significant time. One has to be aware of the fact, however, that limiting war correspondents to nationalities is increasingly difficult as media systems become global. Furthermore, one important area of representation has always been transnational, at least in its reception: In cinema and television culture, the image of the war correspondent has been significantly shaped by Hollywood, and when British correspondents refer to films, as Kate Adie in the following excerpt, these films are often of American provenance:

»Hollywood films have journalists crabbing towards close vantage points which show them precisely who is shooting whom, while villagers who always speak comprehensible English explain how it all started. We were all too appalled to move any nearer, and, as a rather dramatic sunset ensued, against which brilliant flames reared up through blackened rafters – on the end of a long lens – we crept away rather shamefaced and not a little frightened, to deliver our offerings to London« (Adie 2002, 291f.).

For representations in film and television, the book will therefore include a number of American examples apart from British (co-)productions, which are also often made for the international market.

The selection of examples will otherwise be limited to texts and films about wars with relevance to Britain or at least British correspondents. As we will see, the (self-)representations of war correspondents tend to cluster in certain periods and in connection with certain conflicts: the

British imperial wars, the two World Wars and the two intermediate wars in Spain and Abyssinia that attracted the attention of the British public. Vietnam is briefly considered as a war that affected the perception of war correspondents everywhere and as a war that has yielded many representations in the area of film. Since they inspired an especially great number of representations, the civil wars in former Yugoslavia, the 1991 Gulf War and the wars occasioned by 9/11 will receive special attention.

Chapter Overview

Since the war correspondent's representation and performance are interwoven, Chapter 2 first provides an outline of the most significant structural features that define the actual behaviour of correspondents. The chapter begins with a look at the performative element – or theatricality – that correspondents themselves and their observers have noted in this behaviour. This performativity highlights the extent to which the professional demeanour of war reporters is governed by role conceptions and rules of the game, and it suggests that theories of social action provide a useful framework for discussing war correspondents as social players within the field of war journalism. Concepts from two theoretical approaches seem particularly apt for this purpose: Performance Studies permit us to discuss war correspondents as social performers, and as human beings endowed not only with a mind but also with body and feelings, that is, aspects foregrounded in the performative approach (and also of special relevance in the fictional representation of correspondents). Social performers need a ›stage‹ or ›playing field‹, and Pierre Bourdieu's notion of fields of social action suggests itself for conceptualising this area. While a field is defined by certain external parameters that define its characteristic actions, Bourdieu's concomitant concept of ›habitus‹ refers to internal dispositions that enable an actor to play in a field in the first place. The notion of habitus incorporates, among others, the rules and images that guide a war correspondent's behaviour, that is, frames in whose construction representations are centrally involved. Apart from identifying the main parameters that have defined the war correspondent's role and behaviour from the 19th century to the present, Chapter 2 points out how these parameters have always been reflected in correspondents' memoirs and have thus become part of a layered textual system through which correspondents themselves have tried to understand their profession and to explain its significance to the general public.

Chapters 3 to 5 then focus on representations of war correspondents in a historical sequence. Since correspondents' memoirs from various periods are cited extensively in Chapter 2, the other chapters, while also drawing on memoirs, lay their particular emphasis on representations in literature and film and on how they negotiate the respective cultural images of war correspondents. Chapter 3 runs from the Crimean to the South African War (or Second Anglo-Boer War, 1899-1902): a period in which British war correspondents accompanied their country's imperial endeavours and a period in which their self-image and the mode of their perception and representation by others were significantly shaped. Chapter 4 spans the time from the profession's first severe crisis during the First World War to the 1980s, tracing various lines in which the representation of war correspondents developed after this crisis, from a restoration of the image during the Second World War to critical reflection about the (im-)possibility of ›objective‹ reporting. Chapter 5 finally addresses the developments which war reporting and its fictional representation have taken since the 1990s.

Chapter 2: War Correspondents in the Field

>»The war correspondent is a newspaper man
assigned to cover a campaign. He goes into the
field with the army, expecting to send his reports
from that witching region known as ›the front‹.
He is a special correspondent commissioned to
collect intelligence and transmit it from the camp
and the battle ground. A non-combatant, he
mingles freely with men whose business it is to
fight. He may be ten thousand miles from his
home office, but he finds competition as keen as
ever it is in Fleet Street or Newspaper Row. He
is engaged in the most dramatic department of a
profession whose infinite variety is equalled
only by its fascination. If he becomes a
professional rather than an occasional
correspondent, wandering will be his business
and adventure his daily fare«
(Frederick Bullard 1974, 3f.).

Performing the War Correspondent

In his ethnography of war correspondents in El Salvador, Mark Pedelty
notes the conscious display that marked the practice of the group he observed: »[T]he reporters throw around symbols of ›Salvadorness‹, mutu-
ally reaffirming their unique status as war correspondents« (Pedelty
1995, 23). This display included deliberate reference to professional traditions and to representations of war reporters, especially in the context of
Vietnam: »Some SPECA reporters draw upon the lore of Vietnam in order to construct their *Salvador* identity. They quote lines from Herr's
Dispatches (1968 [sic]) and the fictional forms he inspired, including
Apocalypse Now« (ibid., 23). Their tendency to ›perform‹ a professional
identity is also noted by correspondents themselves, whose memoirs

23

abound with descriptions of war correspondents posing as war correspondents and playing up to a certain image. James Cameron, for instance, observed about his colleagues during the Korean War:

»They cultivated an intrepid and mettlesome appearance, loaded with helmets and carbines and with daggers protruding from their boots; several had intimidating beards. The effect was very passable to Hemingway, as of tough but fundamentally sensitive men newly returning from dangerous enterprises behind the enemy's lines. The cynicism of that analogy, however, was hard to maintain, because the plain truth was that that was in many cases precisely what they had been doing. They hurried purposefully in, cast their martial impediments from them, and set to work in what appeared to have been a class for infants, forcing their soldierly frames into the only available furniture, which consisted of miniature desks constructed for diminutive Korean children« (Cameron 1967, 124).

The martial pose of reporters in Iraq in 2003 provoked an ironic comment in *The Independent*:

»Never has fiction seemed feebler. Now that the new technology allows us to follow a Cruise missile as it makes its deadly way down the streets of Baghdad, the special effects of war movies seem flashy and pointless. No actor, however butch and unshaven, can compete with the heroic sight of a real war reporter, kitted up to the nines, interviewing a marine as he lays siege to a house from which enemy sniper fire has been coming.«[1]

Television in particular encourages correspondents to playact because this is the medium, after all, in which their performance is actually seen by an external audience (and not only the internal one of other actors within the theatre of war). Martin Bell explicitly refers to television news as »a theatrical medium« with a »thespian character« (Bell 2004, 67). Thanks to real-time and 24-hour news broadcasting, the performative dimension of war reporting is emphasised as never before. We all have countless images in our mind of reporters speaking at the camera in live scenarios of war, and sometimes they are even injured in front of the running camera.

To a British television audience and the international viewers of BBC World, John Simpson's performance during the war in Iraq, in a BBC news special at 10 am on 6 April 2003, will be particularly memorable. It showed him reporting despite being visibly shocked, his face still stained with blood after a friendly-fire attack to which he had just been exposed.

---

1   Terence Blacker, »Are We Really Witnessing the Reality of War?«, *The Independent*, 25 March 2003, 20.

Other members of his team were seriously hurt, and their translator was killed. Simpson looks back on the incident in his book *The Wars against Saddam* (2003), which he dedicated to »the reporters, cameramen, photographers and translators who died during the Iraq War of 2003.« Simpson may not have deliberately exploited the dramatic impact of the situation during the act of reporting itself, but he did make the most of it in later publications, both in textual and visual re-presentation. Apart from the chapter »Disaster«, which provides a detailed and dramatic narration of the attack and Simpson's doing his »piece to camera while the full force of this terrible business was still around us« (Simpson 2003, 334), *The Wars against Saddam* displays a close-up photo of Simpson's blood-stained face right on its cover. The lasting consequences of Simpson's injuries are mentioned in the preface, which thus also draws the reader's attention to the war correspondent's bodily presence and introduces the physical dimension of performance right at the beginning of the book:

»As I write this, it has been exactly six months since that moment: six months of putting my life back together, of getting used to the constant, low-level pain in my leg and coming to terms with deafness. I've long ceased to be bitter about what happened to me; after all, if someone had come to me a minute before and asked me to choose between being burned to death myself or going round with a bit of a limp and not hearing terribly well, I would have gone down on my knees begging for the limp and the deafness« (ibid., vii).

Interestingly, in a book published just one year before the incident, Simpson had criticised other correspondents' inclination to perform to the audience:

»There is something embarrassingly look-at-me, something distinctly self-referential about the idea of journalists in danger. Of course, real danger is genuinely enthralling if you survive it, and it makes excellent pictures – if, that is, you are lucky enough to catch it on camera. Unfortunately, such moments are pretty rare: either the camera isn't running at the time, or else it isn't pointing in quite the right direction at the key moment. Television can sometimes be the most frustrating business on earth.
And so there is always a temptation to underline the sense of menace by, say, kneeling down to do your piece to camera (which gives the feeling that you might be shot if you stood up) or waiting to begin it until a gun goes off nearby, in case there are no other shots or explosions while you are talking. These are tricks of the trade, not necessarily false or illegitimate at all, since the bangs are real enough and so, often, is the sense that you might get your head blown off if you peer out of your shelter. [...] The wearing of a flak jacket [...] on camera is sometimes done for effect too« (Simpson 2002, 350).

Simpson's colleague at the BBC, Kate Adie, depicts such performances with irony when remembering her colleagues' behaviour during the Gulf War of 1991. All accredited correspondents permitted to visit troops at the front were requested to wear uniform, and Adie notes how some of her male colleagues adopted not only military habit but also military habits with greater flourish and credibility than others:

»By now ꞌwe were in uniform, an unlikely band of Official War Corres-pondents. Some took automatically to the role – Martin Bell instantly appeared officer-like and soigné, adjusting his desert scarf as a cravat and looking as if he'd been in and out of sandy trenches for years. [...]
It was fascinating to see how the rest of the hack-pack seemed to be surrepti-tiously realising boyhood dreams, festooning themselves with colourful keffiyeh and sporting an array of water-bottles and large watches with many dials for telling you where you were and what the time was in Baghdad« (Adie 2002, 385).

However ironic, such comments reveal how war correspondents often act according to a heroic image that derives from their involvement in the dangers of war and association with the military community.

›Dressing up‹ for war and posing as a correspondent ready to face the risks of the profession is an element one finds in accounts since the days of the Crimean War. 19th-century correspondents even went so far as to create their own kind of uniform: »[Russell] had decided that he should wear some sort of uniform and had got together a gold-banded commis-sariat officer's cap, a rifleman's patrol jacket, cord breeches, butchers' boots with huge spurs, and a large sword« (Knightley 2004, 7).[2] Remem-bering the Battle of Khartoum (1898), the war artist Frederic Villiers emphasised that he and his fellow correspondents had then acted as bravely as their military ›comrades‹ and accordingly suffered their own casualties:

»In this expedition which had been so destructive of man and beast the war cor-respondents suffered no less severely than their brethren in uniform. Out of eight who started with Stewart four were killed and one was wounded, making our casualties more than 50 per cent – a circumstance which alone is quite in-dicative of the character of the fighting« (Villiers 1921, II, 73).

The dangers for – and implied heroism of – war correspondents were not only displayed in verbal monuments. Plaques in the crypt of St Paul's

---

2   See also Wilkinson-Latham (1979, 45) on Russell's uniform and those of
     other correspondents.

cathedral in London commemorate, among others, correspondents killed in the Sudan campaigns and those who died during the South African War. The most recent tribute to journalists killed in war (and peacetime), a glass and light sculpture on top of the BBC's broadcasting house, was unveiled in London in June 2008.

Indeed, it can be claimed that the heroic image still has great impact on the public perception of war correspondents as well as on their actual performance. As Paul Moorcraft notes in his memoirs: »Despite the generally poor rating of journalists [...] war correspondents are often seen as heroes, the good guys (and girls) in flak jackets who risk their lives to expose the lies of politicians and generals« (Moorcraft 2001, 368). After the war in Iraq, the Newseum, an American museum devoted to journalism, presented an exhibition on war correspondents that was clearly aimed to monumentalise their performance in past and present wars. The catalogue proudly claims that

»[t]he war correspondents trail clouds of glory. The names of the pioneers of the trade are stardust: Ernest Hemingway, Alexandre Dumas, Henry Villard, Winston Churchill, Stephen Crane, John Reed, Arthur Conan Doyle, Rudyard Kipling, Richard Harding Davis, John Dos Passos, John Steinbeck, Jack London, George Orwell, Philip Gibbs, Luigi Barzini. The names from World War II, Korea and Vietnam, the Gulf War and Kosovo are likewise as redolent of adventure and derring-do, with photojournalists, and radio and television commentators crowding the pantheon.
They are the eyes of history – when they are allowed to be« (Evans 2003, 29).

Publications about war correspondents are also explicitly marketed in terms of heroism. The cover of a recent book about the British television agency Frontline, for instance, puts the stories of its real protagonists on a level with adventure literature of the Victorian age: »Their story reads like a latter-day Rudyard Kipling adventure. [...] Part Bang Club, part Flashman, Frontline is the gripping story of lives lived full in some of the worst places on earth« (Loyn 2005). Some correspondents have rejected an interpretation of their actions as heroism. Martin Bell, for instance, complained about being turned into a hero after he had been hit by a mortar in former Yugoslavia, in front of the running camera:

»For a short while after what happened to me there were little features and articles in the press based on the total fiction of the reporter as hero. It was nonsense, of course. We are not heroes but just journalists doing our job and sometimes in harm's way more than is good for us. But we have so many advantages that real people, facing equal dangers, do not. We are there of our own free will, they are not. We can escape, they cannot« (Bell 1995, 82).

However, the incident *is* mentioned in Bell's own memoirs shortly before the excerpt quoted here, and in physical as well as dramatic terms that re-stage the event for the reader:

»I had always wondered what it would be like to be wounded and now I knew – end of curiosity, for a lifetime. It was like an acute pain in the abdomen, though somewhat numbed by the shock of it. I had been struck by two or three frag-ments of shrapnel, falling (fortunately for me) near the end of their trajectory. They penetrated exactly at the spot where the flak jacket ended. [...] In the split second of the fall I knew that I had been hit, but I was lucky. I called out to the others, ›I'm all right. I'll survive.‹ I did not wish to alarm them. [...] Don con-tinued the shooting of what would be my last news story for a while« (ibid., 81).

Since the behaviour of war correspondents and their self-perception is so strongly associated with ›acting‹ and role-play, it seems appropriate to conceptualise this behaviour in terms of theories of social action that em-phasise its performative dimension.

Performance, Habitus and Fields of Action

Notions of ›performance‹ have proliferated with the diversification of Performance Studies (or Performance Theory) over the past decades. Performance Studies are not a clearly defined discipline and have gener-ated a whole spectrum of definitions of ›performance‹ and ›performativ-ity‹ that cover forms of behaviour in everyday life as well as ritual or act-ing in the theatre. For the purpose of the present book, Richard Schechner's elementary definitions of ›performance‹ and ›performativ-ity‹ provide a sufficient basis:

»The underlying notion is that any action that is framed, presented, highlighted, or displayed is a performance. [...]
›Showing doing‹ is performing: pointing to, underlining, and displaying doing«
(Schechner 2002, 2 and 22).

»»Performativity‹ is an even broader term, covering a whole panoply of possi-bilities opened up by a world in which differences between media and live events, originals and digital or biological clones, performing onstage and in or-dinary life are collapsing. Increasingly, social, political, economic, personal, and artistic realities take on the qualities of performance« (ibid., 110).

The examples above have shown that an element of ›showing doing‹ marks the behaviour of war correspondents quite frequently, and even where the element of ›showing‹ is toned down, the doing alone will often have a trace of performativity (as in Schechner's last definition).

Performance Studies assume a close relationship between performance and the construction of identities. In a basic understanding, identities are constituted in or through performative acts,[3] and we can also see this in the behaviour of war correspondents. ›Playing‹ the war correspondent according to certain images and established cultural frames aligns the individual correspondent with traditions and role models of his trade and thus with important elements of a professional identity. In this respect, the performance approach bears an affinity with Pierre Bourdieu's notion of habitus.[4]

Bourdieu assumes that people act socially according to routines which are not always wholly conscious but essentially determine their practice. In *Outline of a Theory of Practice*, Bourdieu defines habitus as »an acquired system of generative schemes objectively adjusted to the particular conditions in which it is constituted« (Bourdieu 1977, 95); the habitus thus predisposes individuals to act in certain ways in certain social situations. Discussing Bourdieu's definition, Richard Jenkins emphasises the relationship the habitus has with the body; this physical ›embodiment‹ constitutes another affinity with the notion of performance:

»The dispositions and generative classificatory schemes which are the essence of the habitus are embodied in real human beings. This embodiment appears to have three meanings in Bourdieu's work. First, in a trivial sense, the habitus only exists inasmuch as it is ›inside the heads‹ of actors (and the head is, after all, part of the body). Second, the habitus only exists in, through and because of the practices of actors and their interaction with each other and with the rest of their environment: ways of talking, ways of moving, ways of making things, or

---

3   Schechner notes that performance can serve to »mark or change identity«, or to »make or foster identity« (Schechner 2002, 38).

4   Bourdieu's theory of social action is also generally related to Performance Studies. Like other theories explaining social action, it employs the metaphors of game and the theatre. See, for instance, Bourdieu's definition of habitus in *In Other Words* as the »practical mastery of the logic or of the imminent necessity of a game – a mastery acquired by experience of the game« (Bourdieu 1990a, 61). As Jenkins (2002, 70) points out in a critical introduction, Bourdieu had predecessors here, in particular Erving Goffman, whose influential comparisons between social life and games or the theatre were first developed in *The Presentation of Self in Everyday Life* (1959). Goffman, in turn, is often counted among the representatives of Performance Studies.

whatever. In this respect, the habitus is emphatically *not* an abstract or idealist concept. It is not just *manifest* in behaviour, it is an integral *part* of it (and vice versa). Third, the ›practical taxonomies‹ [...] which are at the heart of the generative schemes of the habitus, are rooted in the body. Male/female, front/back, up/down, hot/cold, these are all primarily sensible – in terms of making sense and of being rooted in sensory experience – from the point of view of the embodied person.
The embodiment of the habitus finds another expression in Bourdieu's use of the word ›hexis‹. Originally Greek, with a meaning not dissimilar to the Latin ›habitus‹, in Bourdieu's work it is used to signify deportment, the manner and style in which actors ›carry themselves‹: stance, gait, gesture, etc. The similarity of the original meanings of the two words, habitus and hexis, is an indication of the centrality of the body to Bourdieu's conceptualisation of the habitus. It is in bodily hexis that the idiosyncratic (the personal) combines with the systematic (the social)« (Jenkins 2002, 74).

We have already seen that the habitus of war correspondents is quite pronounced in physical terms (both demeanour and dress). It is when the bodily (or embodied) aspects of the correspondent's behaviour are emphasised that the sense of performativity is most intense.

All players need a playing field or stage, and in Bourdieu's theoretical framework, habitus is therefore conceived back-to-back with the idea of fields of social action. A habitus is field-specific and, as Bourdieu explicates in *The Logic of Practice* (1990b), disposes a person to behave according to the field in which he or she is presently situated. A field confronts actors with specific structures (for instance power structures), co-actors, demands and constraints while they pursue certain interests and profits to be gained in the particular field. The most immediately relevant field for a war correspondent is the journalistic one, that is, a field within the larger field of cultural production. The journalistic field is discussed, above all, in Bourdieu's highly critical essays on contemporary television, published in *Sur la télévision* (1996). Here, Bourdieu characterises the journalistic field as a microcosm with its own laws:

»Le monde du journalisme est un microcosme qui a ses lois propres et qui est défini par sa position dans le monde global, et par les attractions, les répulsions qu'il subit de la part des autres microcosmes. Dire qu'il est autonome, qu'il a sa propre loi, c'est dire que ce qui s'y passe ne peut pas être compris de manière directe à partir de facteurs extérieurs« (Bourdieu 1996, 44).

These laws are determined by, among other things, the forces of media markets which create, for instance, strong competition among the actors in the field; it is manifest, for example, in the journalist's proverbial hunt for scoops. However, even though the journalistic field is autonomous in the way it determines the actions of its players, its boundaries are porous and shifting. The journalistic field is affected by other fields and affects other fields itself. It is subjected, for instance, to economic interests, and has a significant impact on the political field. War journalism specifically influences, and is determined by, the military field; in an actual war scenario, a correspondent finds himself ›in the field‹ in quite the traditional understanding of that phrase. Since this book is not a sociological study, it takes the liberty to adapt Bourdieu's original concept of the field loosely and to understand the war correspondent's ›field‹ of action as a social space defined by various parameters that provide the outward setting for his or her practice.[5] Several of these parameters are points where the journalistic field intersects with other fields.

Bourdieu's notion of intersecting fields is also useful for conceptualising this study's main interest: the *representation* of war correspondents and their practice. Representations are products of what Bourdieu calls the field of cultural production. The journalistic field itself forms a subfield of this larger field, and when correspondents are represented in memoirs, novels or films, these products are created in other subfields from which it is possible to observe the (war-)journalistic field with its actors and practices. When representing war correspondents, these products subordinate them to their own interests, be it entertainment, reflection or critique. Accordingly, it is not uncommon for representations of war correspondents to highlight certain features deemed interesting for an audience at a given time, or suitable to the demands of a certain genre. Representations select aspects of the war correspondent's professional habitus and field or, in other words, the war correspondent's performance. Indeed, representations, even where they are not performative themselves, are always a way of *showing* doing, to use Schechner's term, and where they show war correspondents who are ›doing the war correspondent‹, the performativity of that behaviour is particularly pronounced. As has been indicated before, representations also have repercussions on the journalistic field, and the final section of this chapter will elaborate how correspondents consume and engage with memoirs, films and other modes of representation. First, however, the following sections will identify key elements of the war correspondent's habitus and some important parameters that determine the war reporter's professional field.

---

5   McLaughlin (2002) also names some of the most relevant structural elements that define the war correspondent's field of action.

Role Conceptions

We have already seen that the cultural image of war correspondents is associated with an expectation of adventure and heroism which some correspondents absorb into their habitus. While such expectations shape the popular image and the behaviour of war correspondents, they are a secondary effect rather than an element inherent in the journalistic profession itself. More essentially, the professional habituation of journalists includes an understanding of their responsibility towards the public and the public's right to be informed, for instance about an ongoing war. Like other journalists, war correspondents regard themselves as witnesses and watchdogs in the public's service. They see their job as a vocation and declare themselves dedicated to telling the truth, raising consciousness and revealing what war means in human terms, like John Simpson in the following excerpt from one of his memoirs:

»I would say [...] that those of us who have the job of providing people with information have a duty – the very word sounds embarrassing and outmoded in most ears nowadays – to tell them as much, as widely, as deeply, and as honestly as possible about what is going on in the world around them« (Simpson 2002, 107).

Being an ›objective‹ observer has been an ideal in Western journalism for much of the 20th century. It has become part of the journalistic code of honour, especially in the English-speaking countries. John Simpson for instance demands that good war reporting should be critical but never take sides and cross the »invisible yet somehow always clear-cut line which divides the observer from the participant« (ibid., 37). Looking back to the beginnings of his profession, Simpson sees his ideal embodied by William Russell, while Archibald Forbes overstepped the line between observer and participant:

»Archibald Forbes was desperate to participate. He longed for British victories in all those sad little wars he covered, in which Gatling guns wiped out entire Afghan tribes, entire Zulu impis, entire armies of Egyptian fellahin. It didn't matter to him how the victories were won, just so long as the final scoreline was right. William Howard Russell, by contrast, understood that by observing correctly and reporting back what he saw, rather than what his patriotism or the generals in command wanted him to see, he was doing his country a much greater favour. When he reported from India in the aftermath of the Mutiny he revealed that some British and Indian troops were carrying out savage acts of vengeance on captured and defeated mutineers. For Russell, honesty came be-

fore comfort. [...] To keep quiet when you know things are not right is the reverse of patriotism: it is to cover up for those interests that stand to gain from
silence. It is to be a partisan of inefficiency and stupidity and mindless cruelty.
[...] Journalists, it seems to me, have a duty to resist being simply corralled into
obedient silence: it isn't good for journalism, and it isn't good for government«
(ibid., 37).

This commitment to impartial and critical reporting is shared by many of
Simpson's British colleagues such as Paul Moorcraft, who maintains that

»[o]f course, total objectivity is clinically impossible, especially after witnessing a massacre or two, but journalists should strive for it, and reject the tempta-
tions of advocacy journalism. War correspondents may bond (or pretend to
bond) with the warriors who share their food or armoured vehicle; ultimately,
however, hacks must refuse to take sides, especially when they are covering
wars fought by their own nationals. This is the prime imperative of war reportage« (Moorcraft 2001, 368f.).

Total objectivity is not only difficult to achieve in all circumstances, it
has also not always been a guiding principle of (war) journalism, and it is
sometimes deliberately violated. In the excerpt above, Simpson refers to
19th-century correspondents' open patriotism. The Spanish Civil War
provides us with classic examples of war journalism committed to a
political cause.[6] In the recent war in Iraq, some American journalists no-
toriously did not hide their sympathies and received a bashing from some
of their British colleagues who felt they had managed better to maintain
impartiality and journalistic integrity. John Simpson raged about Fox
News and its »loud, combative, ultra-patriotic stance« (Simpson 2003,
68) as well as CNN's »embarrassingly nationalistic« broadcasting in Iraq
(ibid., 339). Martin Bell expressed a general verdict on the American
press in the campaigns after 9/11: »If you were looking for impartial, en-
quiring journalism, the land of the free and home of the brave was not the
place to find it« (Bell 2004, 40). Bell's comment is particularly interesting in this context because he himself is often cited for the view that absolute objectivity is almost impossible to achieve nor is it desirable when
the human cost of war is taken into account (see p. 35).

Indeed, human concerns motivate a correspondent's partiality quite
frequently. James Cameron, for example, the most famous British reporter to cover Vietnam, confesses that he was very often emotionally
involved when ›observing‹ human suffering – also in North Vietnam,

---

6   Significantly, Knightley's chapter on the reporters of the Spanish Civil War
     is entitled »Commitment in Spain 1936-1939« (Knightley 2004, 207-235).

33

which Cameron was the first Western journalist permitted to enter: »My feelings were tremendously engaged in this uniquely brutal and muddled war, though they might have had no more value than anyone else's, but for the fact that I had seen both sides« (Cameron 1967, 301). His memoirs include a lengthy passage about why he felt unable to report impartially:

»I cannot remember how often I have been challenged, and especially in America, for disregarding the fundamental tenet of honest journalism, which is objectivity. This argument has arisen over the years, but of course it reached a fortissimo [...] when I had been to Hanoi, and returned obsessed with the notion that I had no professional justification left if I did not at least try to make the point that North Viet Nam, despite all official Washington arguments to the contrary, was inhabited by human beings. [...] objectivity in some circumstances is both meaningless and impossible. I still do not see how a reporter attempting to define a situation involving some sort of ethical conflict can do it with sufficient demonstrable neutrality to fulfil some arbitrary concept of ›objectivity‹. It never occurred to me, in such a situation, to be other than subjective, and as obviously so as I could manage to be. I may not always have been satisfactorily balanced; I always tended to argue that objectivity was of less importance than the truth, and that the reporter whose technique was informed by no opinion lacked a very serious dimension« (ibid., 71f.).

During the 1990s, crimes against humanity in former Yugoslavia gave rise to a particularly intense debate, among both media practitioners and academics, about how humanly committed journalists should become. A prominent figure in this debate was British ITN correspondent Michael Nicholson who, during the war in Bosnia, not only reported from the enemy side (refusing to be content with the information provided at NATO press conferences), but also took direct action on behalf of the war's victims. Nicholson used his status as a prominent television reporter to raise help for an orphanage. His book about the events, *Natasha's Story* (1993), enjoyed wide public attention and was turned into the fiction film *Welcome to Sarajevo*.[7] In a Channel 4 programme, Nicholson confirmed his belief that journalists should strive to be committed rather than to keep their emotions out of their professional behaviour:

»All the great journalists that I've admired [...] were people who weren't afraid to show their emotions, afraid to show their humanity. [...] you've got to get as close to a story as you can and sometimes that means becoming a casualty

---

7   For a discussion of this film, see pp. 137-139.

yourself, a physical casualty or, as I was in Sarajevo, an emotional casualty. But I see nothing wrong with that« (qtd. in McLaughlin 2002, 154).

This view is also clearly expressed in Nicholson's memoirs:

»If we [war correspondents] were troubled, it was because it was sometimes hard to know what it was that separated the observer from the participant; to distinguish how you thought from how you felt and to know the difference between what you thought you saw and what you knew you had to say. And to resist the temptation not simply to report the story but to assume a role in it« (Nicholson 1991, xii).

Nicholson's colleague Martin Bell, another television reporter (for the BBC) and later Member of the British Parliament, had strong reservations about Nicholson's open engagement in Bosnia and crusading journalism in general,[8] but he too found it increasingly difficult to follow the »tradition of objective and dispassionate journalism« in which he had been trained:

»From where I have been since and what I have seen, I would describe objective journalism as a sort of bystanders' journalism, unequal to the challenges of the times. What I do believe in still [...] is fairness and impartiality and a scrupulous attention to the facts and a determination to pay heed to the unpopular spokespeople of unfavored causes« (Bell 1998, 102).

Bell coined the phrase »journalism of attachment« to characterise the kind of non-detached journalism that became his own ideal. This is a journalism committed to both facts *and* ethics. To Bell, the journalism of attachment is »aware of the moral ground on which it operates, that cares as well as knows, and that will not stand neutrally between good and evil, the victim and the oppressor« (ibid., 103).[9] Like his original television

---

8   In his memoirs Bell writes that while reporting from Bosnia himself, he felt that he had to »avoid having to match ITN in what I felt to be a mawkish and exploitative story about the rescue of Sarajevo's orphans« (Bell 1995, 69).

9   On the discussion about attached vs. detached journalism see also Hume (1997) and McLaughlin (2002, Chapter 8). To Hume, »[t]he Journalism of Attachment uses other people's wars and crises as a twisted sort of therapy, through which foreign reporters can discover some sense of purpose – first for themselves, and then for their audience back home. It turns the life and death struggles of others into private battlegrounds where journalists who have lost faith in the old values of their profession can fight for their souls« (Hume 1997, 18). Philip Seib, by contrast, explicitly demands journalists to

coverage of the war in Bosnia, Bell's memoirs of this war repeatedly dwell on the reporter's emotional and ethical challenge in face of suffering civilians. Bell emphasises that this was the general attitude among Western correspondents who covered this specific war: »In such conditions, detached and dispassionate journalism was out of the question. We were drawn into this war as something other than the witnesses and chroniclers of it. We were also participants« (Bell 1995, 129). As the later chapters will show, commitment and attachment not only concern journalists in their own memoirs. They are also a prominent theme in many fictional representations of war reporters in the 20th century. Fictional treatments frequently introduce the character of the war *photographer* to underline the reporter's dilemma between witnessing and participation, taking up the belief that the objective of a camera must present an objective view. This is demonstrated to be a deceptive assumption, however, since there is always a human being behind the camera, and photographs therefore capture a personal, that is, subjective perspective on reality.[10]

The statements of war correspondents in interviews and in their memoirs suggest that the attitude with which they fulfil their role as the public's witnesses is an aspect of their habitus that keenly interests themselves. After all, it is this attitude which most obviously engages them as specifically human mediators of war and which entails the ethical challenge of their profession. Their memoirs reveal just as clearly, however, that war correspondents, just like other journalists, are also driven by a strong sense of professional competition, that is, a disposition generally created by the journalistic field:

»La concurrence économique entre les chaînes ou les journaux pour les lecteurs et les auditeurs ou, comme on dit, pour les parts de marché s'accomplit concrètement sous la forme d'une concurrence entre les journalistes, concurrence qui a ses enjeux propres, spécifiques, le *scoop*, l'information exclusive, la réputation dans le métier, etc. et qui ne se vit ni se pense comme une lutte purement économique pour des gains financiers, tout en restant soumise aux contraintes liées à la position de l'organe de presse considéré dans les rapports de force économiques et symboliques« (Bourdieu 1996, 46).

---

act out of their conscience: »journalists should recognize that their coverage may affect opinion and policy. [...] Where cameras go, attention and aid are much more likely to follow. That makes journalists actors, not merely observers, and there is no escaping the responsibilities that accompany that role« (Seib 2002, 4).

10 See the discussion of the films *Salvador* (pp. 126-127) and *War Stories* (pp. 156-158) as well as Pat Barker's novel *Double Vision* (pp. 141-142).

Landing a scoop is a frequent theme in the self-representation of war journalists (as well as in novels and films). Pride in having been the first in a theatre of war or getting an exclusive interview is expressed sometimes with slight irony, but even then with undisguised satisfaction about having ›beaten‹ one's colleagues:

»Such is the irony, or the wretchedness, of the reporting trade, any hard newsman who really wants to shine is always in pursuit of the big one. A big murder. A big fire. A big plane crash. A big anything where there is death and suffering and the emotions of man are bared. And none is more newsworthy than a war, where every emotion of man is exposed: cynicism to sentiment, hatred to harmony; calamity to kindness, horror to happiness; lust to love, warmth to wickedness; bravery and banality, courage and cowardliness; saintliness, sinfulness; dying and death, duty and devotion. All of them unfolded right before you, a lexicon of life on parade in the Big Story that has none bigger, with the catchline, War« (Burrowes 1982, 86).

This statement indicates how the disposition to get a scoop may clash with the role conception of committed or attached reporting, thus creating a potential for ethical dilemma in the correspondent's behaviour that is, as later chapters will reveal, of particular interest to writers of fiction and filmmakers.

As far as the self-representations of war correspondents are concerned, satisfaction with professional success seems independent from the kind of war that is reported. This satisfaction is a recurrent motif in accounts from the 19th century to the present. In the Second World War, Leonard Marsland Gander, Special Correspondent for the *Daily Telegraph*, rejoiced at being the only journalist on the Greek island of Leros »at the cable-head with one of the finest stories of the war« (Gander 1945, 213). Max Hastings, who had struggled hard »to win a passage to the South Atlantic« (Hastings 2000, 272) and for whom joining the Falklands Task Force in their landing was »the greatest romantic adventure of [his] life« (ibid., 300), experienced his finest hour when he was the first man in Stanley, even ahead of the British force:

»I knew that I had sent the greatest story I should ever know. ›British forces are in Port Stanley‹, I began. ›At 5.45 p.m. British time today, as men in the Parachute Regiment halted on the outskirts at the end of their magnificent drive on the capital pending negotiations, I walked through the Argentine lines with my hands in the air, and met the first of the town's civilian population ...‹ The *Evening Standard*'s front page banner headline on 15 June, crowning my dispatch, read: THE FIRST MAN INTO STANLEY. It was the happiest moment of my career« (ibid., 379).

John Simpson remembers a similar moment of triumph when he and his team were the first journalists to report the liberation of Kabul from the Taliban in 2001. In his description, the event and experience are literally staged, re-performing in distinctly physical terms Simpson's enthusiastic reception by grateful civilians and his own elation:

»After all the waiting, all the fear, all the anxiety about failure and being beaten by our opposition, a superb sense of elation built up inside me, and I raised my arms to greet the crowds, forcing my way through them. A bus was stuck in the throng, and everyone inside it who could get an arm through the windows tried to touch me. I grabbed as many hands as I could, laughing with the relief and pleasure of it all. To be the first journalists out of so many to enter the most closed and difficult city on earth: it was a superb moment« (Simpson 2002, 10).

Competition is, of course, encouraged by the media organisations for which journalists work, and their subjection to market forces. These forces may pertain even more to war journalism than to other forms of journalism since war can be ›big‹ news and thus of high commercial interest in the media (as long as a war holds the audience's attention). Apart from economic parameters, the practice of war correspondents is affected by all other aspects of the media complex, both infrastructural and technological. A scoop is only a scoop, after all, when it does reach the intended audience.

The Media. Technologies and Infrastructure

Changes in communication technology have affected war reporting since its beginnings. »The telegraph, the camera, the radio all had their day on the battle front and each in its own way appeared to bring new qualities of immediacy and authenticity to the reporting of war« (McLaughlin 2002, 25). In the late 19th century, Archibald Forbes beat William Russell by first using the telegraph to send dispatches from the Franco-Prussian War. This did not only alter the transmission speed of a report, but also its style and content:

»The telegraph [...] lent reports immediacy and freshness. It increased the popularity of the war correspondent as hero. But it also fuelled the growth of the popular press and yellow journalism, encouraging a style of journalism that favoured the drama and sensation of war over truth and accuracy. The new technology improved the means of reporting war but not the quality and reliability of the journalism« (ibid., 29).

In one of his books, Forbes himself looked back to the change the tele-graph had brought to war correspondence as »a fine art«, paradoxically deploring the emphasis on speed in contemporary reporting on which his own reputation had been built: »The war journalists who, previous to the Franco-German war of 1870 made for themselves name and fame, achieved their successes by the vivid force of their descriptions, by their fearless truthfulness, by their staunchness under hardships and disease« (Forbes 1895, 218). He also explicitly noted the new requirements which the telegraph made on war journalism:

»At a casual glance it might seem that the chief qualification requisite in the modern war correspondent is that he should be a brilliant writer, able so to de-scribe a battle that the reader may glow with the enthusiasm of the victory, and weep for the anguish of the groaning wounded. The capacity to do this is ques-tionless a useful faculty enough; but it is not everything – nay, it is not even among the leading qualifications. For the world of today lives so fast, and is so voracious for what has come to be called the ›earliest intelligence‹, that the man whose main gift is that he can paint pictures with his pen is beaten and pushed aside by the swift, alert man of action, who can get his budget of dry, concise, comprehensive facts into print twenty-four hours in advance of the most graphic description that ever stirred the blood« (ibid., 225).

The satellite technology of the late 20th century caused a similar water-shed, making instantaneous broadcasting a new standard in the television reporting of war. CNN used a satellite dish during the 1991 Gulf War, satellite phones have been in use since Kosovo (1999), and now in the early 21st century, reporters are being equipped with videophones. Paul Adams comments on the rapid advance of technology between the 1991 Gulf War and the war in Iraq:

»It wasn't just the military whose technological advances made this a very dif-ferent conflict from the first Gulf War, a dozen years earlier. With the internet, mobile phones and satellite dishes able to broadcast on the move, the media have taken their own great strides« (qtd. in Beck/Downing 2003, 111).

These recent changes also have repercussions on the quality of the re-porting. On the one hand, technologies for instant transmission provide the opportunity for immediacy that sells well in today's media markets. On the other hand, they confront correspondents with new demands. They are expected to be available around the clock for comments and re-ports, at the cost of time they might otherwise have invested in research-ing their stories more extensively. Kate Adie comments cynically on this development:

»Increasingly, hacks were tethered to the satellite dish, always on hand to de-liver the ›live spot‹, in a curious belief that rabbiting on live is a more relevant and informed kind of reporting; in reality, someone stuck next to a dish for hours on end is the last creature on earth to have learned anything new, and probably unaware of a corpse twenty yards away« (Adie 2002, 415).

Real-time reporting also increases the risk for correspondents who are expected to convey not only information but war action and thus to get as close to the front as possible. Greg McLaughlin diagnoses a veritable »tyranny of the satellite uplink and the demands of the 24-hour ›real-time‹ news agenda« (2002, 23).

With regard to the media formats in which correspondents work, the report and illustration for newspapers are the earliest and most enduring ones, even if the war artist's sketch has been replaced by the photograph. Roger Fenton's work in the Crimean War is often cited as the first war photography; however, as a medium of front reportage, this early photog-raphy was not yet significant. »[P]hotographers appeared to have had lit-tle success in capturing battle action pictures until the Omdurman cam-paign of 1898 and the Boer War (1899-1902) and the illustrated news-papers still continued to rely mainly on the talented skill of their war art-ists to portray events« (Wilkinson-Latham, 1979, 18). War artists like Frederic Villiers and Melton Prior thus enjoyed a high reputation in war journalism until the early 20th century.

The film camera also was already used in the 19th century, though likewise with small success. Villiers experimented with the new medium and took a camera with him to the Greco-Turkish war (1897), but was frustrated by the result, as he remembered in his memoirs:

»When this little war broke out I had ingenuously thought that cinema pictures of the fighting would delight and astonish the public. The cinema camera was then in its infancy, so at considerable expense I took one to the front, as I have already mentioned. It was a laborious business in those early days to arrange the spools and change the films; and I sweated a good deal at the work, but managed to get touches of real warfare.
It was a great disappointment, therefore, to discover that these films were of no value in the movie market« (Villiers 1921, II, 181).[11]

That his footage had no material value is explained by the fact that the contemporary movie market had already been saturated with re-enactments of battles that were able to show the fighting more close-up

---

11 On Villiers's attempts as a war cameraman, see also Bottomore (1980), and on early attempts to capture war on film in general, Bottomore (1995).

and in a more dramatic manner than Villiers's authentic material shot with a cumbersome camera at the actual front. Later, in the Sudan with Kitchener, Villiers's camera failed entirely and he had to go back to the reliable medium of the sketch (ibid., 264). The first professional newsreel cameraman made his appearance in the South African War, William Dickson of the Biograph company.[12] Dickson entitled his memoirs *The Biograph in Battle* (1901) but also had to concede that filming battle was a major problem. Nevertheless, the films he shot »were widely watched« (Hudson/Stanier 1999, 36) since they captured, if not the fighting, many of the more filmable moments of life in camp, the protagonists of the British army and the general scenario in which the war took place. Cameramen were more widely used in the First World War, where their main task consisted in gathering material for instructional and documentary films such as the famous *Battle of the Somme* (1914). In the Spanish Civil War and the Second World War, the newsreel report as such became significant, but another medium was the main competition for the press as far as day-to-day reporting was concerned.

Radio was the first medium to make live reporting from the war zone possible, and its reporters, such as Richard Dimbleby of the BBC or the American celebrity Edward R. Murrow, brought the Second World War into people's living rooms:

»For the first time in war, because of technological improvements in the equipment made during the war, the civilian population in Britain was able to hear, if not to see, the authentic sounds of the fighting. BBC war correspondents became household names in Britain and, indeed, sometimes almost throughout the world« (Hudson/Stanier 1999, 70).

Immediately after the Second World War, the BBC published a selection of its best radio broadcasts in which the reporters' role was praised as »a link between the civilian and the services, a window on the war through which the combatant and the folk at home could catch a glimpse of each other« (Hawkins/Boyd 1946, 9). But radio not only provided a new connection between the front and the public at home, it also offered »a new style in reporting. [...] Radio forced the reporter to describe what was going on in a way that supplied the listeners with both words and images with a new intimacy, to communicate with the mass audience and the audience of one at the same time« (McLaughlin 2002, 36). Along with the press, radio has remained a significant medium of war reporting, and

---

12 »The biograph was a moving picture camera taking its name from the American patent company which exhibited the camera in London in 1897« (Wilkinson-Latham 1979, 252).

it experienced a notable revival in Britain during the Falklands War, when television coverage was highly restricted:

»Instead, radio reporters such as Brian Hanrahan and Robert Fox became household names. [...] At the time of Cold War tensions and intercontinental missile technology, it was striking to see a territorial conflict unfold through a medium that was thought to have reached its pinnacle in World War II« (Conelly/Welch 2005, xiii).

Television reporters like Michael Nicholson also did radio work again because video tapes took too long to get back to Britain, and Nicholson remembers enjoying the experience of working without a camera team:

»Now with my newly acquired tape recorder [...] I could move on my own, travelling on impulse from unit to unit, hitching lifts on a passing helicopter, standing in the middle of nowhere thumbing the sky – without the hindrance of a camera – recording interviews, capturing the natural sound of an air attack or an artillery bombardment and writing my words around them. Suddenly I was creating word pictures and it was altogether a new sensation« (Nicholson 1991, 247).

In general perception, however, television is now *the* medium in which war is brought to the mass public.[13] Vietnam is often designated as the first ›television war‹, and since it was also a largely »uncensored war« (Hallin 1986), it engendered the myth that the United States lost this war at home, through a loss of common support based on ›unsympathetic‹ television coverage.[14] While this view is now contested, there is no doubt that television is a medium with a special impact on the public, especially in the age of 24/7 news.

The media determine the practice of war correspondents not only through technologies and technological change. Correspondents are also

---

13 In this context, see also Bourdieu on the general power of television and its dominant position in relation to the press: »Avec les années [...], la relation s'est complètement renversée et la télévision tend à devenir dominante éco-nomiquement et symboliquement dans le champ journalistique« (Bourdieu 1996, 47).

14 Allegedly, reporters in Vietnam were »free to roam the war zone unham-pered by military restrictions, to criticise and challenge and question, and to fatally undermine military morale and the American will to win« (McLaughlin 2002, 71). Although this assertion cannot go unchallenged, the myth that journalists were responsible for America's defeat in Vietnam affected political and military attitudes towards war correspondents for many years to come, not only in the United States.

affected by the structure of media organisations (with editors and news desks) or the market factors already mentioned. This dependence of the reporter on organisational frameworks is, once again, noted by Kate Adie: »All reporters work on the end of a piece of string which leads back to an editor or proprietor. Away with romantic ideas of the Hack Raging Against The World. Hacks have to eat. And they have to get on air, or published, too« (Adie 2002, 168). News texts and their ideological content are thus influenced by »stockholders, executives, owners, and especially, advertisers who produce, manage and profit from news production« (Pedelty 1995, 6). The trend towards infotainment is a clear example of this influence, and such pressures are particularly strong in privately owned media, where many newspapers and broadcasters are now part of big commercial organisations that operate globally. Public broadcasting may be under less pressure here,[15] but it has to compete with private broadcasting and accordingly adopts some of its strategies. The internet has begun to provide alternative, independent outlets for reporting war, for instance in blogs,[16] but the established media retain their power to influence a wide cross-section of the public, and attempts to influence war reporting by politics and the military are still strongly focused on these media.

Politics and the Military

As Bourdieu observes, the power of the journalistic field to grant access to the public gives it influence in a number of neighbouring fields, especially the political one:

»Les journalistes – il faudrait dire le champ journalistique – doivent leur importance dans le monde social au fait qu'ils détiennent un monopole de fait sur les instruments de production et de diffusion à grande échelle de l'information, et, à travers ces instruments, sur l'accès des simples citoyens mais aussi des autres producteurs culturels, savants, artistes, écrivains, à ce que l'on appelle parfois ›l'espace public‹, c'est-à-dire à la grande diffusion. [...] Bien qu'ils occupent

---

15 See, for instance, John Simpson's claim that the BBC has no editorial line (Simpson 2002, 91).

16 The role of blogging in the war in Iraq was widely noted in the established media, for instance in *The Guardian* (Jane Perrone, »Conflict of Interests: The Sites You Need to See«, 27 March 2003, 6). A particularly famous blog was that of the Iraqi Salam Pax – so famous, in fact, that it was later published as a book (Pax 2003).

une position inférieure, dominée, dans les champs de production culturelle, ils exercent une forme tout à fait rare de domination: ils ont le pouvoir sur les moyens de s'exprimer publiquement, d'exister publiquement, d'être connu, d'accéder à la notoriété publique. [...] Et ils peuvent détourner une part de ce pouvoir de consécration à leur profit [...].

Mais surtout, étant en mesure d'accéder en permanence à la visibilité publique, à l'expression à grande échelle, tout à fait impensable, au moins jusqu'à l'apparition de la télévision, pour un producteur culturel, même très célèbre, ils peuvent imposer à l'ensemble de la société leurs principes de vision du monde, leur problématique, leur point de vue« (Bourdieu 1996, 52f.).

There are more cautionary views on the media's influence on politics. Johanna Neuman, for instance, argues that this influence should not be over-estimated since the media are not in a position to make the political decisions themselves: »The photograph is a powerful weapon, television images even more compelling, invitations to intervention all. But none of these weapons of communicate [sic] do any more than flag a problem, or focus attention. They are a lens, not a prism« (Neuman 1996, 243). Nevertheless, an impact of the media on the makers of political decisions and, by implication, military decisions, cannot be denied: »the media within democracies has influenced public opinion, which, in its turn, has influenced political decision-making in the making of war: indeed, that is partly what democracy is about« (Hudson/Stanier 1999, 303).

Television has a particular power to make politicians act, especially where it operates globally. The phenomenon has been discussed as the so-called CNN effect, here described in the words of Martin Bell:

»In the 1990s much ink was spilled in media journals on the so-called CNN effect – the tendency of governments to adjust their policies to cope with the something-must-be-done demands generated by TV coverage of a humanitarian crisis. This especially applied to Somalia, Rwanda and Bosnia where the Western democracies essentially had no policies, but policy vacuums waiting to be filled. In Somalia, it was the media that got the United States into it and then, gravely damaged on CNN, out of it. [...] In Bosnia, belated and remedial actions were taken which, without television, would not even have been considered« (Bell 2004, 37).

Even before the days of 24-hour news channels, television had political impact, as Michael Nicholson experienced early in his career, when he and his team were covering the Nigerian civil war. In his memoirs, Nicholson devotes considerable space to the fact that one of his pieces (made for British television) became interference in the war itself. Nicholson and his team had filmed an illegitimate execution, and after the report had been broadcast in Britain, the executor was executed himself. In retrospect, Nicholson is aware not only of the power of television images, but also of the fact that this power is often utilised by politicians:

»With hindsight I doubt the Biafrans would have made us leave if they had had the slightest fear we would not return. Our camera was too important a weapon not to use. We already had dramatic footage for their propaganda cause and the best and worst pictures, depending on the point of view, were still to come« (Nicholson 1991, 28).

While filmed images have the impact of (perceived) immediacy and authenticity, an interrelationship between war reporting and political decision-making has a long tradition. It is a well-known fact that William Russell's reports about the British army's insufficient supplies in the Crimean caused a public outrage and induced politicians to improve conditions for the troops.[17] A correspondent of the First World War, Ellis Ashmead-Bartlett, proudly claimed in his memoirs that his letter to Prime Minister Asquith about »the true state of affairs« in the Gallipoli campaign had exerted some influence on the British decision to withdraw from this theatre of the war (Ashmead-Bartlett 1928, 240). This claim may be somewhat exaggerated,[18] but it reveals a correspondent aware and proud of his role as a player in the political field. Jon Snow, a long-time presenter of Channel 4 news and before that an experienced correspondent, even sees a special obligation for (war) journalists to engage in political matters: »I'd like to think that my next period as a working journalist will be challenged less by the need to survive on a battlefield than by the search for the new international order that has eluded us since the wall came down« (Snow 2004, 379).[19]

---

17 See Wilkinson-Latham (1979, 49) and Knightley (2004, 11f.).

18 The letter is also fully reprinted in Ashmead-Bartlett's book. However, Asquith never read Ashmead-Bartlett's original letter, which the correspondent had given to his Australian colleague Keith Murdoch in an attempt to circumvent the military censor. The letter was intercepted and confiscated, and Murdoch thus had to restore its main points, adding a few ideas of his own. It was in this version that the letter reached the Prime Minister (see Knightley 2004, 198). Ashmead-Bartlett subsequently published his opinion in *The Times* and eventually became an icon of investigative war journalism (see also Daniel 2005, 121).

19 In this context, see also Graham Spencer's study on the neglect of peace-oriented reporting in the media: »Television news coverage of Vietnam, Rwanda, Bosnia, the Middle East, Northern Ireland and Iraq, reveals a notable lack of attention to voices of moderation and conflict prevention, as elite positions determine the parameters of debate and policy direction. Without access to counter-arguments which challenge dominant parties, news discourse not only legitimizes that discourse, but renders alternative

While journalists are aware of the media's impact on politics, they are also keenly aware of how their practice is subjected to control by politics and the military and how this control interferes with their self-image as witnesses for the public. The most immediate control of war correspondents is exerted by representatives of the military with whom they interact directly in the war zone. Because of the divergent aims of their respective professions, the relationship between war correspondents and the military has never been entirely stress-free, and it has always comprised an element of negotiation:

»In a period of a hundred years from the Crimean War to the Korean War, reporters and the military have fought on contradictory principles: the military's need for secrecy and the journalist's need not just for facts and information but also news. [...]
For their part, reporters learned that it was pointless adopting a purist, principled position of independence. As in all major wars since Crimea, many war correspondents learned to strike a deal with the military that would guarantee all-important access to ›authoritative‹ information« (McLaughlin 2002, 71).[20]

In *Going to the Wars* (2000), Max Hastings, who personally had a positive attitude towards the (British) military and bonded closely with the soldiers he accompanied during the Falklands War,[21] explores the complexity of this relationship in the opening sentences of his preface:

»Soldiers and journalists make uneasy bedfellows. Members of any decent army, navy or air force are formed in a tradition of duty, discipline, honour, teamwork, sacrifice. Journalists are individualists, often even anarchists. Whoever heard of a successful reporter respectful of regulations and hierarchies? To the eye of your average regimental officer, correspondents are irresponsible, disloyal, undisciplined. [...]
My experiences among warriors have been among the most important of my life. On their side, it is compulsory to express disdain for publicity. Yet it is only natural for men who are risking their lives for their country to appreciate recognition. However much they dislike the media, commanders of Western armies have been obliged to acknowledge that soldiers in modern war want to

---

articulations incidental, even worthless. [...] The idea of a journalism which is peace oriented begins to look at this situation from the other way around« (Spencer 2005, 2).

20 See also Moorcraft/Taylor (2008) for a more recent and detailed investigation of military-media relations.

21 His chapters on the Falklands War abound in the use of the first-person plural. The first chapter of *Going to the Wars* is, rather outspokenly, an account of his »first love affair with the British army« (Hastings 2000, 1).

know that their efforts and sacrifices are being reported at home. They need journalists to tell their story. I am one of those who has often been happy to do so, although this book also records plenty of occasions when I have caused trouble by wilfully disobeying or deceiving military authority in various parts of the world. That has been my job as a journalist and, to be honest, great fun too. Even when we admire soldiers, it is not our business to record their doings on their terms. Of course, I have often been frightened and run away. I have seen soldiers do some terrible things. I have also, however, seen them do fine and even great ones« (Hastings 2000, xviif.).

Since the ability to report a war as autonomously as possible is a prime concern for a war journalist, it is not surprising that censorship and other forms of media management are a frequent theme in their self-representations. Some control to protect sensitive military information or troop morale is usually accepted by correspondents. Sir Arthur Conan Doyle (who also produced propaganda for the British government during the First World War) visited the Western Front in 1916 as an »independent observer« and in his subsequent account mentioned censorship as a necessary matter of fact: »You know that there are several courteous but inexorable gentlemen who may have a word in the matter [...]. But above all you have the twin censors of your own conscience and common sense, which assure you that, if all other readers fail you, you will certainly find a most attentive one in the neighbourhood of the Haupt-Quartier« (Doyle 1916, 9). Christopher Bellamy, who covered the 1991 Gulf War as a defence correspondent for *The Independent*, draws attention to the thin line between control accepted and rejected by journalists in a war:

»We all knew a lot more than we reported. [...] That was not a function of censorship by the military, but of our own professional ethics. If, on the other hand, we had discovered that British troops were being sent into battle with inadequate training, equipment, poor leadership, or had been let down in any other way, and that senior officers or politicians were about to risk lives unnecessarily, then we would have been very impartial indeed« (Bellamy 1993, xxxi).

Complaints about restrictions of mobility and censorship of dispatches have been a staple of war correspondents' memoirs since the 19th century. Journalists in the Crimean War were not censored at first, but when Russell's reports became too embarrassing, restrictions were introduced (Knightley 2004, 15). They became common in all later wars, also because developments in communication technology necessitated stricter control. Archibald Forbes gave vent to his frustration about censorship in his essay »My Campaign in Pall Mall«:

»The journalist who now accompanies an army is a war reporter. He dances in the fetters of the censorship, whose power over him is absolute; it may not only detain or withhold his work, but at discretion may alter it so that he may be made to say the direct reverse of what he wrote« (Forbes 1891, 307).

When writing about the former glamour of war corresponding in his *Memoirs and Studies of War and Peace*, Forbes even held military censorship responsible for his profession's gradual decline:

»[I]ts conditions are being so altered that it may be said, I fear, to have ceased to be the fine art into which zeal, energy and contrivance elevated it for a brief term. It is now an avocation at once simplified and controlled by precise and restraining limitations. In all future European wars, by an international arrangement the hand of the censor will lie heavy on the war correspondent« (Forbes 1895, 216).

A comment by Forbes's colleague in many campaigns, Frank Scudamore, goes in the same direction:

»Of course, war corresponding has long been a dead trade, which nothing in this world can ever revive. Its demise was inevitable as a consequence of the development of telegraphy all over the world, with the resultant necessary strict censorship on all press communications. The slow death song began in 1882, when genial Lord Methuen was our censor at Kassassin and Tel-el-Kebir« (Scudamore 1925, 223).

Frederick Bullard's short history of the ›famous war correspondents‹ sings a veritable swan song for the profession, likewise because of censorship. Its preface predicted in 1914 that the new war would have to be reported with greater restrictions »than in any previous war and this because of the new conditions brought about by modern science«:

»Methods of communication are so nearly instantaneous, and means of travel so swift, that governments will not permit reporters to enjoy the intimate touch with armies in the field which gave such men as William Howard Russell, Archibald Forbes and Januarius A. MacGahan the materials for their thrilling narratives. The tendency to apply the muffler has been apparent for years [...]. Today the cables of Europe are controlled by the war departments of the Powers. No such rigid censorship has before been known« (Bullard 1974, viif.).

In historical overviews as well as in the eyes of many correspondents, the First World War is assessed as the final death-blow to a
Golden Age of war reporting.[22] The British military's control of correspondents in this conflict, through strictly limited accreditation and a
pooling system, accompanied by severe censorship, was perceived as a
particularly harsh interference with the journalists' self-image as guard-
ians of the public's right to be informed. Ellis Ashmead-Bartlett's *The
Uncensored Dardanelles* (1928) includes many passages of outspoken
criticism of these restrictions as well as demands that the military should
consider correspondents as allies rather than enemies:

»At the commencement of the war no Special Correspondents were allowed in
the field, a state of affairs which speedily led to discontent amongst the public,
who felt that they were entitled to hear of the gallant actions of our soldiers and
sailors on land and sea. This veto on the Press gave rise to a widespread belief
that the truth was being concealed, and that many grave events were taking
place which were being purposely hidden by the authorities.
The main obstacle to overcome was the hostility of Lord Kitchener, who was –
as he had ever been throughout his career – bitterly opposed to War Correspondents. Sir John French took an entirely different view. He desired to utilise
the Press, believing that descriptive accounts of their actions, subject to an in-
telligent censorship to prevent information from reaching the enemy, encouraged the troops in the field and the public at home. For many months Lord
Kitchener remained adamant. [...] All propositions, however reasonable, were
invariably turned down by that great man, who entirely failed to realise, at this
stage, that if he wished to make the war a national one, and to induce the whole
nation to take part in it, it was necessary to interest the people and to employ an
extensive propaganda for this purpose.
Neither were precedents lacking which should have warned Lord Kitchener and
his advisers that they were pursuing a policy which had been tried before, and
had singularly failed. Since the days of Russell, Kinglake, and Archibald
Forbes, War Correspondents have played an honourable and valuable rôle in
every campaign, and no British Army has ever had cause to regret their presence at the front. A long line of illustrious writers have added prestige to British
arms from Afghan snows to the South African feldt« (Ashmead-Bartlett 1928,
23).

In the Second World War, military-media relations were more relaxed
since, in this ›people's war‹, conditions at the front were not meant to be
hidden from the public at home. British journalists were expected – quite
in the manner outlined by Ashmead-Bartlett – to support their country's

---

22 See, for instance, Furneaux (1964, 218) and Knightley (2004, 83-120).

war effort, and they usually complied. In some cases, however, they felt too obviously ›guided‹ in their practice. In *Dyonysia*, an account of his experiences as a BBC radio correspondent in the Middle East, Denis Johnston mentions how he was sometimes unnerved by requests to shape his reports according to political necessity: »I have been followed out by many exhortations from the News Room to mention British troops as much as possible in order to offset enemy propaganda that England is fighting the war to the last drop of Dominion and Indian blood« (Johnston 1949, 30).

During the Falklands War, the British once more adopted a policy of firm control over the media, influenced by the myth that ›uncontrolled‹ reporting from Vietnam had cost the United States their victory. Journalists who were permitted access into the Falklands war zone were handpicked, forced to co-operate in a pool and restricted in transmitting their reports. Significantly, »[i]n the weeks immediately after the war, correspondents back from the front rushed into print with ›the untold story‹, incidents that the MoD censors had refused to pass at the time« (Knightley 2004, 480).[23] Memoirs of the Falklands reporters often comment on their restricted working conditions. Michael Nicholson, for instance, emphasises how he and his colleagues often felt misinformed (»We coined a new phrase: information oppression«), and he remembers that »[w]e became more and more depressed at being employed simply to confirm what was being announced by a minister or his spokesman in London« (Nicholson 1991, 215 and 225).

After the Falklands, however, relations between the British military and the media took a new course, following the United States' new strategies. These strategies acknowledge the public's right to be informed about wars in which their country is involved, and they recognise that the media are essential for creating public support for a war. Not least, they react to the fact that advances in communication technology have made it increasingly difficult to suppress or manipulate reports in the first place. The wars of the late 20th and early 21st centuries are fought in the media as well as at the battle front, and in the age of Information War, military-media relations have become a complex and sensitive area. Information Operations is high on the military's agenda: »IO represents, for the military at least, a flexible set of guidelines that sets out the importance of good military-media relation particularly with a view to influencing adversaries« (Connelly/Welch 2005, xv). Strict measures of control have

---

23 See, for example, Hastings/Jenkins (1983) and Fox (1982). On the handling of the media in the Falklands War by the British government and armed forces, see also Harris (1983) and Mercer et al. (1987, part II).

thus given way to more subtle means of ›managing‹ the media, providing them with information and opportunities for images.[24]

PR officers have become increasingly significant in recent years, such as NATO's Jamie Shea during the Kosovo crisis in 1999, whose strategies of spin have been perceived as successful media management:

»It is true that a good majority of British and American journalists accepted the fundamental rationale for bombing Serbia and Kosovo; an observation that can be extended to many left-of-centre intellectuals and academics who waved the NATO flag for bombing on behalf of Kosovar Albanians in spite of the rather dubious legal grounds on which the bombing campaign was carried out. There was a liberal, humanitarian consensus abroad that squeezed out radical dissent more effectively than was the case in the Gulf War in 1991 [...]. It is also the case that most journalists at the briefings were too willing to be fed information and digest it as transparent accounts of events on the ground rather than as selective and self-serving presentation of those events« (McLaughlin 2002, 119).

Television has a privileged position in the new military-media relationship, as Martin Bell observes:

»In the new, bleak and lawless landscape of armed conflict, TV does indeed have military purposes. It manages perceptions and shapes the battlefield. Wars can be won by television as well as by precision-guided missiles. Indeed they cannot be won *without* television. The missiles alone will not deliver victory. To win a war, you have in the first place to be *seen* to be winning it« (Bell 2004, 56).

Means to ensure the ›complicity‹ of correspondents practiced in recent years include pooling and embedding. The former, which was used systematically during the 1991 Gulf War, permits a group of pre-selected journalists to accompany troops on selected military operations, thus granting them access to »some otherwise unavailable source of information.« In exchange, they have to »pool their reporting with that of other news agencies, so that no exclusives or scoops can be claimed« (Paul/Kim 2004, 66).[25] Embedding as practiced in the Iraq War at first sight appears to grant unrestricted access to troops at the front, but is, of course, just as much subject to military control: »While an embedded press system provides access, the military retains a large measure of control over that access, determining, for example, which journalists receive

---

24 On details of Information Warfare and how it affects journalistic practices, see also Tumber/Webster (2006).

25 On the management of journalists in the 1991 Gulf War, see, among many other publications, Smith (1992).

the most desirable embedding assignments« (ibid., 67). More than 700 journalists were embedded with allied troops in Iraq, and all of them had signed the military's ›ground rules‹. In exchange the media got pictures and occasions for dramatic reports that would boost their viewing figures.[26]

Pooled and embedded journalists risk being instrumentalised and, in the worst case, used for propaganda purposes.[27] To preserve their integrity as impartial journalists, many reporters during both wars in the Gulf thus rejected the privileged access through pooling and embedding and preferred to act as unilaterals:

»Unilateral journalism is as closely akin as possible to the ›standard‹ day-to-day model of news reporting and collecting. Unilateral journalism has historically taken two forms: freedom to travel with troops (but without the sort of official assignments used with the embedded press) and ›cowboy‹ or ›four-wheel-drive‹ journalism, in which journalists do not travel with specific troops, but travel on their own, and at their own risk« (Paul/Kim 2004, 67).

Unilaterals can also decide to report a war from behind enemy lines. Some of the most famous war reporting in recent decades was conducted from enemy ground, such as the reporting from Baghdad in 1991. In pub-

---

26 On embedding and military-media relations in Iraq see, among others, Miller (2004), Tumber/Palmer (2004), Kamalipour/Snow (2004) and Sylvester/Huffman (2005). Like pooling in the Gulf, embedding caused a high level of media self-reflexivity. See, for example, the contributions in Katovsky/Carlson (2003). Articles in British papers varied in the drama and adventure they tried to convey of the embeds' experience. Not surprisingly, tabloids rated highest in this respect; articles in the *Sun* on the war against Iraq usually had sensational captions such as »Desert Storm: Sun's man lashed by sand in 60mph gale« (26 March 2003, 9), or »How I Dodged Sniper« (24 March 2003, 9). But the broadsheets hit the same vein: Chris Ayres, while embedded in Iraq, filed many articles to *The Times* in the first person, commenting on his feelings and his own condition: »Long and Grinding Road to Battle: The battle for Baghdad has begun, writes Chris Ayres, who endured a slow trek north with US Marines« (25 March 2003, 4). There were also many meta-articles on the role of the media, particularly in *The Guardian;* see, for instance, »Television agendas shape images of war« (27 March 2003). Phillip Knightley, as an expert on the history of the war correspondent, wrote about the reporting of the war in the *Daily Mail*, for example under the caption »Truth and the war secrets they'll never let you see« (21 March 2003, 17).

27 See Willcox (2005) on propaganda themes in the British press during the 1991 Gulf War.

lic perception this is associated, above all, with CNN, but British reporters, like John Simpson, Brent Sadler (for ITN) and Robert Fisk (*The Independent*) were also based there. During the war in Iraq, Fisk also reported unilaterally for *The Independent* and expressed his criticism of war cruelties candidly, for instance on the front page of the paper on 27 March 2003: »It was an outrage, an obscenity. [...] Two missiles from an American jet killed them all – by my estimate, more than 20 Iraqi civilians, torn to pieces before they could be ›liberated‹ by the nation which destroyed their lives. Who dares, I ask myself, to call this ›collateral damage‹?« Fisk's reporting, and that of other unilaterals, came under fire from politicians (above all the British Defence Secretary at the time, Geoff Hoon) for being too critical or even ›unpatriotic‹. Similar criticism of unilaterals has been voiced in other contexts.[28]

The large-scale embedding in Iraq redirected attention to the way in which personal relationships between media representatives and the military affect the reporting of a war. As such, however, the idea of embedding is not new. 19th-century war correspondents commonly practiced a kind of self-embedding and displayed their military affiliation by wearing a self-created kind of uniform (see p. 26). George Lynch, a reporter in the South African War, openly expressed his admiration for the soldiers he accompanied: »That close contact with the men of this struggling world, and the men who *do* things, and shove these life-wheels round, warms up in one a great love for one's kind – a comrade feeling, like that which comes from being tent-mates in a long campaign« (Lynch 1903, xiii).

Since the First World War it has been common for the military to request accredited journalists to wear uniform, also for their own protection. This stands in a certain contradiction to their official status as civilians who report for other civilians. The Geneva Convention explicitly »insists upon reporters staying out of the fighting. It protects them and it

---

28 See Knightley (2004, 492f.). See also John Simpson (2003, 279f.) on the British government's reaction to his critical reporting from Belgrade in 1999 on the NATO bombings of Serbia: »I came in for a good deal of trouble from the British government's press machine, which seemed to want to bludgeon everyone into accepting the view from Downing Street, and to undermine anyone who provided a different version of things. [...] In fact, I had no sympathies whatever for Milosevic, any more than I did for the Taliban in Afghanistan or Saddam Hussein in Iraq. But I did have a great deal of sympathy for the ordinary people of all three countries, and if you bomb a country, as opposed to an army, then the taxpayers back home who pay for the war have a right to know where the bombs are landing, and what results they have when they explode.«

protects the ability to report conflict at all. [...] When war correspondents become warriors they risk not only their own lives and the lives of their colleagues but the very institution they serve« (Evans 2003, 15). However, when correspondents accompany troops, the line between civilian and soldier is easily crossed. Interestingly, Alex Vernon's study of autobiographical war writing considers correspondents' memoirs as a variety of *military* autobiography:

»War correspondents are firsthand witnesses and participants: they interact with the soldiers, form relationships with them, they risk their lives; they observe events from a different vantage; they sometimes get involved in the action, tending to the wounded, getting in the way, even sometimes firing off a couple of rounds (Hemingway and Michael Herr both admitted to firing weapons as correspondents). The line between journalists and soldiers is particularly complicated when the journalist wears a military uniform, as was the case with most American correspondents in World War II (Hemingway included); such journalism can slip or be pushed into propaganda (another kind of weapon)« (Vernon 2005, 7).

Indeed, a pooled or embedded correspondent's identification and solidarity with the soldiers is an effect calculated by the military, and it is acknowledged to occur by correspondents themselves. Reporters of the Second World War who accompanied British and American troops were outspoken about their sympathies for the fighting men and seem not to have identified this as a problem for their self-image as witnesses. James Lansdale Hodson, for instance, writes in his account of the evacuation of Dunkirk:

»In spite of our situation of considerable peril, in spite of two evacuations of our B.E.F., in spite of lack of equipment and pieces of organization not always up to the mark, my predominant feeling on looking back over these past weeks is one of pride that I belong to the same people as our soldiers« (Hodson, 1940, 189).

Role transgressions do not only occur where reporters wear an official uniform. Scottish Vietnam reporter John Burrowes, for instance, remembers his confusion when an American soldier with whom he had hitched a ride forced him to carry a rifle:

»Riding shotgun, at least, gave me a memorable intro for my first report from Saigon which made the ›splash‹ the next day in the *Sunday Mail*. I used the incident as a scene-setter for an on-the-spot report on the war. But carrying the gun had me in a state of considerable mental confusion« (Burrowes 1982, 38).

Martin Bell's reminiscences of the 1991 Gulf War include a long reflexive passage on how the pooling system affected his stance towards the allied military:

»The fiction held that we were *with* the army but not *of* it [...]. For all practical purposes we were soldiers without the means of self-defence. We were thrust into desert camouflage uniforms topped with a choice of steel helmets or sun hats. [...]
We were under army command and discipline, we took battlefield first-aid courses, we were trained and equipped against chemical warfare, and we dug trenches. Did we ever dig trenches! [...]
At the time I suspected that these media response teams were no more than an ingenious scheme to raise the morale of the troops in the field and take their minds off the forthcoming war. We were the pick and shovel brigade, the Desert Storm cabaret act: we gave them something to laugh and write home about. But what this was in fact [...] was the army's new way of dealing with the press.
[...] The new way was not only to allow us full access under controlled conditions, with a travelling censorship system operating alongside, but to invite us to share the dangers and hardships of the front-line soldiers in such a way that we could hardly fail to identify with them. The process was called ›bonding‹, and – unusually for an army plan – it worked« (Bell 1995, 10f.).

In a similar manner, memoirs of embedded correspondents in Iraq weigh the pros and cons of close contact with the troops. Oliver Poole, who covered the war for the *Daily Telegraph*, provides a perceptive analysis of the strategies behind embedding in his memoirs:

»There was however one other factor motivating the American authorities to embrace a closer relationship with the press. In unguarded moments Pentagon officials would privately admit that they were betting on journalists ›going native‹. The war in Afghanistan had demonstrated that the military could no longer control the battlefield – correspondents were often on the ground before American combat troops – or the flow of information, as satellite communication was now so easy and inexpensive. Planners had concluded that if you couldn't simply stop journalists, it was at least worth trying to ensure that they told your side of the story and not the enemy's. What better way to do that than by placing them in units, so they formed a bond with the soldiers, and as a result found it harder to write negative things about them? The army knew it would be a challenge for any of us to maintain objectivity about the troops with whom we were living. Few of the assembled press pack had ever been on a battlefield before. We could end up so in awe of the weaponry we were witnessing, and so in debt to those we were relying on for protection, that it would prove emotionally impossible to express criticism« (Poole 2003, 13).

Poole indeed begins his book with an expression of his good understanding with the soldiers of the unit he had been embedded with, and of his hope that they would not be offended by some of his critical remarks:

»I am sure there are parts of this book the soldiers I was with will not like. I am sure there are conclusions they will disagree with. But this is meant to be their story, and I trust that they will recognise that I have tried to tell it as objectively as possible. [...] My hope is that by describing what happened, candidly and unflinchingly, I can help people understand what it was really like to be in Iraq during those long, hot days of fighting« (ibid., xx).

Such remarks show that the relationship between the military and the media is not one of basic and general antagonism. Apart from maintaining good working relations with the military, journalists may also share and support the military's aims, not only in wars of their own nation, but also, for instance, during peacekeeping missions. Martin Bell, for instance, comments about the media's relationship to United Nations troops in Bosnia:

»[I]n peacekeeping, we in the press were engaged in an entirely new relationship with the military – that is, the blue-helmeted military. Of course we had our differences with the UN – usually over interpretations of its mandate – but we were fundamentally its partners and not its antagonists. We shared its dangers and frustrations. We were to some extent responsible for its deployment in the first place. We wished it to succeed« (Bell 1995, 29).

How correspondents relate to the military also depends on their individual background. Up to the early 20th century, British war correspondents and officers had been socialised in similar contexts: They were members of the educated upper class or upper middle-class and shared attitudes, including patriotism and a generally affirmative view of war as a necessary and legitimate means to enforce political aims.[29] When remembering the Zulu War, the Victorian war artist Melton Prior explicitly mentions the cordial treatment he received from the officers in camp: »Hospitality to the correspondents was the rule in camp. I dined with the General and Staff and the clergymen.« And Prior made every possible effort to return this hospitality and fasten his bond with the military:

»My tent in the daytime was looked upon as an artist's studio, and became the rendezvous of all the best fellows in camp during the lazy hours. There was a little cupboard love as well, I think, added to it, for my servant had a wonderful

---

29   See Daniel (2006b, 13), and Steinsieck (2007).

knack of making the most lovely Indian-corn porridge, and very often, instead of the afternoon cup of tea, this stuff went round and the fellows ate it with condensed milk or jam« (Prior 1912, 99).

Social connections of this kind came to be loosened in the further course of the 20th century when many journalists developed war-critical and anti-military views. After the Second World War, Britain ceased conscription and British war correspondents began to lack military training and sometimes any insight at all into how the military works, as Martin Bell remarks in his memoirs:

»[T]hanks to more than fifty years without a global conflict and forty without conscription, we are almost all civilians. We depend for our front-line reporting on a generation of war reporters who, like the politicians, lack personal experience of soldiering. With the distinguished exception of the unkempt Anthony Loyd of *The Times*, who does not look at all like the Royal Green Jackets captain he used to be, they have never worn the uniform, held a rifle, dismantled a machine gun or suffered the close attentions of a sergeant major. In individual cases this may not matter. [...] But in general soldiers would rather work with reporters who know the difference between a brigade and a battalion, a tank and an armoured personnel carrier, a brigadier and a bombardier« (Bell 2004, 43f.).[30]

Chris Ayres, who belongs to a younger generation than Bell, even characterises himself as a »war virgin«:

»The children of Thatcher and Reagan – my generational brothers and sisters, on both sides of the Atlantic – are war virgins: never drafted into military service; never invaded by a foreign army; never expected to defend their countries with their lives. The few conflicts we've lived through – the Falklands, Gulf War I, Bosnia – lasted only a few days, or weeks, and were fought by volunteers, not schoolyard conscripts. [...] As teenagers watching television at home, it was tempting to regard these latter-day conflicts as entertainment: real-life

---

30 Bell also remembers how Max Hastings became a hate figure for his fellow correspondents during the Falklands War, among others because of his excellent relationship with the officers: »Max was a would-be soldier who had once been an officer cadet with the Parachute Regiment, until they parted by mutual agreement, because of his Maxocentric character and lack of the team spirit that goes with soldiering; but he looked and sounded officer class, and of all the press gang on the Falklands he had the best contacts with the military, which he was able to exploit to his tactical advantage, especially in hitching rides on helicopters« (Bell 2004, 47).

video games. Perhaps it was because we had grown up being told that a *proper* war would involve 50-megaton nukes« (Ayres 2005, 53f.).

The parameters looked at so far (media technology and organisation, and military-media relationships) determine the war correspondent's field of action in a structural way. Their manifestation in a war correspondent's actual behaviour is adapted, of course, to the specific war scenario and shaped by the correspondent's individual traits.

Individual War Scenarios and Individual Actors

Each war confronts correspondents with its specific conditions. In a war of their own nation, journalists are likely to get a chance to accompany their own or allied troops, while in others they may be reduced to the role of a mere spectator. The Irish journalist Francis McCullagh comments on the special difficulties of reporting a civil war (in this case, the Spanish Civil War):

»A Civil War is hard on the war-correspondent because nobody wants to see him. He is like an inquisitive stranger in a house where a domestic squabble is in full blast. If he is on the Insurgent side, he finds that there is no Press Bureau, no organization for dealing with his despatches. If he is on the Government side, he finds that the regular censor has actually resigned his comfortable post and taken up arms, a thing which no regular officer, in full possession of his faculties, would do in an ordinary war« (McCullagh 1937, viii).

Individual wars even differ in what can be seen of them in a quite literal sense. In 1871, Archibald Forbes envisioned perfect working-conditions for a war correspondent, that is, universal access, unrestricted visibility and direct means of communication:

»If the millennium does not intervene through the zealous efforts of the Peace Society, we may anticipate gigantic strides in this department of catering for the avidity of the public, culminating perhaps in opposition-balloons with a war correspondent in each hanging in the air over the centre of the battle-field, and having a ›special wire‹ [...] leading direct into each Foreign Editor's room. But such appliances are for posterity« (Forbes 1871, 143f.).

The reality for posterity, however, is that it has become increasingly difficult to obtain a ›full‹ picture of any war. In the Second World War,

Richard Dimbleby reported from the Middle East and visited the historic site of the Battle of Omdurman (1898), which Winston Churchill had still been able to observe from a position on top of a hill. Dimbleby remarks that such visual privilege would be unattainable for the modern reporter:

»We took advantage of our visit to Omdurman village to drive out to Kitchener's battlefield, so vividly described by Winston Churchill in *The River War* [...]. Churchill was lucky to have such an ideal grand-stand view of the battle of Omdurman. The modern war observer would not live for five minutes if he stood on such as hill to watch the fighting. Nowadays it is a business of camouflage and cover, holes in the ground, a hill behind which to shelter and not for observation, except perhaps for a wretched artillery officer who must expose himself to the enemy fire« (Dimbleby 1943, 113f.).

The most recent technological advances – such as fighting with long-distance weapons – have made wars even more difficult to survey and report. In the 1991 Gulf War and in Kosovo in 1999, much of the fighting took place in the air and through computer-guided missiles, so that journalists on the attacking side had little to ›witness‹.

Like war scenarios, war reporters too have their individual features and are more or less personally affected by the war(s) in which they participate. Jim Willis, himself an experienced journalist, has emphasised, for example, how the witnessing of catastrophes and atrocities can cause a trauma which some journalists have difficulties to overcome:

»Talking with fellow journalists or writing down the narrative can help to validate and place the events in context. Usually, transient reactions dissipate and a new equilibrium is established. At times, however, the disquieting feelings and thoughts do not go away and the past continues to intrude into the present. The increased use of alcohol to numb the pain, increased risk taking, social isolation, and other actions can lead to increased suffering and professional and interpersonal problems« (Willis 2003, 147).

War correspondents may not only become personal victims of their profession, they also derive private gratifications from it: »a privileged view of history in the making« (Bell 1995, 272), or the opportunity for extreme forms of travel.[31] To Antony Loyd, reporting war became the defining ex-

---

31 A travel element is emphasised in a number of correspondents' memoirs, especially where they attempt to understate the dangerous nature of participation in war. See, for example E.F. Knight's *Reminiscences: The Wanderings of a Yachtsman and War Correspondent* (1923), Richard Busvine's *Gullible Travels* (1945), or the subtitle of Paul Moorcraft's books (1995 and 2001): »Travels with an Occasional War Correspondent.« Evelyn

perience of his whole life, as he suggests at the end of *Another Bloody Love Letter*:

»Staring out again at the Tigris, I watched the last of my youth meander away with the river's current, and felt life burn hard.
And I thought that I should write of the places and the people that had given me so much, whose lessons could perhaps never have been learned one without the other; who had gone but would never leave me. I could have known no better« (Loyd 2007, 303).

When Paul Moorcraft wonders about his reasons for being a war correspondent, hedonism comes into consideration:

»What was the point in risking so many dangers for so little news coverage? Mere entertainment for couch potatoes back home, or revealing horrors and injustice to make the world a better place? Was it healthy adventure or morbid voyeurism? Merely a personal exploration of the boundaries of my own courage, or lack of it? Or was I following the herd in seeking to topple dictators and uncover unjust wars in the name of professionalism, pride, Pulitzers, and personal gain?
It was all about guns and poses. Getting shot at for that great video sequence or still photograph. But did the pictures make any difference? Or was I in the end just a war tourist, a poseur?« (Moorcraft 2001, 3).

Undoubtedly, some journalists are ›war junkies‹ in need of adrenalin, and enjoy the glamour of the profession and the escape it provides from the routines of everyday life.[32] In any case, correspondents' memoirs frequently convey a strong compulsion to go to war, independent of the specific conflict in question. Almost eighty years lie between the two following excerpts, by Philip Gibbs and Michael Nicholson respectively, but their similarity in conveying the excitement and exhilaration of going to war is striking:

»In Fleet Street, which is connected with the wires of the world, there was a feverish activity. Walls and tables were placarded with maps. Photographs, gazetteers, time tables, cablegrams littered the rooms of editors and news editors. There was a procession of literary adventurers up the steps of those buildings in the Street of Adventure – all those men who get lost somewhere between one

---

Waugh was asked to report the war in Abyssinia not because of any prior experience as a reporter of war but because he had written about his travels in Africa; on Waugh's reporting of the war in Abyssinia see pp. 107-108.

32 See also McLaughlin (2002, 6-19) and Tumber/Webster (2006) on the personal motivations of war correspondents.

war and another and come out with claims of ancient service on the battlefields of Europe when the smell of blood is scented from afar; and scores of new men of sporting instincts and jaunty confidence, eager to be ›in the middle of things‹, willing to go out on any terms so long as they could see ›a bit of fun‹, ready to take all risks. Special correspondents, press photographers, the youngest reporters on the staff, sub-editors emerging from little dark rooms with a new excitement in eyes that had grown tired with proof correcting, passed each other on the stairs and asked for their Chance. It was a chance of seeing the greatest drama in life with real properties, real corpses, real blood, real horrors with a devilish thrill in them. It was not to be missed by any self-respecting journalist to whom all life is a stage play which he describes and criticises from a free seat in the front of the house« (Gibbs 1915, 5f.).

»The worst moment in a war was my fear I should not be sent to it. The expectation, the sight and sound of gunfire never failed to exhilarate. Risk spiced my life, but then I had the return ticket, the paper promise to lift me alive and away from the killing fields and dangerous living. There was only ever one answer to the repeated question why did I go to war: it was because I wanted to. [...]
In my generation the same newsmen went to war, the regulars, who missed one only by accident or if they were dead. You were bound to see the same faces at one or other end of the flight. We were an eccentric club of privileged globetrotters who held our meetings in the most bizarre places. When we were together was the only time we talked of our wars, and even then warily. Our adventures seemed so unlikely in retrospect.
Was it machismo or masochism that encouraged us so compulsively and repeatedly to risk our lives? Probably both, but there was really no choice. Having done it once we had to do it again« (Nicholson 1991, xi).

Despite their excitement about participating in the great spectacle of war, both Gibbs and Nicholson are known as correspondents with a high ethical commitment. They thus exemplify how war reporters will often have to navigate between private gratification, human engagement and a professional role image. As mentioned at the beginning of this book, reporting a war involves the correspondent as a human being with all faculties: physically, emotionally and intellectually. This engagement of the war correspondent as a ›whole‹ human being is also emphasised by many experienced war reporters. In one of his books, John Simpson talks explicitly about the »humanity« of the war reporter (Simpson 2002, 34), and Kate Adie dismisses the view that »you are an impervious embodiment of objectivity« and claims, rather, that »[y]ou can properly appreciate what you witness only if your intellect, observation and emotions are in play« (Adie 2002, 167). Being personally and wholly involved in a war may be one reason (apart from the market appeal of such products) why journalists, and particularly war journalists, write their memoirs. Tensions between their professional role and their personal experience certainly render war reporters interesting as characters represented in novels and films.

Representations

Representations highlight certain aspects of the war correspondent's behaviour and relegate others to the background. The excerpts quoted from correspondents' memoirs in the preceding sections suggest that certain aspects of their profession – role images, working conditions and ethical considerations – have preoccupied war journalists since the 19th century and are reflected in their self-representations. Like fictional representations in literature and film, memoirs help to shape the public image of war correspondents and the self-image that is part of their professional habitus. In Bourdieu's conception, habitus in general has a historical dimension:

»The habitus as a shared body of dispositions, classificatory categories and generative schemes is, if it is nothing else, the outcome of collective history: ›The *habitus*, a product of history, produces individual and collective practices – more history – in accordance with the schemes generated by history‹ [*The Logic of Practice*, 54]. Here, once again, we have people creating their own history, albeit not in circumstances of their own choosing. The habitus cannot in any simple sense, however, be considered the cumulative ›collective wisdom‹ of the group (although this is doubtless true). Bourdieu is arguing that the objective world in which groups exist, and the objective environment – other people and things – as experienced from the point of view of individual members of the group, is the product of the past practices of this generation and previous generations. History culminates in an ongoing and seamless series of moments, and is continuously carried forward in a process of production and reproduction in the practices of everyday life« (Jenkins 2002, 80).

To a considerable extent, however, a sense of professional tradition is also constructed through the representations that confront correspondents with images of their trade. Correspondents not only observe each other carefully – a trait possibly encouraged by professional competition[33] –

---

33 Bourdieu observes that the competition inherent in the journalistic field causes journalists to carefully observe their competitors: »la concurrence incite à exercer une surveillance permanente (qui peut aller jusqu'à l'espionnage mutuel) sur les activités des concurrents, afin de profiter de

but they are also avid readers of their colleagues' books, and they are familiar with the careers and self-representations of their predecessors. Winston Churchill's account of the Sudan campaigns, *The River War*, for instance, is mentioned by Richard Dimbleby as »the book we had brought as our bible on the first visit to the Sudan in 1940« (Dimbleby 1943, 113). Alan Moorehead, Dimbleby's colleague in the desert war, also remembers in the first volume of his *African Trilogy* (1944) how they read Churchill's book:

»Richard Dimbleby of the B.B.C. found a chaise-longue and a grass fan. I stripped to the waist and read through *The River War*, that classic book on the Omdurman campaign, written by Kitchener's young second-lieutenant in the Twenty-first Lancers, Winston Churchill. Churchill, already beginning his career as a war correspondent, records with powerful accuracy just what the Upper Nile was like when he went up it at the end of last century to take part in the Lancers' great charge at Omdurman. The description holds still, will always hold« (Moorehead 1965, 32).

War correspondents are also aware of their representation in novels and films. Indeed, as far as Martin Bell is concerned, one novel »should be mandatory reading in our journalism schools«: Evelyn Waugh's *Scoop*, which was published in 1938 (Bell 2004, 181). In the eyes of Max Hastings, *Scoop* »remains the definitive work on foreign correspondence« and »[s]chools of journalism might be taken more seriously by journalists if Evelyn Waugh was a set text« since it reveals so much about the absurdities a correspondent will be confronted with (Hastings 2000, xix). John Simpson mentions that he reread *Scoop* in the days before the battle in Afghanistan.[34]

An awareness of representations is particularly pronounced in Chris Ayres's bestselling book about his time as an ›embed‹ in Iraq, *War Reporting for Cowards* (2005).[35] Working for the London *Times* as their Los Angeles correspondent, Ayres found himself, quite unexpectedly, as an »accidental war correspondent« (Ayres 2005, 75) among a unit of American marines, facing the dangers of real war instead of Hollywood celebrities. Ayres departs from the typical war correspondent's memoirs by striking a mock-heroic note. Over long stretches his account reads like a burlesque of the genre because Ayres draws himself as an anti-hero – a young man of ordinary courage (and thus probably resembling the major-

---

leurs échecs, en évitant leurs erreurs, et de contrecarrer leurs succès« (Bourdieu 1996, 86).

34 Simpson (2002, 11). *Scoop* is discussed on pp. 107-110.

35 At the time of writing, a film based on this book is under development.

ity of his readers[36]) who should not have participated in the war in the first place but felt compelled to do so in order not to jeopardise his career. Ayres withdrew from the war earlier than most of his embedded colleagues, taking the first opportunity that offered itself (the confiscation of his satellite phone by the US military). Ayres may have felt somewhat humiliated by this act of ›desertion‹ (although he did not lose his job), but all in all, his reaction is understandable and his alleged ›cowardice‹ seems closer to his readers' everyday experience than the ›heroism‹ displayed by some his colleagues. Most of all, Ayres's self-deprecation is a pose meant to ex-pose a stereotyped perception and performance of the war correspondent.

The text stages Ayres's alleged failure through consistent comparison and intertextual references. Ayres constantly measures his own behaviour against that of the icons of his profession, from Winston Churchill through Robert Capa, Ernest Hemingway and Ernie Pyle, to the star correspondents of his own time, such as Janine di Giovanni, John Simpson and Martin Bell:

»Growing up, the enduring image I had of a war correspondent was Martin Bell, the BBC man in his trademark white linen suit, who took a direct hit from mortar shrapnel while reporting live from Sarajevo in 1992. ›I'm all right, I'll survive‹, were Bell's stoic words as he collapsed into a pool of his own blood. There was a thrilling, implicit machismo to Bell's work, betrayed by the title of his memoirs: *In Harm's Way.* Bell, always the self-deprecating hero, could barely bring himself to mention the incident in the book. I hated to think of the piercing, girlish squeal, followed by the involuntary bowel movement, that would have been broadcast into the homes of BBC viewers if it had been me in Sarajevo instead of Bell. The profanity I would have unleashed upon being hit, however, would probably have ensured that the satellite feed was cut long before it reached London« (ibid., 17).

The technique of ironic juxtaposition used in this passage also exists between Ayres's two epigraphs. One is a Robert Capa quote (followed by the information that he was killed by a landmine in 1954): »The war correspondent has his stake – his life – in his own hands, and he can put it on this horse or that horse, or he can put it back in his pocket at the very last minute ... being allowed to be a coward, and not be executed for it, is

---

36 As Ayres writes in his preface: »Most war reporters are brave, selfless types – more interested in the news story at hand than their own physical discomfort and fear. Not me. Which is why the book is dedicated to those who find themselves running in the opposite direction to the action. Yes, *you* know who you are: my fellow cowards out there« (Ayres 2005, xi).

his torture.« This contrasts sharply with a remark that prepares for Ayres's own less-than-brave performance: »The events described in this book really happened. I wish they hadn't. Some conversations have been written from memory. (It's hard to take notes when you're running away).«

Ayres as narrator concedes with envy that not all journalists of his generation failed the great models. As described by Ayres, his colleague and competitor Oliver Poole (normally also stationed in Hollywood) wore his flak jacket with manly grace and delivered a flawless performance of the heroic type:

»I later saw a photograph of Oliver Poole as an embed. Shirtless beneath an unzipped Army flak vest, he was casually smoking a cigarette in front of a blackened mural of Saddam Hussein. To his right, an Iraqi truck was on fire. His Goa necklace, I noticed, was still intact. He looked good – dashing almost« (ibid., 251).

By contrast, the photo on the cover of his own book shows Ayres as a pale, short-sighted young man quite unsuitable for active ›service‹: His helmet does not fit, and his jacket seems much too big – an outfit appropriate for a ›war coward‹.

Ayres's notion of a typical war correspondent has not only been shaped by the real role models of his profession and their autobiographical texts, but also by fictional representations. Generally, Ayres claims to know war only from television, literature and cinema:

»War films were my only references, and gore-soaked scenes from *Saving Private Ryan*, *Three Kings* and *Apocalypse Now* flickered in my imagination like a private horror show. I saw Humvees and tank trenches; grenades and M-16s. And I remembered a line by Private Joker, the war correspondent in *Full Metal Jacket*: ›A day without blood is like a day without sunshine‹« (ibid., 120f.).

Ayres takes Graham Greene's *The Quiet American* with him to the front, a novel whose protagonist is himself a *Times* correspondent in the Indochina War:

»I reconsidered my reading list. Perhaps it was a bit on the heavy side. Graham Greene's *The Quiet American* was depressing the hell out of me. It was, after all, about a war-weary, opium-addicted and borderline suicidal *Times* correspondent in Indo-China, who keeps putting himself in mortal danger only to get just a single paragraph, if that, printed in the paper. I had reached the part where the hero's girlfriend (his marriage had failed) leaves him for a rich American« (ibid., 162).[37]

At the front, however, films prove the most significant influence on the journalist's and the soldiers' mutual perception: »The only reporters they'd ever seen, after all, were in the movies; and most of them were scumbags. Likewise, the only marines we'd ever seen were also in the movies; and they were mostly scumbags, too« (ibid., 201). One Marine in Ayres's unit even wants to re-enact a well-known scene from *Full Metal Jacket* with him (between Private Joker and a mad gunner in a helicopter),[38] and Ayres is – eventually – able to join in because he knows this film just as well as the soldier. The exchange between the Marine and the correspondent is presented as an extensive comic scene that reveals film as a significant frame for both men's behaviour and as a means to resolve their obvious communication problem:

>»Hey, media dude, you should do a story about me sometime.‹
[...]
›Oh, right, of course‹, I said. ›Can we do an interview later?‹
›No‹, he said, shaking his head. I noticed him ball his fists with frustration. ›That's not what you're supposed to say.‹
Then he repeated, at a dunce's pace, ›You ... should ... do ... a story about *me* sometime.‹ He gave me an expectant look – like a dog waiting for a stick to chase. I wondered what the hell was wrong with him.
›OK‹, I said, trying to resolve the issue. ›I *definitely* will.‹ I could feel the sun on the back of my neck, like a branding iron.
›Jesus CHRIST!‹ grunted the Marine. ›Ain't you never seen *Full Metal Jacket*?‹
[...]

---

37 For a discussion of Greene's novel see pp. 115-118.
38 For a discussion of the film see pp. 122-123. As a matter of fact, the scene in the helicopter was transferred to the film from a real reporter's book, Michael Herr's *Dispatches*: »»You guys ought do a story on me suntahm‹, the kid said. He was a helicopter gunner, six-three with an enormous head that sat in bad proportion to the rest of his body and a line of picket teeth that were always on show in a wet, uneven smile. [...] He was from Kilgore, Texas, and he was on his seventeenth consecutive month in-country. ›Why should we do a story about you?‹ ›Cause I'm so fuckin' good‹, he said ›'n' that ain' no shit, neither. Got me one hunnert 'n' fifty-se'en gooks kilt. 'N' fifty caribou.‹ He grinned and stanched the saliva for a second. ›Them're all certified‹, he added« (Herr 1978, 179).

There was a long, hot silence. The Marine's blue eyes, like pilot lights, continued to set me ablaze. Then I realized what I had to do. He wanted me to play the part of Private Joker, the fictitious war reporter.

›Why should we do a story about you?‹ I asked, triumphantly.

The knot in the Marine's brow unravelled. He beamed at the chance to deliver the next line. I almost passed out with relief.

›BECAUSE I'M SO FUCKING GOOD!‹ he shouted. Then he turned on his heels and high-fived a buddy behind him.

The two of them bellowed with laughter.

›*Shit* yeah!‹ said the Marine. ›I've *always* wanted to say that to a media dude‹«« (ibid., 187f.).

The scene shows that the mutual perceptions of correspondent and soldier are significantly shaped by cinematic representation, and it might suggest to Ayres's readers that their own perception, both of soldiers and correspondents, is also a product of such and other representations. Incidentally, Oliver Poole's memoirs of the war in Iraq include a similar reference to a war reporter in film and his relationship with the military:

»*We Were Soldiers*, a recent film starring Mel Gibson, tells the story of the 1965 battle between 450 Americans and two thousand Vietnamese in the la Drang Valley. It was an early and particularly brutal action in that war [...]. Among the fighting men was a reporter, Joe Galloway, who at the time worked for United Press International. In the film, as the Viet Cong break through American lines, he is depicted picking up a rifle and starting to fight. A large number of the men in 1st Battalion had seen the movie, as the scenes depicting the American soldiers training prior to their deployment in Vietnam had been shot at a 3rd Infantry Division base camp in Georgia. This had partly worked to my advantage. My arrival in the company just days before the invasion had been seen as a confirmation that what they were doing was important, that like the men at la Drang, their deeds would not be forgotten. However, it also meant that I was regularly asked when I was going to ›tool up‹ and join them in taking out some of the Hajji, as Galloway had been shown doing against the VC« (Poole 2003, 158).[39]

The image of the war correspondent seems inextricably bound up with representations and a tradition of these representations – for correspondents themselves, the military and the public.

Moving from performance to representation, this chapter has shown how these aspects are closely interwoven, both in the cultural perception of war correspondents, and in their actual practice. The memoirs quoted

---

39 The real Joe Galloway co-wrote his memoirs, on which the film is based, with Hal Moore: *We Were Soldiers Once ... and Young* (1992).

here indicate the general self-reflexivity of war correspondents, and they show which aspects of the war-journalistic habitus and field are perceived as pertinent by correspondents themselves for their performance and their perception by self and others: conceptions of the war correspondent as a hero or as a humanly challenged witness, an awareness of the media with which correspondents work and the media structures to which they are subjected, the relationship with the military and in particular the measures with which the military tries to restrict journalistic autonomy. Correspondents' memoirs reveal personal facets of their respective authors, but they are strongly focused on their professional lives.

For their historical outline, the subsequent chapters will also draw on self-representations. They lay their particular emphasis, however, on fictional representations in literature and film, which are treated as indices for the general cultural perception of war correspondents. A question to be taken up at the end of the book is whether fictional representations differ from memoirs in the aspects they emphasise. First of all, however, the focus in the following chapters will be on how stories, novels and films for cinema and television engage with the dominant perceptions of war correspondents during their respective time.

Chapter 3: Setting the Trend. Representations of the Golden Age

>»However, the war – when it came – suited me
very well, for I was able to sandwich it in very
nicely between the Cretan revolution, in which I
had been engaged since January, and the second
phase of the advance into the Sudan, for which I
was due on the Nile in early August«
(Frank Scudamore 1925, 183).

>»During the heat of the fight I was out in the
centre of the plain behind some rocks making
sketches of what was going on all round me, not
realising the dangerous position I was in. When I
found the troops falling back I also retreated
from my position in double-quick time. Dr. Stark
afterwards sent a sketch of me to my office
representing me hard at work«
(Melton Prior 1912, 290).

Self-Representations.
The War Correspondent as Adventurer

The second half of the 19th century is often referred to as a Golden Age
of war correspondence in which persistent images and modes of representation of the profession were generated. It is a well-known fact that
William Russell's dispatches from the Crimean War caused an early
media sensation, and as such they became a subject of representation
themselves. A cartoon in *Punch*, for instance, reacted to the wide attention that Russell's dispatch from Balaclava received among British
newspaper readers. It shows the »Enthusiasm of Paterfamilias on reading

the report in the *Times* of the Grand Charge of British Cavalry.«[1] Russell's admiring biographer Rupert Furneaux attributed this unprecedented success to Russell's style, which presented such vivid and dramatic impressions of the war that the readers in their armchairs were turned into ›witnesses‹ themselves:

»When Russell's letters were received from the Crimea their impact was terrific. Nothing like them had ever been written from the front before. For the first time the newspaper-reader was presented with a realistic and factual account not only of battle and siege, but of the everyday life in camp and base, previously available, if at all, only when the historian had completed his researches. Russell's particular brand of journalism lay in the descriptive letter, and in comparison with the later rush to the telegraph to get news home as speedily as possible, this more leisurely method gave far greater possibilities to a man who possessed the power to fully make use of this medium. To Russell was given the opportunity to break new ground – and he seized the occasion with both hands, writing letter after letter which enabled his readers to hear the thunder of battle and see the details of every tent and bivouac as they read« (Furneaux 1944, 11).

When Russell returned from the Crimea, he was a famous man and could profit from that fame: »After the war Russell's dispatches were published in book form, and while awaiting new battles to cover he went on a lecture tour« (Knightley 2004, 15).

Indeed, conditions were most favourable for the profession to flourish as soon as it had been invented. The second half of the 19th century was a time of many wars, especially for British correspondents who, apart from covering other conflicts worldwide, followed their ›own‹ troops into a whole array of imperial wars. Technological advances in transport (the railway and steamships) as well as communication made it possible for correspondents to reach wars in remote corners of the world and still to get their dispatches home in relatively short time, especially after the telegraph had become available. The first epigraph to this chapter conveys the image of a war correspondent almost embarrassed by the rich choice of wars to be covered and perplexed as to how they might all be accommodated in his tight schedule. Another factor responsible for the war reporter's rise to fame was the media system for which he worked, with a »rise of the popular press, the increasing use of the telegraph, and the tardy introduction of organised censorship. The newspaper expansion in the two major newspaper-reading countries was explosive«

---

1   The cartoon is reproduced in Hankinson's biography of Russell (1982, opposite 55).

(Knightley 2004, 43). Especially the British press, spurred by an increasing number of readers after the 1870s Education Reform,[2] had expanded dramatically and become a medium with considerable power to form public opinion. War reporting was particularly attractive for its readers; in a volume of his memoirs, Archibald Forbes notes »the popular appetite with what has come to be known ever since the Crimean times as ›War Correspondence‹« (Forbes 1871, 9). Dispatches from ongoing wars helped to sell the newspapers, which in turn invested a considerable amount of money in this branch of journalism. News agencies like Reuters also thrived in this climate.

Among his readers, the war journalist came to enjoy a public reputation as being »at once a chronicler and mentor, preceptor and guide, diplomat and adventurer, and even, on occasion, a warrior in his own right« (Hohenberg 1995, 41).[3] In the footsteps of William Russell and Archibald Forbes, the correspondent celebrities of the 19th century included Frank Vizetelly, George Warrington Steevens, Melton Prior, John Cameron, Frederic Villiers and Frank Scudamore, to name only a few. In the public perception and their own self-image, these journalists were heroes as much as the soldiers they accompanied, whose habitus they adopted and with whom, as was shown above (pp. 56-57), they were often closely affiliated. With troops of their own country, Victorian correspondents could share life in camp as well as the heat of battle, at a time when war was still widely perceived in terms of patriotism, honour and heroism. The Victorians were aware of the brutality of war and its human casualties, but they regarded war as a necessary means to pursue political aims. Engaging in a war was an opportunity to prove one's patriotism and, at the same time, one's capacity for ›manly‹ performance. War was a bloody but also glorious spectacle, and correspondents conveyed both aspects in their dispatches, their campaign books[4] and their memoirs. The

---

2 The number of newspapers »doubled between 1880 and 1900. During the Franco-Prussian War the *Daily News* trebled its circulation« (Knightley 2004, 43).

3 Rupert Furneaux's popular history of the Golden Age of war reporting is celebratory, announcing in its Foreword »the adventures of the men who made war sound so exciting that it appeared worth playing for the game's sake« (Furneaux 1964, 7).

4 Campaign books trace the history of a war and its fighting; the correspondent as persona is in the background or has retreated entirely. The narrative stance adopted oscillates between that of a participant and that of a historian. See, for example, *The Ashantee War* (1874) by the *Daily News'* Special Correspondent, Sir John F. Maurice, declared on its title page to be a »popular narrative« of that war, or Winston Churchill's *The River War*

following excerpt by the *Daily Graphic*'s war artist in the South African War, George Lynch, compares the war correspondent to the theatre critic watching war as a gripping performance:

»In stirring times the drama of life is to him like the first night of a play. There are no preconceived opinions for him to go by; he ought not to, at least, be influenced by any prejudices; and the account of the performance is to some extent like that of the dramatic critic, inasmuch as that the verdict of the public or of history has either to confirm or reverse his own judgment. There is a peculiar and unique fascination about this reading of contemporary history, as it grows and develops while one peers with straining eyes through one's glasses. There is something like a first night, too, about the way the critic views things« (Lynch 1903, xif.).

However, the role conception of the Victorian war correspondent entailed much more than viewing and depicting war because he also saw himself as a player in the performance, acting with the same patriotism, honour and heroism as the soldiers. Not least, an attitude of heroism was also spurred by the fact that the competition for scoops, between newspapers and individual correspondents, defined the correspondent's professional life. For good stories (or, in the case of war artists, good pictures) correspondents had to be close to the fighting, and when the fighting was over, they often took further risks to get their dispatches (or sketches) on the way ahead of their competitors.[5]

(1899). By contrast, Churchill's book about the South African War, *London to Ladysmith* (1900), is highly personalised since it is written in the ›letter‹ style of his original dispatches.

5   The risks for Victorian war artists specifically were acknowledged even in a contemporary scholarly publication on the history of the periodical press. It comments, among other perils, on the war artist's risk of being arrested as a spy: »When the great war of 1870, between France and Prussia, broke out, the illustrated newspapers had special artists on both sides, who encountered all sorts of hardships, and passed through all kinds of adventures in fulfilling their duties. Besides being frequently arrested as spies, and undergoing the privations of beleagured [sic] places, they had also to run the risk of shot and shell, and sometimes they were obliged to destroy their sketching materials under fear of arrest. One of them was in custody as a spy no less than eleven times during the war. The danger of being seen sketching or found with sketches in their possession was so great that on one occasion a special artist actually swallowed his sketch to avoid being taken up as a spy. Another purchased the largest book of cigarette papers he could obtain, and on them he made little sketches, prepared in case of danger to smoke them in the faces of his enemies« (Mason 1885, 331f.).

The adventurous nature of their profession, and not only that of war itself, was expressed in dispatches from the front and in memoirs, but also in public lectures or in sketches and photographs that displayed correspondents in heroic poses. With their depiction of adventure and patriotism in war, often in ›exotic‹ scenarios, the accounts of British war correspondents shared features with another popular genre of their time – the adventure fiction for young readers that also thrived after the Education Reform and the resulting increase in literacy:

»To cater for this growing young market, eager for adventure stories, various magazines were produced; the *Boy's Own Paper*, perhaps the most famous of all, appeared first in 1879. It was soon followed by a host of others such as the *Union Jack*, edited by George Alfred Henty, one-time war-correspondent of the *Standard*, *Sons of Britannia*, and the *Young Englishman*, all filled with heroic ›sun drenched, blood-stained prose‹. This love of adventure at second hand pervaded all classes and all ages and helped to create the many preconceived ideas of the late Victorians and Edwardians with regard to Imperial right, and the attitude to foreigners, especially natives.
To the reader in England, the most urgent priority was that every battle and every adventure was described by an eye-witness and the fact that the writer brought more of his personal adventures into the dispatch than actual news was neither here nor there« (Wilkinson-Latham 1979, 136f.).

The writing of adventure fiction and war correspondence seemed to stand in a natural affinity, not only in the case of the prolific Henty. As Phillip Knightley notes, public demand for war reports in the newspapers was »immense – providing they were written mainly as narratives of adventure, without too much political comment or moralising to interrupt the narrative« (Knightley 2004, 44). And, as Knightley goes on to observe, some correspondents at least were chosen by their papers because they had already proven to be good storytellers: »It is significant that two of the big-name correspondents of this period, the *London Daily News'* representative, Archibald Forbes, and Stephen Crane of the *New York Journal*, got their jobs because their editors had been impressed by their fictional descriptions of battles« (ibid.).

William Russell in the Crimean had not yet turned himself into the hero of his own texts, but his younger colleague and competitor Archibald Forbes did.[6] Already during the American Civil War it had become more common for newspaper correspondents to report »their own adventures and exploits as well as news of the fighting that they were sent to

---

6   See also John Simpson's comparison of these two correspondents, quoted on pp. 32-33.

cover« (Wilkinson-Latham 1979, 84), and from the 1870s it was custom-ary for correspondents of the British imperial wars to stage themselves as heroes:

»While the newspapermen were ready to face the dangers and hardships of campaigning to satisfy their editors, to produce enough stories of high adven-ture to earn their bonuses, they were also keen to relate their own adventures in published books. After every campaign in the late Victorian era, a large number of correspondents published their own vivid, but on occasion inaccurate, ac-count of the fighting« (ibid., 129).

One of the legendary feats of a Victorian war correspondent is Archibald Forbes's »ride of death« after the Battle of Ulundi in the Zulu War (1879),[7] occasioned, above all, by Forbes's sense of competition. Under great personal danger and hardships, Forbes rode to a telegraph station in order to be the first to let the British know about their troops' victory (and his own participation in the event). Forbes himself perceived this performance as a heroic service for the military and the public at home and would have liked to be decorated for his heroic action; his essay »My Campaign in Pall Mall« (1891) includes a bitter complaint that he was not awarded a medal. He received much praise and gratitude from an-other side, however. Since a war artist was no immediate rival (sketches could not be telegraphed), Forbes had taken a sketch by his friend Melton Prior with him, and the latter paid due respect to his colleague in his memoirs, since he thus also enjoyed a scoop in his own line of reporting: »Arrived in Maritzburg, he took post cart and rail for Durban, where he arrived in record time, very much done up. But he telegraphed his ac-count and posted my sketch, which arrived and was published in the *Il-lustrated London News* a clear week ahead of any other« (Prior 1912, 124).

Prior's reminiscences also do justice to his own daring, for instance when he narrates how he took his sketch of the Battle of Ulundi. As pre-sented in the text, the opportunity to take a good sketch made Prior oblivious of his precarious situation until it was almost too late:

»I had flames on three sides of me, but I cared not. I was so delighted to be able to obtain a drawing of this savage King's residence, that I only thought of the work, and did not know that Forbes and Beresford had left me to it.
I may have been some four or five minutes sketching, when I saw some black object pop up above the palisade on my left. What can it be? I thought to my-

---

7   On the incident, see also Wilkinson-Latham (1979, 154f.) and Knightley (2004, 55).

self, and clambering up, I actually saw a real live Zulu, with spears and shield. Then I suddenly took the situation: I was alone with fire on three sides of me and the Zulu running to get round the courtyards, so as, if possible, to cut off my retreat.
With sketch-book in one hand and pencil in the other, I started on a run for my life. Great Scot! how I ran to try and get out of this frightful trap« (ibid., 121).

In this self-representation the first-person pronoun occurs densely; the passage is focalised through the experiencing (rather than the narrating) self and reads like a lively re-performance of Prior's adventure. In another passage too Prior depicts himself in the middle of a fight. This is done in a dramatic scene of a kind one might also find in contemporary adventure fiction:

»All those who were not actually engaged in fighting were ordered to keep as low down as possible, and I was doing so kneeling, when I discovered the Rev. Gore, who was Principal Chaplain to the Forces, was by my side.
›It's very warm, Prior‹, he said.
To which I readily agreed, as a bullet banged into one of our native allies close to us and rolled him over. By the way, it was very funny to see these men lying flat on the ground, with their shields covering their backs.
Another bullet killed a horse behind us and made him jump at least three feet in the air. Then all at once there appeared to be a perfect hailstorm of bullets in our direction, and we both wriggled on our knees, until one in particular passed between us with a nasty ›phew‹, and my friend exclaimed, ›My God, Prior, that was close.‹
This sort of thing went on all the time, until I heard the Zulus were said to be preparing to rush one of our corners« (ibid., 118).

Prior's flippant remark about natives lying ›funnily‹ flat on the ground exposes the racist ideology which the Empire often engendered and which also marks the texts of many Victorian correspondents. In general, however, Prior and his colleagues were not blind to the human cost of war. Prior describes a massacred British regiment with deep compassion, not hiding the cruelty and indignity of the men's deaths:

»In all the campaigns I have been in I have not witnessed a scene more horrible. I have seen the dead and dying on a battlefield by hundreds and thousands, but to come suddenly on the spot where the slaughtered battalion of the 24th Regiment and others were lying at Isandlwana was appalling. Here I saw not the bodies, but the skeletons, of men whom I had seen in life and health, some of whom I had known well, mixed up with the skeletons of oxen and horses, with wagons overthrown on their sides, all in the greatest confusion, showing how furious had been the attack of the enemy. [...] Skeletons of men lay on the open ground, bleaching under a tropical sun, along miles of country. The individuals could only be recognised by such things as a ring on a finger-bone, a letter or knife, an armlet or neck-chain (which, considered as a fetish, the Zulus would not touch). This identification could only be made with much difficulty, for either the hands of the enemy or the beaks and claws of vultures tearing up the corpses, had, in numberless cases, so mixed up the bones of the dead that the skull of one man, or bones of a leg or arm, now lay with parts of the skeleton of another« (ibid., 101f.).[8]

However, for the war artist such sad occasions are also material for a potential scoop, as Prior openly admits. He hurriedly draws sketches of the field and rushed his servant off to post them:

»My best horse was saddled, and my man, with my sketches in the regulation red envelope of the office, was only waiting for daylight to start and gallop to Landman's Drift to save the post, which he succeeded in doing, and my sketches were the only ones that appeared in London in connection with that sad event« (ibid., 107).

Prior's memoirs cover his experiences in many theatres of war, from the Ashanti War in 1873/4 to the war in South Africa (1899-1902). In the latter he experienced, among others, the siege of Ladysmith, which provided him with a special opportunity to emphasise the sense of community and comradeship among the correspondents. One of his colleagues, G.W. Steevens, caught typhoid fever and died during the siege. Prior builds a monument to his esteemed colleague when he describes how gallantly Steevens accepted his death verdict:

»With less effort than one would have thought under such circumstances, Steevens gave his final instructions to [the war artist] Maud and his final wishes, and then said, ›Well, Maud, we have been very good chums, and if I am going to die let's have our final drink together. Get that last bottle of champagne that I have reserved for the relief of Ladysmith.‹ Maud assured me it was awful, but he opened the bottle, and pouring out two tumblers gave one to Steevens. He, raising himself as well as he could, touched Maud's glass with

---

8   See also the detailed descriptions of injuries and scenes in field hospitals in Victorian correspondents' memoirs, for instance Villiers (1921, I, 32): »As he [a soldier] lifted his head a moonbeam fell upon a sight I shall never forget. His face – a mere pulp – had been crushed by a fragment of shell and was as black as a negro's with clotted gore.« Or see George Lynch's depiction of soldier's injuries in the South African War (Lynch 1903, 10f.) and his entire chapter on »The Aftermath of War.« For the Russo-Japanese war, see Glossop's depiction of a Japanese field hospital (Glossop 1907, 100-103).

his, saying, ›Well, goodbye, old chap‹; he emptied the tumbler, while Maud, as he afterwards assured me, positively could not swallow his. But Steevens insisted, and thus these two chums bade each other goodbye. Steevens only lived three hours afterwards« (ibid., 301).

Steevens, who worked for the *Daily Mail*, was appreciated by his readers and his colleagues as a man »of distinguished literary artistry« (Bullard 1974, ix). He had become famous a few years before his death with his dispatches from and later his memoirs of Kitchener's campaign against the Dervish Empire that had arisen from the Mahdi rebellion and of the subsequent re-conquest of the Sudan (1896-98). As Steevens remembers in his book about the campaign, he embarked on it as an inexperienced novice, with far too much luggage and no knowledge about the working conditions that would await him in the Sudan.[9] Despite this lack of previous experience, however, Steevens's dispatches and his later memoirs had a high appeal for their readers.

Kitchener's Sudan campaign was one of the most prestigious expeditions in the British imperial wars since it not only defeated the Dervishes, as the Mahdi's followers were referred to, but also avenged the tragic death of General Gordon at Khartoum in 1885, which had caused much concern among the British public. It provided an exemplary stage for the war correspondent to present the war and himself to a highly expectant audience. As Trevor Royle writes: »In no other 19th-century campaign is the golden age of the war correspondent better expressed than in Kitchener's re-conquest of the Sudan. It was far away, romantic and glamorous« (Royle 1987, 41).[10] It therefore attracted a particularly large number of correspondents, many of whom published books about the campaign, such as Steevens's *With Kitchener to Khartum* (1899), Bennett Burleigh's *Sirdar and Khalifa or the Re-Conquest of the Soudan* (1898) and Winston Churchill's *The River War* (1899).

Steevens's rendering of the troops' fighting is highly dynamic, as in the following depiction of the Battle of Atbara, where the narration even switches from the correspondent's perspective to the perception and emotions of the soldiers. This is a device borrowed from fiction in order to let the readers share the perception of the fighters whose excitement is, furthermore, conveyed through shifts into the present tense and a fragmentary syntax. The passage culminates in an emphatic outburst of triumph:

---

9 See Steevens (1899), Chapter 4: »The Correspondent's Progress.« On Steevens see also Royle (1987, 40-77).

10 On the popularity of the Sudan campaign see also Wilkinson-Latham (1979, 186f.).

»Forward and forward, more swishing about them and more crashing from them. Now they were moving, always without hurry, down a gravelly incline. Three men went down without a cry at the very foot of the Union Jack, and only one got to his feet again; the flag shook itself and still blazed splendidly. Next, a supremely furious gust of bullets, and suddenly the line stood fast. Before it was a loose low hedge of dry camel-thorn – the zariba, the redoubtable zariba. That it? A second they stood in wonder, and then, ›Pull it away‹, suggested somebody. Just half-a-dozen tugs, and the impossible zariba was a gap and a scattered heap of brushwood. Beyond is a low stockade and trenches; but what of that? Over and in! Hurrah, hurrah, hurrah!« (Steevens 1899, 147).

Since Steevens, like his colleagues, shared the life of the soldiers, he was able to empathise with them. The extent to which he felt part of the military community, whether in camp, during marches or battle, is reflected in his frequent use of the first-person plural, for example in his chapter on the Battle of Omdurman, where the occasional use of the second person also includes the reader into the collective perception:

»We waited half an hour or so, and then the sudden bugle called us to our feet. ›Advance‹, it cried; ›to Omdurman!‹ added we. [...]
Movement was slow, since the leading brigades had to wait till the others had gone far enough inland to take their positions. We passed over a corner of the field of fire, and saw for certain what awful slaughter we had done. The bodies were not in heaps – bodies hardly ever are; but they spread evenly over acres and acres. And it was very remarkable, if you remembered the Atbara, that you saw hardly a black; nearly all the dead had the high forehead and taper cheeks of the Arab« (ibid., 268f.).

The British public's attention for Kitchener's campaign in the Sudan was even topped by the interest aroused by the war against the Boers. The South African War has been referred to as Britain's first mass media war that attracted all famous correspondents of its time and a number of new ones who wanted to make their reputation there since the demand for war reporting had increased further with new mass circulation newspapers such as the *Daily Mail* and the new medium of film.[11] The correspondents of this war

»brought back to Britain in their dispatches a new kind of journalism which was to change the focus of their reporting. The human interest side of war evolved and became as important as the tactical details of battle. The likes of

---

11 See Farrar (1998, 6). On the use of the film camera in the South African War, see p. 41.

Edgar Wallace at the *Daily Mail* and Winston Churchill at the *Morning Post* became household names in Britain.

To the press this period had demonstrated that wars sold newspapers. However, to the military, the war correspondent had become a nuisance and a security risk in an area it regarded as its own« (Farrar 1998, 6).

The British military's censorship in the South African War was stricter than during earlier wars, but correspondents still found plenty of opportunity to prove their mettle and to present themselves as men of action. In 1901, the popular periodical *Pall Mall* published »The Life of a War Correspondent«, a short account of his experiences by an Australian journalist accredited with the British troops, A.G. Hales. Hales commented on his everyday life in camp, complained about censorship, and depicted his stress once fighting began. Above all, this correspondent too wished to convey the excitement of war and his own daring, hectic performance »in the thick of a battle«, for which he switched into the present tense and included the reader through use of the second person. Indeed, when he »skirmishes« for details, the correspondent's own work is described in martial terms:

»Off you scuttle again, for you *must* see the onward rush of the troops if you mean to do justice to your report. You suddenly find yourself in the thick of it without knowing why. You see fellows fall, and see them picked up and carried away. Then you notice the general's aide-de-camp galloping like a streak of flame across the field; if you happen to know him, and he is a good fellow, you dig the spurs into your horse's flank, and gallop stride for stride with him for a little way, asking him for any news he may feel disposed to give you. Then once more you visit right and left front in turn, and note what effect our guns are having, also what the enemy's guns are doing to our side. Having got through this lot, you ride back to the ambulance waggons and have a chat there, then down to the hospital tents, where the surgeons are busy on their grim tasks. Having picked up all that is lying around loose in the shape of general information, you skirmish round for details, and get hold of non-coms. and privates, and so pick up many an unconsidered trifle, little acts of heroism that the men speak of whilst their blood is hot; next day they won't talk of such things at all« (Hales 1901, 208).

Edgar Wallace, the later author of many thrillers and plays, clashed with the military for smuggling a report past censorship in 1902. The report was badly researched but became a big scoop, although it lost Wallace his right to work as a war correspondent for the rest of his life.[12] Winston Churchill, who acted both as an officer and a correspondent (writing his

---

12 On Wallace's career as a war correspondent see also Royle (1987, 79-108).

dispatches in the form of ›private letters‹), reported the South African War for the *Morning Post* and became a hero when his account of his spectacular escape from a Boer prison in Pretoria was released.[13] Already well-known for his books about previous campaigns, Churchill now became »the idol of the public, the star war correspondent and the subject of a popular music hall song, sung by T.E. Dunville, the Lancashire music-hall comedian: ›You've heard of Winston Churchill / This is all I have to say / He's the latest and the greatest / Correspondent of the day‹« (Wilkinson-Latham 1979, 258).

In his novel about the siege of Ladysmith, Giles Foden pays tribute to the importance war correspondents had in shaping the public image of this historical event, also turning it into a media event. *Ladysmith* (1999) is based on books by several of the correspondents who were besieged in Ladysmith, including the unlucky G.W. Steevens and Henry W. Nevinson,[14] as well as some reporters who joined General Buller's relief expedition, like the flamboyant Churchill and William Dickson, cameraman for the Biograph company. These correspondents also appear as characters in the novel, which includes the stories of Churchill's escape from the Boers (also reprinting his famous account in the *Morning Post*) and Steevens's tragic death (including the champagne drinking). Most important, however, are the correspondents' different reactions to war and its mediation. Significant parts of the action are focalised through the correspondents' perceptions, in particular that of ›Nevinson‹ and ›the Biographer‹, both of whom are keenly aware of the changes in war corresponding. The Biographer is ever conscious of working in a new medium which the other reporters do not take seriously or regard with suspicion,[15] and Nevinson knows that modernisation has also affected his trade:

---

13 Churchill's dispatches are collected, among others, in Churchill (1972), which includes the account of his escape (178-189); it is also recounted in Churchill's *London to Ladysmith* (1900).

14 Nevinson narrated his experiences in Ladysmith in *Changes and Chances* (1923, Chapter XI).

15 »Some of the other correspondents, like Churchill and Atkins, had managed to get themselves a place at the Captain's table with Buller's staff, but the Biographer had not been admitted to this inner circle. He suspected it was because his type of journalism was not taken seriously. Some said it was unnatural to fix life's transitory moments in the way that he did. Well, time would tell whose record of Buller's expedition was the most lasting« (Foden 1999, 27f.).

»Now all was facts and evidence. And moving photography. Other members of the press corps in Ladysmith had heard how a representative of the Biograph Company was headed for the Cape with General Buller, and sneered accordingly; but Nevinson had kept his councel [sic]. He could see it had potential, this new art. Or was it a science?« (Foden 1999, 42).

The characters' awareness of modernisation underlines Foden's presentation of the South African War as a watershed experience that destabilised traditional perceptions of war and Britain's imperial greatness. Arguably, Foden's take on the South African War through the point of view of war correspondents is motivated by the circumstance that *Ladysmith* was written at a time when the mediation of war had entered a new phase of public awareness after the Gulf War of 1991 and Bosnia.

Fictional representations of war correspondents were also produced in the 19th century and already had a strong media-reflexive element.[16] The next section takes a look at two examples written by widely read authors of the time, Sir Arthur Conan Doyle and Rudyard Kipling, both of whom engage critically with the popular perception of war correspondents at their time.

Victorian War Correspondents in Fictional Representation. Doyle and Kipling

Sir Arthur Conan Doyle, famous for his Sherlock Holmes stories that appeared in the *Strand Magazine*,[17] wrote much of his fiction for the periodical market. In the late 19th century, this market had a great demand for stories that would appeal to the general readership, and »The Three

---

16 See also p. 9 on the topicality of newspaper fiction at the end of the 19th century.

17 In 1903, the Strand Magazine published H.G. Wells's science-fiction story »The Land Ironclads«, in which a perplexed war correspondent witnesses the introduction of armoured vehicles to an imaginary war inspired by the conflict in South Africa. The war is won by those who have science and technological progress on their side: Their gigantic, ironclad machines anticipate tanks and defeat their opponents without the least effort. Even the war correspondent is obliged to surrender to them: »»Manhood *versus* Machinery‹ occured to him as a suitable headline. Journalism curdles all one's mind to phrases« (Wells 1966, 137).

Correspondents« (1896),[18] which originally appeared in *The Windsor Magazine*, provided precisely such reading matter. The story emphasises the adventurous nature of war reporting and, above all, the exciting competition between its characters. Furthermore, it exemplifies that information about correspondents' equipment and routine in the field – of the kind also depicted in their memoirs – was likewise of interest to the readers Doyle had in mind for this story. Its very beginning specifies typical props of the profession (such as field-glass, revolver and water bottle), and we also learn that the three correspondents are under hard pressure from their editors: »»What *would* our editors say if we were late for the action?‹« (Doyle 1929, 188). Later, readers are told how correspondents send only very condensed telegrams and how these are then spelt out by their editors at home (ibid., 194f.). The story has a contemporary setting with which Doyle was familiar himself since he had recently covered the early stage of Kitchener's campaign in the Sudan as a correspondent for the *Westminster Gazette*. Frank Scudamore's memoirs include an anecdote about Doyle's spell in the Sudan that illustrates his knowledge of certain details also specified in his story, from the habitus of seasoned correspondents to the difficulties of riding a camel. Scudamore here emphasises the humorous rather than adventurous nature of their experiences:

»In 1896 my friend E.F. Knight and I (with one or two other correspondents) escorted Sir Arthur Conan Doyle and the late Sir Julian Corbett on a camel ride journey from Asswân, where is the First Cataract to Wadi Halfa, thirty miles south of which place begins the turbulent water of the Second, or greatest, of the six Cataracts of the Nile. [...] I had done it before many times during the Gordon Relief Expedition of 1884-85. But to all my companions the ride was a novel experience. To ›Dogger‹ Knight [...], the difficulties of our mountain paths were small beer. [...] But Doyle and Corbett – who declared that till then they had neither of them ever slept out of a comfortable bed beneath a well-planned ceiling – both found the journey somewhat trying. However, they endured all hardships with most genial good humour, and while neither of them was in his first youth, were certainly among the most promising novices I have ever known. [...] As a rule I led the caravan, with a Bishari guide, and usually Sir Arthur Conan Doyle followed immediately behind me. Riding a-camel back, on a native saddle – which is something like a gravy dish – must have been irksome to a man unaccustomed, and somewhat bulky, but he took all happenings in good part. Generally he sang, and we all helped with the chorus. [...] From my position in advance, I would hear the burden of ›Blow the man down‹, or ›Whisky Johnny, whisky‹, suddenly broken by a crash, and looking

---

18 The story is also mentioned in Steinsieck's discussion of military-media relations in the 19th century (2007, 217).

back would see Doyle's camel prone on the track, with the great novelist sitting on the beast's head and still singing blithely« (Scudamore 1925, 101-103).

The three fictional correspondents in Doyle's story work for major London dailies and are waiting for their first fight. They have a Reuters correspondent ahead of them, but they know that their competitors from the penny press are well behind. Mortimer and Scott are hard-boiled veterans who have, between them, covered all important campaigns of their day. The third man, Anerley, is a novice to the profession, and in contrast to Doyle he is a real youngster whom the other two initiate into the secrets of their trade. The story's plot and point revolve around the professional rivalry between the three men:

»Either would have sacrificed himself to help his companion, but either would also have sacrificed his companion to help his paper. Never did a jockey yearn for a winning mount as keenly as each of them longed to have a full column in a morning edition whilst every other daily was blank. They were perfectly frank about the matter. Each professed himself ready to steal a march on his neighbour, and each recognized that the other's duty to his employer was far higher than any personal consideration« (Doyle 1929, 190f.).

Naively, Anerly suggests that the three men could pool their news instead of working against each other, but his colleagues react to this breach of their usual practice and their self-image as individualists with »an expression of genuine disgust upon their faces«:

»›Why, it would take away the whole glory of the profession!‹ cried Scott. ›At present the smartest man gets his stuff first on the wires. What inducement is there to be smart if we all share and share alike.‹
›And at present the man with the best equipment has the best chance‹, remarked Mortimer, glancing across at the shot-silk polo ponies and the cheap little Syrian grey [which belongs to Anerley]. ›That is the fair reward of foresight and enterprise. Every man for himself, and let the best man win‹« (ibid., 195f.).

The novice is instructed accordingly: »›My dear Anerley, I tell you frankly that if you are going to handicap yourself with scruples you may just as well be in Fleet Street as in the Soudan. [...] Do what you can and how you can, and be first on the wires‹« (ibid., 197). In this spirit, when the group are attacked by dervishes and young Anerley receives a wound, his colleagues rush off to the nearest telegraph station to report the incident:

»›Sorry to leave you. We'll be lucky now if we are in time for the morning editions.‹ Scott was tightening his girth as he spoke.

›We'll put in our wire that you have been hurt, so your people will know why they don't hear from you. If Reuter or the evening pennies come up, don't give the thing away. Abbas will look after you, and we'll be back to-morrow afternoon. Bye-bye!‹« (ibid., 205).

But the young man has learnt his lesson. Although seriously injured, he manages to outrun the two veterans on one of the enemy's fast camels and lands the scoop himself in what is a typical surprise ending of the popular magazine story of the time. Doyle uses the adventure and the topicality of war corresponding to provide entertainment for his readers and, at the same time, presents a satire of the war correspondent as a social icon and the dubious ethics of a highly competitive news business.

A more complex and serious treatment of the contemporary war correspondent is found in Rudyard Kipling's novel *The Light That Failed*. It was published in its final form in 1891[19] and also capitalised on the contemporary popularity of journalists in general and war correspondents in particular. At the same time, it intertwines this subject matter with a reflection on the purpose of art, another fashionable topic at the time. Kipling, himself an experienced journalist and a writer intrigued with war and the soldier's experience, takes up existing myths about correspondents and weaves them into a story about *fin de siècle* London bohemia that includes an unhappy love story between his protagonist and a woman artist. As an artist novel, the book (which was Kipling's first attempt at writing a novel after the great success of his early short stories) is considered flawed by some critics,[20] but it is relevant in our context since Kipling's main character, Dick Heldar, is a war artist. Through this protagonist, who becomes a great illustrator of the realities of war, the novel makes a statement in favour of an art committed to realism and against mere aestheticism, that is, a statement located in the lively contemporary debate about the function of art. With this mixture of two topical themes, Kipling's novel became popular with contemporary readers and was also read by correspondents. Frederic Villiers, the probable model for Kipling's fictional war correspondent, refers to the novel in a manner which proves how well-known it still was in the early 20th century: »I recovered from my attack of fever just in time to see a brush with

---

19 The first version was published serially in Lipincott's *Monthly Magazine* in 1890; it was shorter and had a happy ending. My discussion of the novel is based on an earlier article (Korte 2006a).

20 See, for example, Coustillas (1986, 127).

Osman Digna and to be in the fight depicted by Rudyard Kipling in *The Light That Failed*« (Villiers 1921, I, 307).[21]

Villiers was one of the famous war artists of the 19th century. His memoirs, published after a long and distinguished career that continued into the 20th century, emphasise adventure in their very title: *Villiers: His Five Decades of Adventure*. Indeed, an expectation of heroic adventure had brought Villiers to the profession in the first place. During his first campaign in the Balkans (1876), Villiers accompanied one of the idols of his youth, Archibald Forbes, and tried to equip himself adequately (and with a certain performativity) for the adventures in store for him with the legendary correspondent:

»My first thought was to find Archibald Forbes, who was already en route to the front, for I felt that if I met that splendid fellow he would tell me how to set about becoming a war artist at once. Was he not the hero I had worshiped since a boy, to me the central figure of Sedan, Gravelotte, and Le Bourget? I added to my outfit riding boots, spurs and a moderate-sized bulldog revolver to prove myself in his eyes, directly he saw me, a determined young fellow out for adventure« (ibid., 15f.).

The war action of Kipling's novel takes place in the Sudan, but a few years before Kitchener's famous campaign, around the time of the Gordon relief expedition. Britain had occupied Egypt in 1882 and thus had to deal with the unruly Egyptian province of the Sudan, where a rebellion formed around a charismatic leader, the Mahdi. By 1884, the garrison of Khartoum was the last British outpost in the Sudan, and General Gordon (who had previously been governor of the Sudan) was besieged there by the Mahdi and his followers. The Nile Expedition arrived two days after Khartoum had fallen to the enemy and Gordon had been killed. The affair caused great concern in the British public and still occupied a prominent place in public memory when Kipling's novel was published.

Dick Heldar, an amateur artist, is discovered for his profession during his service in the Nile Expedition. While he is sketching scenes for his own pleasure, his talent is noted by the veteran correspondent Torpenhow, who knows all the tricks of his trade like the experienced correspondents in Doyle's story:

»Among the seniors – those who knew every shift and change in the perplexing postal arrangements, the value of the seediest, weediest Egyptian garron offered for sale in Cairo or Alexandria, who could talk a telegraph-clerk into amiability

---

21 Indeed, *The Light That Failed* was still popular enough to be turned into a film melodrama in 1939 (dir. William Wellman).

and soothe the ruffled vanity of a newly appointed Staff-officer when Press regulations became burdensome – was the man in the flannel shirt, the black-browed Torpenhow. He represented the Central Southern Syndicate in the campaign, as he had represented it in the Egyptian war, and elsewhere« (Kipling 1964, 18).

Torpenhow is possibly modelled after Archibald Forbes, even though the latter was no longer active during the 1880s.[22] Torpenhow becomes Heldar's mentor and gets him a job as war artist for his syndicate. Heldar soon builds himself a reputation, but the beginning of his career is also already the beginning of its tragic end. During his first professional assignment, Heldar, like his more experienced colleagues, proves an exemplary Victorian correspondent since he is not a distanced spectator but an active participant in the fight. As a result of this participation, however, he is injured in the head; the injury hurts his optic nerve and will eventually blind him. Readers are enabled to share Heldar's experience of the decisive event when the text renders his perceptions in the midst of fighting, fragmented yet also sharply focused on details:

»Dick was conscious that somebody had cut him violently across his helmet, that he had fired his revolver into a black, foam-flecked face which forthwith ceased to bear any resemblance to a face, and that Torpenhow had gone down under an Arab whom he had tried to ›collar low‹, and was turning over and over with his captive, feeling for the man's eyes. The doctor was jabbing at a venture with a bayonet, and a helmetless soldier was firing over Dick's shoulder. The flying grains of powder stung his cheek. It was to Torpenhow that Dick turned by instinct. The representative of the Central Southern Syndicate had shaken himself clear of his enemy, and rose, wiping his thumb on his trousers. The Arab, both hands to his forehead, screamed aloud, then snatched up his spear and rushed at Torpenhow, who was panting under shelter of Dick's revolver. Dick fired twice, and the man dropped limply. His upturned face lacked one eye. The musketry-fire redoubled, but cheers mingled with it. The rush had failed, and the enemy were flying. If the heart of the square were a shambles, the ground beyond was a butcher's shop. Dick thrust his way forward between the maddened men. The remnant of the enemy were retiring, as the few – the very few – English cavalry rode down the laggards.
Beyond the lines of the dead, a broad bloodstained Arab spear cast aside in the retreat lay across a stump of scrub, and beyond this again the illimitable dark

---

22 On Kipling's great admiration for Forbes see Wilkinson-Latham (1979, 117). That Villiers was the model for Heldar and admired Forbes in his youth (see above), also makes it probable that Torpenhow was inspired by the famous Forbes, who remained popular in the 1880s and 1890s through his memoirs and other books.

levels of the desert. The sun caught the steel and turned it into a savage red disk. Some one behind him was saying, ›Ah, get away, you brute!‹ Dick raised his revolver and pointed towards the desert. His eye was held by the red splash in the distance, and the clamour about him seemed to die down to a very far-away whisper, like the whisper of a level sea« (ibid., 27f.).

In this action-filled depiction of battle, the fact that Heldar is aware of war's brutality, both on his own and the enemy's side, is typical of the Victorian attitude to war as already found in correspondents' memoirs. But the representation in Kipling's novel is more artistically shaped, for instance in its attention to the motif of eyes and visual perception at the very moment when Heldar's capacity to see, on which his whole career and life depends, is damaged. Ironically, in the very moment that determines his own future blindness, Heldar notices how one of the enemies loses an eye, and as a visual artist, he has an eye not only for the butchery of war, but also the aesthetic effect of the blood-stained spear in the blood-red sun. Despite this accent on visuals, however, the passage also conveys the overall effect of the war artist fully involved in the action, also with his whole body.

It is the combination of Heldar's intense participation in and perception of reality, and his eye for pictorial effect which makes him a successful war artist, and *only* military subjects appear to provide him with material on which he can exert his talent to his own and others' satisfaction. For Heldar, art and war go together, and representing war gives his life purpose. The novel makes it quite obvious that this mediator of war not only serves »the British public's bestial thirst for blood« (ibid., 60) – as the novel refers to the mass readership's greed for news of war – but also his own personal need for subject matter on which he can exert his talent and an activity through which he can quench his thirst for virile adventure: »There was colour, light, and motion, without which no man has much pleasure in living« (ibid., 283).

The blind Dick so much longs for the excitement of war and the company of his correspondent ›brothers‹ that he wants to be present when his former colleagues (many equipped with the nicknames of old campaigners) return to the Sudan. The hectic and elated manner in which they prepare for this return intensifies the sense of Heldar's loss:

»Dick was led into a chair. He heard the rustle of the maps, and the talk swept forward, carrying him with it. Everybody spoke at once, discussing Press censorships, railway-routes, transport, water-supply, the capacities of generals, – these in language that would have horrified a trusting public, – ranting, asserting, denouncing, and laughing at the top of their voices. There was the glorious certainty of war in the Sudan at any moment. The Nilghai said so, and it was

well to be in readiness. The Keneu had telegraphed to Cairo for horses; Cassavetti had stolen a perfectly inaccurate list of troops that would be ordered forward, and was reading it out amid profane interruptions, and the Keneu introduced to Dick some man unknown who would be employed as war artist by the Central Southern Syndicate. ›It's his first outing‹, said the Keneu. ›Give him some tips – about riding camels.‹ [...]
›I'll give you one piece of advice‹, Dick answered, moving toward the door. ›If you happen to be cut over the head in a scrimmage, don't guard. Tell the man to go on cutting. You'll find it cheapest in the end. Thanks for letting me look in‹« (ibid., 205).

Heldar's final remark, which is both sad and cynical in its use of the word ›look‹, anticipates that Heldar, having lost the purpose of his life, seeks an honourable way to commit suicide. Under great hardships he follows his colleagues to the Sudan, remembering his former glorious and satisfactory existence:

»There was colour, light, and motion, without which no man has much pleasure in living. This night there remained for him only one more journey through the darkness that never lifts to tell a man how far he has travelled. Then he would grip Torpenhow's hand again – Torpenhow, who was alive and strong, and lived in the midst of the action that had once made the reputation of a man called Dick Heldar: not in the least to be confused with the blind, bewildered vagabond who seemed to answer to the same name. Yes, he would find Torpenhow, and come as near to the old life as might be« (ibid., 283f.).

Eventually Heldar does find the death he desires, a warrior's death, in Torpenhow's arms:

»»No. Put me, I pray, in the forefront of the battle.‹ Dick turned his face to Torpenhow and raised his hand to set his helmet straight, but, miscalculating the distance, knocked it off. Torpenhow saw that his hair was grey on the temples, and that his face was the face of an old man.
›Come down, you damned fool! Dickie, come off!‹
And Dickie came obediently, but as a tree falls, pitching sideways from the Bisharin's saddle at Torpenhow's feet. His luck had held to the last, even to the crowning mercy of a kindly bullet through his head.
Torpenhow knelt under the lee of the camel, with Dick's body in his arms« (ibid., 291f.).

Kipling's portrayal of a late-Victorian war artist incorporates many elements one also finds in the self-representations of contemporary war correspondents: the desire to be with the troops and share the excitement of war, the exhilaration of that participation and, at the same time, an awareness of war's inhumanity that is, however, accepted as a matter of fact and recorded with no sense of moral indignation. The circumstance that Heldar capitalises on war as an artist also disturbs neither Kipling's protagonist nor his narrator. If any doubts are associated with the reporting of war, these are directed not against the correspondent but a war-greedy public whom he serves like a soldier:

»With the soldiers sweated and toiled the correspondents of the newspapers, and they were almost as ignorant as their companions. But it was above all things necessary that England at breakfast should be amused and thrilled and interested, whether Gordon lived or died, or half the British army went to pieces in the sands. The Sudan campaign was a picturesque one, and lent itself to vivid word-painting. Now and again a ›Special‹ managed to get slain, – which was not altogether a disadvantage to the paper that employed him, – and more often the hand-to-hand nature of the fighting allowed of miraculous escapes which were worth telegraphing home at eighteenpence the word. [...]
The syndicate did not concern itself greatly with criticisms of attack and the like. It supplied the masses, and all it demanded was picturesqueness and abundance of detail; for there is more joy in England over a soldier who insubordinately steps out of square to rescue a comrade than over twenty generals slaving even to baldness at the gross details of transport and commissariat« (ibid., 18f.).

Although Kipling here draws a highly critical image of the contemporary press system and how it caters to the taste of a mass audience, the image of the heroic, and war-addicted, correspondent is drawn with sympathy. Dick Heldar is a tragic hero of an age in which war was considered a manly and honourable pursuit and war correspondents were perceived as heroic performers in the theatre of war. Kipling represents the correspondent as an individual who finds the purpose of his life in the pursuit of war and its depiction for others, another image familiar from correspondents' memoirs of the time. Indeed, *The Light That Failed* draws on many of the elements which correspondents themselves foreground in their self-representations, but as a character in fiction Dick Heldar comes across as a more complex figure whose immersion in the business of war depiction is interwoven with his personal tragedy. As far as war correspondence in general is concerned, however, the novel still largely represents the conditions of a Golden Age of adventure and relative autonomy for correspondents.

As mentioned above (p. 48), the end of this Golden Age, caused primarily by strict censorship, was already diagnosed by some correspondents when Kipling's novel was published. The South African War increased correspondents' concerns about military control, and the Russo-Japanese War (1904-05) was noted for its particularly strict censorship on the Japanese side which, as Greg McLaughlin claims, became the »blueprint for modern military censorship«:

»The American journalist and novelist, Jack London, went to report the war with ›gorgeous conceptions‹ of the war correspondent, based on the romantic accounts of journalists who reported General Gordon's fall at Khartoum in the Sudanese uprising in 1885. London became a war correspondent to ›get thrills‹ but instead he and the small contingent of journalists who made the journey to Tokyo found themselves up against nothing but ›delays and vexations‹; a vast military bureaucracy that could not see that journalists could help promote the cause« (McLaughlin 2002, 55).

In this war, British and other Western correspondents were not participants but mere observers, which made it difficult for them to perform according to a heroic template. Nevertheless, traces of perceiving war as a glorious spectacle and a stage for heroism survive even here, for instance in a depiction of the Battle of Port Arthur by Ellis Ashmead-Bartlett, who was later to become one of the prominent reporters of the First World War. Even though the fighting with modern weapons rendered many traditional fighting methods obsolete, Ashmead-Bartlett described the battle in the established mould of a theatrical piece:

»The great assaults on Port Arthur could not have been better witnessed had they been mounted at Drury Lane. The configuration of the ground on which the Russian works were constructed provided an ideal stage for the actors in the drama. The low Suishien Valley, at the foot of the chain of forts, enabled onlookers to gaze up, as it were, from the stalls to the footlights. It would have been impossible to occupy a position in close proximity to the scene of hostilities without some protection from rifle, machine-gun, and artillery. Shelter was provided by the network of trenches which, like the stalls in a theatre, allowed those present to choose their own distance from which to watch the combat« (Ashmead-Bartlett 1906, vii).[23]

---

23 For a similar impression of this war as a sublime spectacle see also the account of Reginald Glossop, who was a war artist for the *Daily Graphic*: »I was sitting on a mountain top with other correspondents, awaiting the approach of this mighty battle. [...] Suddenly the scene changed. ... Shall I ever forget the sight? A startling awe-inspiring transformation, the like of which I venture to say was never portrayed on the barbaric stage of the battlefield before. Picture to yourself a thousand star-bomb-shells, leaping upwards into the darkness of the night, then bursting with a blinding light – brighter and whiter than burnt magnesium, illuminating mountain top and

Ashmead-Bartlett's attitude towards soldiery and the necessity of war still echoes that of his predecessors. He is full of admiration for the Japanese soldiers' bravery and characterises war as »a deplorable evil«, but one without which »nations rapidly deteriorate. It is necessary at times to separate the good from the bad. As long as war is recognised, it is far better to conduct it thoroughly than in a half-hearted manner« (ibid., 492). In all respects mentioned here, Ashmead-Bartlett displays typical traits of the Edwardian war correspondent. In his study of the depiction of war in Edwardian newspapers, Glenn Wilkinson notes the general frequency of an imagery of theatre or spectacle and concludes:

»In examining the Edwardian press and the way in which it presented warfare before 1914, it is possible to determine the perceptions of war possessed by readers. It is clear that these perceptions were for the most part positive and were not challenged or contradicted by images of the horrific and brutal aspects of warfare. These images were not only conveyed in the reporting of *actual* warfare in the news columns and leading articles, but were also evident in other areas of the newspaper, such as cartoons, advertisements, illustrations, drawings and photographs« (Wilkinson 2003, 134).

In Edwardian times, war reporting still followed Victorian patterns and had lost nothing of its attraction for the media and their audiences. It also still attracted many men as a career opportunity.[24] The success of such a career continued to depend on scoops, also against military regulation, which explains the enmity which some military leaders, in particular Kitchener, developed towards war correspondents.

The hunt for scoops among the correspondents of his time is taken up in P.G. Wodehouse's satirical novel *The Swoop!* (1909), which parodies the invasion novel, a popular subgenre of adventure fiction in late Victorian and Edwardian times. In Chapter XI, war correspondents become the object of ridicule as these heroes of foreign wars prove incapable of reporting an invasion of their own country. All famous correspondents of the day – many of whom were veterans of the campaigns in the Sudan and in South Africa – are seriously incapacitated by the English weather, which turns the proverbial fog of war into a pathetic reality. Relentlessly, the novel debunks even the most charismatic figures of the profession, and this parody would have failed if the correspondents

---

crevice, exposing the silent army of Nogi's heroes to the full view of the Russian batteries« (Glossop 1907, 87f.).

24 See Daniel (2005, 117). Villiers describes the new type of freelancer in *Port Arthur* (Villiers 1905, 15f. and 154f.).

mentioned in the following excerpt had not been real heroes in the perception of their time:

»It was hard.
The lot of the actual war-correspondents was still worse. It was useless for them to explain that the fog was too thick to give them a chance. ›If it's light enough for them to fight‹, said their editors remorselessly, ›it's light enough for you to watch them.‹ And out they had to go.
They had a perfectly miserable time. Edgar Wallace seems to have lost his way almost at once. He was found two days later in an almost starving condition at Steeple Bumpstead. How he got there nobody knows. He said he had set out to walk to where the noise of the guns seemed to be, and had gone on walking. Bennett Burleigh, that crafty old campaigner, had the sagacity to go by Tube. This brought him to Hampstead, the scene, it turned out later, of the fiercest operations, and with any luck he might have had a story to tell. But the lift stuck half-way up, owing to a German shell bursting in its neighbourhood, and it was not till the following evening that a search-party heard and rescued him.
The rest – A.G. Hales, Frederick Villiers, Charles Hands, and the others – met, on a smaller scale, the same fate as Edgar Wallace. Hales, starting for Tottenham, arrived in Croydon, very tired, with a nail in his boot. Villiers, equally unlucky, fetched up at Richmond. The most curious fate was reserved for Charles Hands. As far as can be gathered, he got on all right till he reached Leicester Square. There he lost his bearings, and seems to have walked round and round Shakespeare's statue, under the impression that he was going straight to Tottenham. After a day and a-half of this he sat down to rest, and was there found, when the fog had cleared, by a passing policeman.
And all the while the unseen guns boomed and thundered, and strange, thin shoutings came faintly through the darkness« (Wodehouse 1909, 109-111).

Wodehouse's novel illustrates poignantly that notions of war correspondents which had been generated in the course of the 19th century still framed the public's (and writers') perception on the eve of the First World War – despite the fact that conditions both of warfare and war mediation had undergone significant developments. Although works of fiction criticised and parodied the contemporary press system and/or the stereotypical war correspondent, their images of war correspondents also closely resembled the self-representations in contemporary memoirs, and like these self-representations, fiction nourished images of the profession against which the performance of the correspondents of the First World War was measured.

The First World War was reported by a new generation of correspondents, but also by older men who had still been trained in the tradition of the Golden Age. This fact already suggests that the reporting of this war and its consequences for the journalists' self-perception is not quite as radical as is often claimed. Although new attitudes towards war undoubtedly did arise during the First World War and affected correspondents' role conceptions and their representation, traditional patterns also survived – not least because Victorian representations remained in circulation. Heroic notions of the war correspondent survived, for instance, in adventure literature for the young. A.B. Cooper's *Frank Flower: The Boy War Correspondent* (1913) is a typical Edwardian romance that presents war as the great adventure. Its hero is a bright boy from an impoverished family who starts to work for a newspaper. He is abducted to Venezuela, where he gets involved in a revolutionary war and starts to report it for his paper, becoming a celebrity back home and being rewarded with a secure middle-class future for his efforts.

Victorian patterns also linger on in the self-representations of some correspondents who experienced and covered the First World War. Geoffrey Malins, for instance, one of the two cameramen of the war's famous documentary, *The Battle of the Somme* (1914), depicted his performance at the Western Front in a manner familiar from many Victorian accounts – even though Malins worked with new technology and for a modern medium. In *How I Filmed the War* (1920), Malins occasionally stages himself as a combatant. In the following passage, his camera becomes his co-actor and first plays the role of a weapon with which Malins ›shoots‹ the fighting, and then of an injured comrade whom Malins assists. With its focus on action, the passage evokes a strong performative note:

»A quick succession of shell-bursts attracted my attention. Back to my camera position. Another lot of our men were going over the top. I began exposing, keeping them in my camera view all the time, as they were crossing, by revolving my tripod head. [...] I loaded again, and had just started exposing. Something attracted my attention on the extreme left. [...] There was the grinding crash of a bursting shell; something struck my tripod, the whole thing, camera and all, was flung against me. I clutched it and staggered back, holding it in my arms. I dragged it into the shrapnel-proof shelter, sat down and looked for the damage. A piece of shell had struck the tripod and cut the legs clean in half [...]. The camera, thank heaven, was untouched« (Malins 1993, 165f.).[25]

More usually, however, the heroic mould became brittle in the course of the First World War, and correspondents started to represent their role in

---

25 A late-20th century feature film about the Battle of the Somme, *The Trench* (UK 1999, dir. William Boyd), shows the filmmakers at the front in a less heroic way. Led into the trenches by an officer, the cameramen arrange images for propaganda purposes.

new ways. As the following chapter will show, this caesura stands at the beginning of a period during which the (self-)perception and (self-)representation of the war correspondent and the interpretation of his cultural significance underwent continual change, revising traditions but also reviving them.

CHAPTER 4: CRISES AND RE-ASSERTIONS. FROM THE FIRST WORLD WAR TO THE FALKLANDS

»The ideal situation for GHQ would have been a war correspondent who would write what he was told was the truth and not ask questions. This is exactly what the military got with Philip Gibbs, Herbert Russell, William Beach Thomas, Perry Robinson and Percival Phillips. [...] The introduction of journalists to the Western Front could have helped the Home Front in their search for the truth. What was created, however, was a group of correspondents who conformed to the great conspiracy, the deliberate lies and the suppression of the truth«
(Martin J. Farrar 1998, 68 and 73).

»It is generally accepted now that, of the men who wrote contemporary accounts of the war, it was the reporters who told the lies and the poets who told the truths. [...] The dead were ignored by the reporters but not by the poets«
(Martin Bell 2004, 54).

An Image in Decay

While their predecessors were perceived as heroes, the British correspondents of the First World War saw themselves exposed to highly critical assessments of their performance. By the end of the war, the reputation of British war correspondents seemed almost ruined. A satirical poem by Helen Hamilton, »Certain Newspaper Correspondents at the Front« (1918), accuses war correspondents of supporting propaganda and pretending to be at the side of the fighting men when actually they were not. The correspondents' use in their dispatches of the first-person plural, a representational pattern common in the Golden Age, is abruptly deconstructed in the poem's second stanza, which replaces the ›we‹ by a distancing ›they‹:

»»We took six hundred prisoners.
We made a splendid stand,
We did this and we did that,
All deeds of matchless bravery.‹
Etc., etc.

They, of course, is what you mean.
Then why not say so?« (Hamilton 1918, 63).

A.P. Herbert's *The Secret Battle* (1919), an anti-war novel, includes a passage that also suggests that war correspondents failed to do justice to the soldiers' experience. The first-person narrator depicts an exhausting march and then claims that »[n]o war correspondent has ever described such a march; it is not included in the official ›horrors of war‹; but this is the kind of thing which, more than battle and blood, harasses the spirit of the infantryman, and composes his life« (Herbert 1982, 21). C.E. Montague's war-critical essay *Disenchantment* (1922) makes several disenchanted remarks about correspondents, claiming that many of them were too closely associated with the military staff to be on the side of the common soldier and wrote what the staff dictated.[1] Montague was par-

---

1   Interestingly, Montague had acted as an official military censor on the Western Front, that is, he would have had to prevent some of the more critical reporting from reaching people back home in Britain. Montague's practice as censor is described in Philip Gibbs's *The Pageant of the Years* (1946, 166): »One of the censors who joined us later was C.E. Montague, the most brilliant leader writer and essayist on the *Manchester Guardian* before the war. [...] Always, or nearly always in those days when he was with us, he had a film over his eyes and a seal upon his lips. Extremely courteous, abominably brave – he liked being under shell fire! – and a ready smile in his very blue eyes, he seemed unguarded and open. But he was in hiding. Very rarely was it possible to get behind those blue eyes to the inner passion of the man – a smouldering fire – or to his philosophy of life. He was, as his writings prove, a man of fine and subtle humour, and idealist with a spiritual outlook on life, a severe critic of all sham and imposture, a realist in his revelation and loathing of war and its human degradation. All that comes out in his great book *Rough Justice* written after the war. But none of it, or very little, was revealed in his conversation with us.«

ticularly repelled by the cheerful tone of much war reporting that helped to disguise real conditions at the front and angered the fighting men:

»The average war correspondent – there were golden exceptions – insensibly acquired the same cheerfulness in face of vicarious torment and danger. In his work it came out at times in a certain jauntiness of tone that roused the fighting troops to fury against the writer. Through his despatches there ran a brisk implication that regimental officers and men enjoyed nothing better than ›going over the top‹; that a battle was just a rough, jovial picnic; that a fight never went on long enough for the men; that their only fear was lest the war should end on this side of the Rhine. This, the men reflected in helpless anger, was what people at home were offered as faithful accounts of what their friends in the field were thinking and suffering. [...]
The most bloody defeat in the history of Britain, a very world's wonder of valour frustrated by feckless misuse, of regimental glory and Staff shame, might occur on the Ancre on July 1, 1916, and our Press come out bland and copious and graphic, with nothing to show that we had not had quite a good day – a victory really. Men who had lived through the massacre read the stuff openmouthed« (Montague 1928, 101f.).

A field officer's surprise about what he read in the papers is cited in the poet Edmund Blunden's memoirs, *Undertones of War* (1928), at the prominent position of a chapter ending:

»We [Blunden and a fellow officer] also went to a lecture by a war correspondent, who invited questions, whereon a swarthy old colonel rose and said, ›The other day I was obliged to take part in a battle. I afterwards read a war correspondent's account of the battle, which proved to me that I hadn't been there at all. Will the lecturer explain that, please?‹« (Blunden 1935, 264).

All Our Yesterdays (1930), a novel by H.M. Tomlinson, who reported from the Western Front himself, includes several passages in which soldiers express their hatred and contempt for correspondents:

»But there was that lieutenant of the London Rifles at Amiens. Jack could not forget that chap. He had listened to the talk about the great doings, and then he stood up over them, very sad, and they shut up. He had a queer look. Then he spoke. He wanted the blood of all war correspondents – seemed to want to paddle in it. He hated them – he said they were decoy ducks« (Tomlinson 1930, 391f.).

»A civilian guest desired to learn from the young major, who to-morrow was returning to the trenches, how the men were faring. Were they in good spirits? [...]

›Better ask the war-correspondents‹, advised Langham, a little sardonically. ›That's their job, courage and cheerfulness. Isn't that so?‹ he enquired of Phipps« (ibid., 446f.).

Siegfried Sassoon's representation of war correspondents, as expressed in his *Memoirs of an Infantry Officer* (1930), is likewise unfavourable. When his alter ego Sherston is reconvalescing in Britain, he comes across a dispatch in the newspaper from ›War Correspondents' Head-quarters‹ that is identified as straightforward propaganda:

»›I have sat with some of our lads, fighting battles over again, and discussing battles to be‹, wrote some amiable man who had apparently mistaken the War for a football match between England and Germany. ›One officer – a mere boy – told me how he'd run up against eleven Huns in an advanced post. He killed two with a Mills bomb (»Grand weapon, the Mills!« he laughed, his clear eyes gleaming with excitement), wounded another with his revolver, and marched the remainder back to our own lines. ...‹ [...]
I wondered why it was necessary for the Western Front to be ›attractively ad-vertised‹ by such intolerable twaddle. What *was* this camouflage War which was manufactured by the press to aid the imaginations of people who had never seen the real thing?« (Sassoon 1930, 261f.).

Against the newspapers' manufacture, Sherston intends to publish a letter about the true conditions at the Western Front but finds it difficult get it printed:

»With regard to what I'd suggested in my letter, he [the editor of a critical newspaper] explained that if he were to print veracious accounts of infantry ex-perience his paper would be suppressed as prejudicial to recruiting. The censor-ship officials were always watching for a plausible excuse for banning it, and they had already prohibited its foreign circulation. ›The soldiers are not allowed to express their point of view. In wartime the word patriotism means suppres-sion of truth‹, he remarked, eyeing a small chunk of Stilton cheese on his plate as if it were incapable of agreeing with any but ultra-Conservative opinions« (ibid., 275).

The editor's reaction suggests that even if correspondents were willing to act as the soldiers' mouthpiece, their reports would be suppressed.

Such representations of correspondents in war-critical literature indi-cate that after the First World War, correspondents in Britain – as well as in other nations[2] – no longer appeared as the stuff that heroes are made

---

2   A drama by the Austrian playwright Karl Kraus, *The Last Days of Mankind* (*Die letzten Tage der Menschheit*), written during the war and published in

of. As the epigraphs to this chapter suggest, this negative perception was long-lived, both in the view of historians and later war correspondents. In general, the First World War is seen as an event that exploded all notions of the glorious nature of war. Nevertheless, soldiers and front officers retained a positive image and were praised as brave and gallant or pitied as victims of war's cruelty. Correspondents, by contrast, now almost equalled cowards in public perception: They had not participated themselves in the great slaughter and permitted themselves to be manipulated by politicians and the military.

It has to be noted that the scope for correspondents to get to the front and perform heroically was indeed far more restricted than in any earlier war with British participation. If Kitchener had tried to restrict correspondents in South Africa, he was even more adamant to keep them from the front when acting as Britain's minister of war. Having first tried to prevent war reporting by journalists altogether (and leave the task to a military ›official eyewitness‹, Colonel Sir Edward Swinton), the British government, alarmed by American protest, agreed to accredit a limited number of correspondents from mid-1915.[3] Military control of the British correspondents, who were requested to wear uniform and work in a pool, included severe censorship to ensure that the readers of newspapers at home would not be disconcerted. In the regular routine, all dispatches reached the newspapers via the War Office, and journalists were thus bereft of any opportunity to hunt for scoops – not to mention the adventur-

---

1922 in its final form, includes scathing criticism of the war correspondents of his own country, in particular a female war reporter, Alice Schalek who, in the play, stands for the worst kind of sensationalist and jingoistic reporting that is entirely ignorant of the realities of war. In Act I, scene 26, for instance, Schalek revels in the spectacle and danger of war, repeating patterns of the 19th century that are entirely inadequate for capturing the conditions of the war she is presently observing: »Thank God, we came just in time. Now a show is beginning – now you tell me, lieutenant, whether an artist's art could make this spectacle more gripping, more passionate. Those who stay at home – let them go on calling the war the shame of the century – even I did as long as I was back home – but those who are out here are gripped by the fever of actual experience. Isn't it true, lieutenant, you who are right in the midst of the war, you might as well admit it, that many of you wouldn't even want the war to end!« (Kraus 1974, 57).

3   Apart from Philip Gibbs, Herbert Russell, William Beach Thomas, Perry Robinson and Percival Phillips, the literary writers John Buchan, Henry W. Nevinson and H.M. Tomlinson were accredited to report from the Western Front for a limited time. Ellis Ashmead-Bartlett was accredited to report from the Dardanelles.

ous races in which some of their predecessors had got their dispatches on their way:

»The correspondents soon settled down into a routine. On the day that an attack was scheduled, they drew lots to see who would cover which area. Each then set out in his chauffeur-driven car, accompanied by his conducting officer. They went as close to the front as possible, watched the preliminary bombardment, got into the backwash of prisoners and walking wounded, interviewed anyone they could, and tried to piece together a story. Back at their quarters, the correspondents held a meeting, and each man outlined the narrative part of his story, keeping any personal impressions for his own dispatch. They then retired to their own rooms, wrote their pieces, and submitted them to the waiting censors. What the censors left was given to a dispatch rider, who took the messages to Signals at GHQ, where they were telephoned to the War Office and sent from there by hand to the various newspaper offices« (Knightley 2004, 102).

Restoring the Self-Image

Of course, such practice clashed with the traditional perception and self-perception of war correspondents as autonomous journalists and as individualists. It is not surprising, therefore, that the contrast between past and present modes of performance and ways of perception is a frequent theme in correspondents' memoirs. One strategy for facing their post-war image problem was to complain explicitly about censorship and other means of military control that had hindered them to perform in the expected and accustomed manner. Ellis Ashmead-Bartlett's criticism of Kitchener's hostility in *The Uncensored Dardanelles* (see p. 49) is an outspoken example. Another strategy was counter-representation, that is, description of what journalists had tried and managed to achieve *in spite* of control, such as Ashmead-Bartlett's letter about conditions on Gallipoli to Prime Minister Asquith and the subsequent withdrawal of British troops from this theatre of war (see p. 45).

Philip Gibbs is another case in point. His *Realities of War* (published in the United States under the title *Now It Can Be Told*) puts special emphasis on the troubles which Gibbs and his colleagues took in order to report the war for the public and on behalf of the soldiers. In Gibbs's description, these efforts – or struggles, as he phrases it – come close to self-victimisation:

»There were times when I was so physically and mentally exhausted that I could hardly rouse myself to a new day's effort. There were times when I felt faint and sick and weak; and my colleagues were like me. But we struggled on to tell the daily history of the war, and the public cursed us because we did not tell more, or sneered at us because they thought we were ›spoon-fed‹ by G.H.Q. – who never gave us any detailed news and who were far from our way of life« (Gibbs 1920, 21).

The public are here castigated as unappreciative of the correspondent's endeavours, and the military are drawn as an antagonist of autonomous journalism and hence as responsible for the war correspondent's loss of face. Accordingly, in another passage Gibbs explicitly distances correspondents from the military, thus deviating from a perceptual and representational topos of the Golden Age. Although they had to wear uniform, Gibbs emphasises, journalists were »civilians«, and *as such* were able to approach the fighting men »as human beings«, not as brothers in arms. And as human beings, they talked to men of *all* ranks and did not affiliate just with the caste of higher officers and their specific view of the war:

»We were civilians in khaki, with green bands round our right arms, and uncertain status. It was better so, because we were in the peculiar and privileged position of being able to speak to Tommies and sergeants as humans beings, to be on terms of comradeship with junior subalterns and battalion commanders, and to sit at the right hand of generals without embarrassment to them or to ourselves« (ibid., 32).

Furthermore, Gibbs devotes much space to his experiences *early* in the war, before official accreditation in May 1915, when he and some other young colleagues tried to report from France and Belgium against military restrictions, while an old guard of correspondents were still willing to cooperate with the officials and waited for permission. Generational difference is here used to highlight a difference between correspondents who permitted their autonomy to be seriously infringed, and a young subversive group who refused to be kept on leash and thus at least made the attempt to preserve their journalistic integrity:

»We went in civilian clothes, without military passports – the War Office was not giving any – with bags of money which might be necessary for the hire of motor-cars, hotel life, and the bribery of door-keepers in the ante-chambers of war, as some of us had gone to the Balkan War, and others. The Old Guard of war correspondents besieged the War Office for official recognition, and were insulted day after day by junior staff officers who knew that ›K.‹ [Kitchener] hated these men, and thought the Press ought to be throttled in time of war; or they were beguiled into false hopes by officials who hoped to go in charge of them, and were told to buy horses and sleeping-bags, and be ready to start at a moment's notice for the Front. The moment's notice was postponed for months....

The younger ones did not wait for it. They took their chance of ›seeing something‹, without authority, and made wild, desperate efforts to break through the barrier that had been put up against them by French and British staffs in the zone of war. Many of them were arrested, put into prison, let out, caught again in forbidden places, re-arrested, and expelled from France. That was after fantastic adventures in which they saw what war meant in civilized countries; where vast populations were made fugitives of fear; where millions of women and children and old people became wanderers along the roads in a tide of human misery, with the red flame of war behind them, and following them; and where the first battalions of youth, so gay in their approach to war, so confident of victory, so careless of the dangers (which they did not know), came back maimed and mangled and blinded and wrecked, in the back-wash of retreat, which presently became a spate through Belgium and the north of France, swamping over many cities and thousands of villages, and many fields. Those young writing-men who had set out in a spirit of adventure went back to Fleet Street with a queer look in their eyes, unable to write the things they had seen, unable to tell them to people who had not seen and could not understand. Because there was no code of words which would convey the picture of that wild agony of peoples, that smashing of all civilized lands, to men and women who still thought of war in terms of heroic pageantry« (ibid., 3f.).

This extensive passage expresses not only Gibbs's indignation about a government and military who tried to reduce correspondents from actors to mere puppets in the theatre of war. It also conveys a self-stylisation that accords with a new mode of perceiving the war's combatants as victims destroyed if not in body then in their minds. In Gibbs's representation the correspondent returning from the front appears just as traumatised as an actual soldier, and he has similar problems in finding a language for the new kind of war he has witnessed. One might argue that, implicitly, the correspondent is thus also excused for not writing about everything he witnessed because many combatants too refused to communicate their experiences to people at home because they would not have been able to understand them; to Gibbs's contemporary readers, this would still have been a familiar phenomenon.

Above all, Gibbs's self-portrayal also fashions the correspondent as a critic of war – a significant clash with the attitude towards war typically found in reporting of the Golden Age. Gibbs presents himself as a witness *not* willing to accept that brutality and human suffering have to be taken as ›natural‹ side-effects of necessary wars. Rather, like the British so-called trench poets and Siegfried Sassoon in particular, Gibbs portrays himself as a man roused into protest by what he has seen. And in Gibbs's case, this pacifism is not a mere pose in order to defend his performance in the First World War against general criticism. Gibbs's abhorrence of war is already apparent in his early war-time book *The Soul of the War* (1915), which also relates his illegal reporting in Belgium and France. Here Gibbs also focuses on the suffering caused by war, to civilians and soldiers, for example when he describes a field hospital to which he gained access as a stretcher-bearer in an ambulance team:

»But I had a more horrible shock, although I had been accustomed to ugly sights. It was when the wounded seamen came up from below. The lamps on the landing-stage, flickering in the high wind, cast their white light upon half a dozen men walking down the gangway in Indian file. At least I had to take them on trust as men, but they looked more like spectres who had risen from the tomb, or obscene creatures from some dreadful underworld. When the German shell had burst on their boat, its fragments had scattered upwards, and each man had been wounded in the face, some of them being blinded and others scarred beyond human recognition. Shrouded in ship's blankets, with their heads swathed in bandages, their faces were quite hidden behind masks of cotton-wool coming out to a point like beaks and bloody at the tip. I shuddered at the sight of them, and walked away, cursing the war and all its horrors« (Gibbs 1915, 232).

As a consequence of his experiences in the First World War, Gibbs turned into a journalist committed to peace and an early representative of the journalism of attachment:

»If there is any purpose in what I have written beyond mere record it is to reveal the soul of war so nakedly that it cannot be glossed over by the glamour of false sentiment and false heroics. More passionate than any other emotion that has stirred me through life, is my conviction that any man who has seen these things must, if he has any gift of expression, and any human pity, dedicate his brain and heart to the sacred duty of preventing another war like this« (ibid., 359).

Gibbs's *Realities of War* ends with the emphatic demand »Let us have Peace« (Gibbs 1920, 455), and his later volume *The Pageant of the Years* (1946), written after Gibbs had also reported the Second World War, frequently mentions his dedication to pacifism after the First World War. That this is a paradigm shift in war journalism and in the representation of the war correspondent becomes obvious when one reads Gibbs's self-presentation against that of a member of the ›old guard‹ of correspondents who took part in the early ›wild‹ reporting of the war (disclaiming Gibbs's assessment that only the young had opposed the military's restrictions). Julius M. Price was a seasoned war artist for the *Illustrated London News*. In the manner of a Victorian correspondent, he presents his foray into France as an adventure that is thrilling and not traumatising as in Gibbs's account. In the familiar 19th-century pose he also understates the risks of his trip into the field; his account occasionally reads like a curious sporting excursion although Price, too, was sensitive to the devastation of war. In the following passage from his reminiscences of a long career, *On the Path of Adventure*, the narrative of his adventure in the First World War blends into the description of a destroyed landscape littered with the relics of heavy fighting, albeit without any trace of human casualties. Unlike Gibbs, Price never voices outrage at the cruelty of the war:

»I had done a lot of cycling in my younger days and it would be an easy matter to take it up again, and I should thus be independent of every one for getting about. But the difficulty, of course, would be to find a machine, as it was scarcely likely there would be any spare ones in the village.
My luck, however, was still in, and during the morning I came across a man who had one he could lend me. There was only one slight drawback, which was that it was a lady's bicycle, but it would answer my purpose very well, so I took possession of it at once. [...]
There was a glorious feeling of freedom as I bowled along, for it did not take me many minutes to get into the ways of my unaccustomed mount, and luckily I had a straight level road for some distance and pretty well all to myself. [...]
Gradually there were signs around me that the scene of the fighting was close at hand: shell holes – broken telegraph poles – shattered tree-trunks, till at length the road emerged into open undulating country with cornfields and grass land. A short distance ahead were the smoking ruins of the picturesque village of Sommeous in an oasis of sheltering trees.
From here on the battlefield extended on both sides, and there was grim evidence everywhere of the fierceness of the fighting: crops trampled down, sheaves of corn rotting in the fields. The countryside was absolutely littered with the awful débris of war: broken rifles, shattered caissons, accoutrements of every description, fragments of big shells« (Price 1919, 98f.).

The obvious difference in tone and attitude between the memoirs of Gibbs and Price indicates that the First World War was a watershed not only in the representation of war in general, but also in the perception and representation of war's mediators. Journalists like Gibbs and Ashmead-Bartlett introduced new patterns for the self-representation of war correspondents: the correspondent as investigator and independent critic of the military and government, his own as well as the enemy's. This role conception would become prominent again in later decades of the 20th century.[4] However, the example of Julius Price shows that residual modes of seeing and presenting war correspondents were also still in use. Even the heroic template for perceiving and depicting war correspondents had not been entirely deactivated, as the excerpt from Geoffrey Malins's memoirs (see p. 93) exemplifies. Under more favourable working conditions for war correspondents than in the First World War, the profession regained a positive image that was fully restored in the Second World War. In Spain and Abyssinia, war correspondence acquired some new icons, but the profession was also satirised, albeit for different reasons and in a different tone than after the First World War.

New Icons and a Parody. Evelyn Waugh's *Scoop*

New paragons of the profession were created in the Spanish Civil War (1936-39), including the maverick Ernest Hemingway, Martha Gellhorn and the idol of war photographers until today, Robert Capa. A collection of personal accounts by reporters in the war emphasises the participatory

---

4   The critical correspondent is thus the type one frequently finds in popular novels about the First World War written since the late 20th century. In Claire Rayner's *Flanders* (1988), a novel from her Poppy series, which tells English history from the point of view of female characters, Poppy falls in love with the war correspondent Bobby Bradman, who is an idealised truth-seeking journalist: »The war correspondents were supposed to be bear-led always by someone from Staff and to be told where to go, but she knew from his dispatches to the paper, which she read avidly, that he was far too independent a man to tolerate that. He was everywhere, she found, sometimes at an airfield and reporting what was happening with the dog fights the pilots involved themselves in when they went up ostensibly to reconnoitre and take photographs over the enemy's lines; sometimes well up to the Front where the shelling was thickest; occasionally behind the lines at Headquarters, pestering senior officers for opinions, news and comments. A good journalist, she thought with a glow, when she put the paper down. He's a *good* journalist. And I wish he wasn't. I wish he was here at home, with me. I wish. I wish – « (Rayner 2001, 215). Indeed, Bobby is seriously injured in a gas attack. The First World War series by crime writer Anne Perry (2003-2007) also features a war correspondent as a subsidiary character who, like Ellis Ashmead-Bartlett and Philip Gibbs, is appalled by the casualties of Gallipoli and the Western Front and has developed strong pacifist sentiments.

nature of the correspondents' presence, and their generally committed position:

»He [the correspondent] found himself personally involved in something cosmic which quite dwarfed his brave little by-line. [...] After he had been there a while the queries of his editor in far-off London or New York seemed like trivial interruptions. For he had become a participant in rather than an observer of the horror, tragedy, and adventure which constitute war« (Hanighen 1940, 5).

With newsreel reports and illustrated magazines apart from the newspapers, the Spanish Civil War was a media war, but it was also a literary war that engaged the interest and active participation of many literary writers,[5] such as Hemingway or, on the British side, George Orwell. Orwell's *Homage to Catalonia* (1938) is one of the best-known memoirs resulting from this war, written immediately after the author had returned from his engagement in the war as a fighter against the Fascists. However, the book is a combatant's memoir and a political essay rather than a reflection about how the war was reported. In general, despite its many prominent participants and their open commitment, the Spanish Civil War generated little reflection about the role of the war correspondent and only few correspondents' memoirs.[6] In novels and films too, the *correspondents* of the Spanish Civil War left hardly a trace, perhaps because the Second World War, with its own perceptions and representations of war reporters, was soon to follow.

---

5   Taking up this literariness of the Spanish Civil War, William Boyd's novel *Any Human Heart* (2002) lets its protagonist, an old writer, reminisce about his time as a correspondent in this conflict.

6   Francis McCullagh's memoirs of reporting the conflict (in his case with little sympathy for the ›Reds‹) begins with an expression of disgust about its cruelties and explains why the author decided to retire from his profession after he had been in Spain. McCullagh, an Irish correspondent, was in his sixties and had participated in earlier wars both as a combatant and a reporter, but felt unable to accommodate the Spanish Civil War into his notions either of war or war-time journalism: »It is this sinister aspect of the new warfare that frightens me. It seems that we are on the eve of a throwback to those appalling wars of extermination, so common in antiquity, wars in which women and children were slaughtered as a matter of course, and whole nations literally wiped out. Not for a hundred years may we again see one nation fighting another nation; all wars may be between groups, one group anti-Christian and the other calling itself Christian; and whichever group wins, Christianity will lose. We shall be back in the Wars of Religion. Such wars I am going to keep out of« (McCullagh 1937, ix).

The only major piece of British fiction referring to the correspondents of the war in Spain, Evelyn Waugh's *Scoop* (1938), amalgamates them with the reporters of Mussolini's invasion of Abyssinia in 1936, and it is far from heroising its correspondent characters who evoke neither Hemingway nor Phillip Gibbs (whose well-known *Realities of War* had been re-published in 1929). Indeed, there is no trace in Waugh's novel that the First World War might ever have shaken the correspondent's (self-)image, nor that Spain had generated new reporter celebrities. Rather, Waugh's characters remind us of the hunters for scoops in Sir Arthur Conan Doyle's »The Three Correspondents«, but with the important difference that the journalists in Waugh's novel only *pose* as heroic adventurers and are feeble caricatures of the Golden Age type. What Waugh's novel shares with Doyle's story most obviously is its harsh critique of a press system greedy for news and reckless in the means of obtaining them. *Scoop*, still frequently read by correspondents today (see p. 63) and a model for later humorous and ironic portrayals of war correspondents,[7] is a satire about Fleet Street and journalistic (mis-)demeanour based on Waugh's own experiences in reporting the war in Abyssinia for the *Daily Mail*. In the preface to a later edition of the novel, Waugh remarked that »[a]t the time of writing public interest had just been diverted from Abyssinia to Spain. I tried to arrange a combination of these two wars. Of the latter I knew nothing at first hand« (Waugh 1964, n.p.).

Scoop exposes Fleet Street's greed for news and resulting need for correspondents. *Waugh in Abyssinia* (1936), the author's reminiscences of his short spell as a war reporter, had already shown how the media were almost hysterical about the new war, even though hardly anybody in Britain – or Fleet Street – knew anything about the country and its conflict with Italy:

»But Abyssinia was News. Everyone with any claims to African experience was cashing in. [...] In the circumstances anyone who had actually spent a few weeks in Abyssinia itself, and had read the dozen or so books which constituted the entire English bibliography of the subject, might claim to be an expert, and in this unfamiliar but not uncongenial disguise I secured employment with the only London newspaper which seemed to be taking a realistic view of the situation, as a ›war correspondent‹« (Waugh 1984, 49).

---

7   See, for instance, Richard Busvine's *Gullible Travels* (1945) and recently Chris Ayres's *War Reporting for Cowards* (see pp. 63-67).

The papers' and film companies' enthusiasm waned, however, as soon as the public got tired of the war, and correspondents were hastily withdrawn:

»Meanwhile in Europe and America the editors and film magnates had begun to lose patience. They had spent large sums of money on the Abyssinian war and were getting very little in return; several journalists had already been recalled; the largest cinema company was beginning to pack up; now a general retreat began. I received my dismissal by cable on the day after the Emperor's arrival« (ibid., 209f.).[8]

This view of media only interested in news that sell is also addressed in *Scoop*. Keen to participate in a war – as real writers were in the Spanish Civil War – the novelist John Courteney Boot asks his influential friend Mrs Stitch to use her connections and get him the job of foreign correspondent for the *Beast* in ›Ishmaelia‹, where a civil war is waged between communists and fascists. Through a curious mistake, however, not John, but William Boot, who writes the paper's country column, is sent to Ishmaelia although he would rather stay in England. This Boot is naive and gullible; he has trouble getting a passport, buys far too much equipment and hence travels with a cumbersome load of luggage. He also does not at first realise the fierce competition between his fellow correspondents, who do not hesitate to fake news and lead each other astray. One of them lays a false trail to a remote place, and everybody rushes off, fully equipped and dressed for adventure like a correspondent of the Golden Age. The exaggeration of parody highlights the correspondents' role performance when they don their gear and pose for each others' cameras:

»For three days the town was in turmoil. Lorries were chartered and provisioned; guides engaged; cooks and guards and muleteers and caravan boys and hunters, cooks' boys, guards' boys, muleteers' boys, caravan-boys' boys' and hunters' boys were recruited at unprecedented rates of pay; all over the city, in the offices and legations, resident Europeans found themselves deserted by their servants; seminarists left the missions, male-nurses the hospital; highly placed clerks their government departments, to compete for the journalists' wages. The price of benzine was doubled overnight and rose steadily until the day of the exodus. Terrific deals were done in the bazaar in tinned foodstuffs; they were cornered by a Parsee and unloaded on a Banja, cornered again by an

---

8   In 2003 W.F. Deedes, one of Waugh's colleagues in Abyssinia, published his own memoirs, *At War with Waugh*. Deedes is believed to be a model for Waugh's portrayal of William Boot in *Scoop*.

Arab, resold and rebought, before they reached the journalists' stores. Shumble bought William's rifle and sold a half-share in it to Whelper. Everyone now emulated the costume of the Frenchmen; sombreros, dungarees, jodhpurs, sun-proof shirts and bullet-proof waistcoats, holsters, bandoliers, Newmarket boots, cutlasses, filled the Liberty [hotel]. The men of the Excelsior Movie-Sound News sporting the horsehair capes and silk skirts of native chieftains, made camp in the Liberty garden and photographed themselves at great lengths in attitudes of vigilance and repose« (Waugh 1964, 141f.).

Only William Boot stays behind because he has fallen in love with a German woman. Thanks to this circumstance he is therefore present where the action really takes place and lands a scoop that makes him famous – fame then further exploited by his paper, which announces a public lecture on his return:

»Boot is Back
The man who made journalistic history, Boot of the *Beast*, will tomorrow tell in his own inimitable way the inner story of his meteoric leap to fame. How does it feel to tell the truth to two million registered readers? How does it feel to have risen in a single week to the highest pinnacle of fame? Boot will tell you« (ibid., 213).

Boot is also offered a very good contract, a literary agent, a book serial and cinema rights (ibid., 214). As he finds out on his return, however, all reports from Ishmaelia published under his name were practically invented by his editor who had to ›spell out‹ the scanty dispatches Boot was allowed to telegraph because of the enormous cable rate.[9] Since he is an honest man, William refuses to be celebrated, but the *Beast* then simply engages his namesake again, who is also knighted in William's stead.

Waugh's satire presents war correspondents as a bunch of men who lack ethical standards and are driven only by professional ambition and their papers' need to compete on the market. The innocent Boot, familiar only with a humble niche of domestic journalism, has to be initiated into this sad truth about the ›noblest‹ kind of journalism by his colleague Corker:

»›You know, you've got a lot to learn about journalism. Look at it this way. News is what a chap who doesn't care much about anything wants to read. And it's only news until he's read it. After that it's dead. We're paid to supply news. If someone else has sent a story before us, our story isn't news. Of course there's colour. Colour is just a lot of bull's-eyes about nothing. It's easy to

---

9   Cable rates in Abyssinia had indeed been exorbitant (Knightley 2004, 188).

write and easy to read but it costs too much in cabling so we have to go slow on that. See?‹« (ibid., 79).

Waugh's novel unmasks a profession that has lost its dignity, but this bad image arises from Waugh's analysis of the journalistic field of his time, and the competitive nature of war journalism in particular. It is unconnected to the image disaster caused by the First World War. However, this disaster was not generally forgotten. A British correspondent of the Second World War, James Landsdale Hodson, had participated in the First World War as a young soldier. Remembering his own negative perception of correspondents in that war, he asked himself if he would deliver a better performance:

»There was the winter's morning on the Cambrian Front in 1915 when C. found an old top hat and came down the trench wearing it a-tilt. ›Love a duck‹, said M. (though not so politely), ›that must be blankety blank, blank‹, naming a war correspondent whose messages were known to us – and not always admired. I thought of it now because, this time, it was wearing the badges of such a one that I was to go. The outlook was uncertain. What new notes would be struck? All that was sure was that the mud would not differ – that filthy, cloying, devilish exhausting stuff that took as much stamina out of men as the dangers that encompassed them. How close to the men during battle should I be – would they be no more than tiny figures far-off amid clouds of smoke and the murderous leaping of disembowelled earth? Should I see no more than the strewn and torn arena, defiled with the evidence? Should I be very afraid – for it had always seemed to me that I did not like war better, but less, the more I saw of it. Bombardments do not strengthen your nerves. Nor do the years. No answer to all this; but the urge to seek an answer« (Hodson 1941, 9f.).

Indeed, Hodson did get close to the men during battle, and praised their courage in his reports and the popular books he published during the war – with the same patriotic attitude he also demanded from his audience:

»We shall not have reached the highest pitch of our war effort till each of us realises, and agrees, and lives on the basis, that none of us has the right to be safer than anybody else, or more comfortable than anybody else; that there's no reason why Tom Harris should die in his ship, or James Watson in his tank, or Harry Brownrigg in the jungle unless we are equally ready to die for them. We cannot all do what they do; other tasks are equally important. But the acceptance of the idea must be in us, the readiness to do all and dare all, and to suffer all. We haven't all reached that pitch yet. But who among us dare deem himself set aside by Fate (combined with himself) to survive while others perish to save him?« (Hodson 1942, 392).

The Second World War's note of patriotism and a strong sense of affiliation between soldiers, correspondents and readers at home fully restored the standing of the war correspondent in public perception and representation.

Heroes Once More. The Correspondents of the Second World War

Richard Collier, a young correspondent during the Second World War, later wrote a glorifying collective biography of his famous British and American »warco« colleagues of the time, who, on the British side, included Richard Dimbleby, the radio correspondent, and the Australian Alan Moorehead (Collier 1989). The restoration of the correspondent's image was effected, among others, by working conditions for journalists that differed significantly from those in the previous conflicts. Unlike the wars in Abyssinia and Spain, the Second World War gave British and American correspondents an opportunity to write about their ›own‹ soldiers again, and in contrast to the First World War, the military *wanted* correspondents to be among the troops and experience the war first-hand. Philip Gibbs, who covered both conflicts, claimed in *The Pageant of the Years* (1946, 168) that the Second World War provided more favourable conditions for correspondents because it was »a war of movement and enormous drama« in which journalists were permitted to play a major part instead of being mere observers. They were frequently ›embedded‹ with soldiers, identified with them and were in turn accepted as comrades rather than antagonists, especially on the American side. Robert Capa took his famous D-Day photographs while landing with his country's troops, and Ernie Pyle, the best-loved American war correspondent of the time, was killed ›in action‹ in the Pacific, among the GIs who regarded him as their best interpreter. In fact Pyle was so popular with the American public as well the soldiers that even before his death he became a figure in a war-time Hollywood film, *The Story of G.I. Joe* (USA 1945, dir. William A. Wellman). It shows a fictionalised version of Pyle covering the Italian campaign, always in close interaction with the soldiers of ›his‹ company and finding ›human interest‹ in their stories for readers at home.

For the British correspondents, Phillip Knightley notes a special importance of covering the desert war. This was, according to Knightley, a particularly significant theatre of war for a nation whose status as a world leader was soon to be taken over by the United States, and the media helped to direct the British public's attention to North Africa:

»Thus, although for Hitler it was never more than a side-show, the desert campaign became for Churchill and the British the greatest theatre of war. It attracted the best war correspondents, produced some of the best writing, and was given a disproportionate amount of space in British newspapers. It threw up more heroes, more household names, and more legends than any other front. It became the most romanticised part of the war, ›a correspondent's paradise‹, ›the last gentlemen's campaign‹. [...]

For the correspondents, the war had everything they could desire. They were free to go wherever they wished [...]. Stories were there for the asking, censorship – with some glaring exceptions – was reasonable, communications were good, and the desert bred a strange spirit of kinship. When Sir Archibald Wavell began his offensive, in December 1940, he announced it to six correspondents. Eighteen months later there were ninety-two, and more were arriving daily. On a personal level, many found the desert campaign the most profound experience of their lives« (Knightley 2004, 332).

The sense of support for the fighting men, which marks the reports and most books by British correspondents published during and after the Second World War, is especially pronounced in memoirs of the North African campaign. Alan Moorehead became particularly well-known for reporting the desert war. He dedicated his *African Trilogy* (1944), which collects three earlier books relating to the war in Africa,[10] »To the Men Who Fought«, and it ends with the sentence »All Africa was ours« (Moorehead 1965, 580), which imparts both a gesture to Britain's former imperial glory and, above all, a sense of common achievement.

Throughout his books, Moorehead presents himself as the correspondent who knows the soldiers well since he accompanies them in battle and shares their experiences on the ground as well as in the air. In his closeness to the fighting men and sometimes active participation in the fighting itself, the ›warco‹ of the Second World War resembles the reporter of the Golden Age. More strongly than the latter, however, he explicitly frames himself as the common soldier's interpreter and mouthpiece rather than a hero in his own right. When depicting his own experiences, Moorehead's intention is not to step into the limelight himself but to give his readers an impression of what the soldiers were doing for Britain and the Commonwealth. In the depiction of a flight with Canadian fighter pilots, for instance, Moorehead's rendering of his own sen-

---

10 *The Mediterranean Front, A Year of Battle* and *The End in Africa*; together these books cover the period from 1940 to 1943.

sations and emotions substitutes for the pilots' experiences and permits his readers to imagine what the pilots went through, not only once, as the correspondent did, but again and again. In this manner, Moorehead shows the bravery of men who would never consider themselves particularly brave:

»I sweated in the hot flying kit as I walked over the far side of the field smoking a last cigarette with the flying officer who was leading our flight. I will give this man a fictitious name, Watson. He was perhaps twenty-two or twenty-three. He was six foot, unusually slim and boyish with dark hair and a serious shy face, and he had been very gay last night at the rest-house. Someone had said to him, ›I hear you are going to do something pretty intrepid to-morrow.‹ ›Yes‹, he had said, ›pretty intrepid.‹ They had got the word out of some newspaper report and it was a joke among them to use it. I do not think that they ever felt brave. They felt tired or exhilarated or worried or hungry and occasionally afraid. But never brave. Certainly never intrepid. Most of them were completely unanalytical« (ibid., 41).

Moorehead's description of the flight expands over a whole page and is focused on his own disorientation and physical discomfort, thus providing a foil for what the pilots achieve under the same conditions:

»There was Kassala breaking through the ground mist. There the jebels, there the town, there the railway yards. And in a few seconds we were going down to bomb. It wasn't necessary to wait any more. With huge overwhelming relief I leaned over for a fuller view. As I moved, the three aircraft dipped in a long easy dive and, inexplicably, I was suddenly lifted with a wave of heady excitement, more sensuous than release from pain, faster than the sating of appetite, much fuller than intoxication. I felt keyed to this thing as a skier balancing for his jump or a surfer taking the first full rush of a breaker. There was no drawing back nor any desire for anything but to rush on, the faster the better.
Now the roar of the power-dive drowned even these sensations, and with the exhilaration of one long high-pitched school-boy's yell we held the concrete huts in the bomb sights and let them have the first salvo. I saw nothing, heard no sound of explosion, as the machine with a great sickening lurch came out of the dive and all the earth – jebels, township, clouds and desert – spun round and sideways through the glass of the cockpit. Then, craning backward, I glimpsed for a second the bomb smoke billowing up from the centre of the compound. It all looked so marvellously easy then – not a human being in sight on the brown earth below; all those ten thousand men huddled in fear of us in the ground. [...] Then again the earth was turning and pitching as we came out of it and I felt sick. Sick, and nursing a roaring headache. Like that I was borne up and out of it into the pure air beyond the ground-fire, beyond harm's way. I experienced pleasure then, calmer but deeper than my earlier excitement. To have had that

dread, to have lost it in excitement at the crisis, and now to have come sailing back safely into this clean open sky – that was much and more than one could ever have foreseen. In a lazy pleasurable daze I sat back through the journey home. I could have laughed at anything then. It was all very intrepid« (ibid., 42f.).

In this long depiction, the correspondent is the focus of perception, and the way the passage is narrated, it is unavoidable that he also holds the stage. Significantly, however, this effect is then deliberately undermined in order to signal an essential difference between correspondent and warrior proper. After all the excitement and exhilaration, the passage ends with a comic performance: »We made an easy landing. My Canadian slid back the transparent roof. I stepped out along the wing, caught my foot in a piece of splintered fuselage and fell flat on my face on the ground« (ibid., 43). With this anticlimax, Moorehead counters any impression that he might now be considered a hero himself; the glory belongs to the fighting men, not the reporter, who sees himself as an interpreter of their experience for the public. That the British war correspondent's image was restored during the Second World War thus seems not only a matter of his own participation in the war – which often meant significant courage on his part – and of outspoken patriotism. It must also be ascribed to the fact that, more modestly than their predecessors of the Golden Age, the British reporters of the Second World War imparted their sympathy and respect for the men who really fought, and eventually won, the war for their country.

It is largely through their reporting and self-representations that British correspondents became well known to their audience and enjoyed a good reputation during the Second World War. They were rarely portrayed in novels and films of the time. The first British novel of note about a war correspondent since Evelyn Waugh's *Scoop* is Graham Greene's *The Quiet American* (1955). It portrays the war correspondent in a manner quite distinct from the image that can be constructed from the self-representations of correspondents who covered the Second World War. In part, this difference is explained by the fact that Greene depicts the correspondent confronted with a foreign war – a war in which his own country is not involved and in which patriotic sentiment is not an issue. Rather, Greene's fictional correspondent is challenged by the dilemma whether to maintain an impartial distance or to allow his reporting to be influenced by his emotional engagement.

The Quiet American.
Detachment and Engagement in a Foreign War

Greene's novel reflects the post-Second World War order with new kinds of war and challenges for war mediation. It responds to the contemporary war in Indochina, where French influence was coming to an end and the United States got involved, providing financial and military aid in order to maintain Vietnam as a Western sphere of influence in Southeast Asia. *The Quiet American* is set in Vietnam between 1952 and 1954, that is, the final phase of the French Indochina War that was followed by an increasingly Americanised war, the Vietnam War, in the 1960s.[11] Greene's main character is a British correspondent, Thomas Fowler, who works for *The Times* and is based in Saigon. It is essential for the novel that its correspondent figure covers a war in which his own nation is not involved and in which he can therefore – at first – maintain the stance of a ›neutral‹ observer. Following Fowler's development, Greene explores the general question of professional ideals which should guide a correspondent. This issue has become increasingly important since the Second World War, and it is not surprising that *The Quiet American* is one of the novels still read by correspondents today (see pp. 65-66).[12] Greene had some journalistic experience in Indochina himself,[13] but the novel is not autobiographical, and neither did Greene have a real-life model for Fowler. He uses the character of the correspondent to explore a basic ethical question focused in war journalism: How long one can remain a mere observer of human suffering and human wrongs without being

---

11 Robert Capa died while photographing the conflict for *Life* in 1954, stepping on a mine, thus adding to the myth around his person that he was the first American reporter killed in Vietnam.

12 It was also read by correspondents of the Vietnam War. Michael Herr's *Dispatches*, for instance, refers explicitly to one of the novel's characters when reflecting on the beginning of the war for the United States: »You couldn't find two people who agreed about when it began, how could you say when it began going off? [...] Maybe it was already over for us in Indochina when Alden Pyle's body washed up under the bridge at Dakao, his lungs all full of mud; maybe it caved in with Dien Bien Phu. But the first happened in a novel, and while the second happened on the ground it happened to the French, and Washington gave it no more substance than if Graham Greene had made it up too« (Herr 1978, 49).

13 Greene visited Indochina several times between 1951 and 1955 with commissions for articles from *Le Figaro*, *The Sunday Times* and *Life* (see Christie 1989, 20).

challenged to act. Fowler believes in objectivity as an ideal of journalism, but the novel then depicts how this ideal becomes increasingly difficult to maintain as the ›foreign‹ correspondent is torn into the conflict between the war's different factions.

The novel follows its protagonist from cynical detachment to deep personal involvement. Fowler as a character is never just the ›correspondent‹. We learn about his disrupted marriage and a Catholic wife who refuses to agree to the divorce that would make it possible for Fowler to marry a young Vietnamese girl, Phuong, whom he considers his last chance to escape a lonely old age. This love relationship is bound up with Fowler's relationship to war, and the link is Alden Pyle, the novel's ›quiet American‹, who is employed in his country's covert »Economic Aid Mission« (Greene 2001, 17). Despite his outward unobtrusiveness, Pyle deprives Fowler of his lover, and, through supplying the anti-Communist side of the conflict with explosives, causes human suffering that Fowler eventually cannot bear to merely watch any more.

In the novel's constellation of characters, Pyle also serves as Fowler's opposite in that he has a completely different approach to politics and life in general. Pyle may look unobtrusive and be politically naive, but he wants to get engaged and take action. He therefore serves as an agent for his country's secret service and actively supports the anti-Communists, quite aware of the fact that the explosives he delivers will cause the death of many people. By contrast, Fowler's motto at the beginning of the novel is that he does *not* wish to become engaged, either as a human being or as a reporter:

»›I'm not involved. Not involved‹, I repeated. It had been an article of my creed. The human condition being what it was, let them fight, let them love, let them murder, I would not be involved. My fellow journalists called themselves correspondents; I preferred the title of reporter. I wrote what I saw. I took no action – even an opinion is a kind of action« (ibid., 28).

But then Fowler *does* get involved and develops an opinion about war when, for the first time, he sees war's casualties close up. In a decisive episode, Fowler experiences a sudden role change from mere observer to participant in the killing of innocent civilians. While usually journalists are only permitted on ›horizontal‹ flight missions that take them over battlefields in a remote distance,[14] Fowler here finds himself accompany-

---

14 See, for instance, the depiction of the flight in Alan Moorehead's memoirs quoted above (pp. 112-114). There the correspondent does not mention the damage caused by the bombs dropped by ›his‹ plane, and the use of the

ing a fighter pilot on a ›vertical‹ mission that brings him close to the ground and turns him into the pilot's accomplice:

»Down we went again, away from the gnarled and fissured forest towards the river, flattening out over the neglected rice-fields, aimed like a bullet at one small sampan on the yellow stream. The cannon gave a single burst of tracer, and the sampan blew apart in a shower of sparks: we didn't even wait to see our victims struggling to survive, but climbed and made for home. I thought again as I had thought when I saw the dead child at Phat Diem, ›I hate war.‹ There had been something so shocking in our sudden fortuitous choice of a prey – we had just happened to be passing, one burst only was required, there was no one to return our fire, we were gone again, adding our little quota to the world's dead« (ibid., 150).

Linguistically, Fowler's engagement is reflected in his use of the first-person plural which identifies him as a co-agent and not just a voyeur of the attack, while, at the same time, his outrage and sympathy with the victims are also expressed. As a result of his newly discovered hatred of war and what it does to innocent victims (also with the explosives that Pyle delivers), Fowler betrays Pyle to men of whom he knows that they will kill the quiet American.

Greene's correspondent is shocked into moral awareness to such an extent that he permits his own behaviour to become morally tainted when he delivers Pyle to his certain death. *The Quiet American* thus draws a completely different image of the war correspondent than Kipling's *The Light That Failed*, where Dick Heldar's attitude towards war remains morally detached even where he watches others dying. Victorian war correspondence is explicitly addressed in Greene's novel and contrasted with the present: »›The spice has gone out of the dish, hasn't it?‹ Wilkins said. ›We ought to have lived in the days of Russell and the old *Times*. Dispatches by balloon. One had time to do some fancy writing then‹« (ibid., 181). Not only has the excitement gone; Fowler realises that Victorian war representation also worked on another ethics. While watching a combat himself from a Cathedral tower, Fowler remembers the pictures of Victorian war artists and associates them with spatial and moral distance: »From the bell tower of the Cathedral the battle was only picturesque, fixed like a panorama of the Boer War in an old *Illustrated London News*. [...] The war was very tidy and clean at that distance« (ibid., 46). This is not an interpretation which Victorian war artists themselves would have shared, whose first-hand experience of war was often ex-

---

first-person plural signifies comradeship between reporter and warrior in a common cause.

tremely close. Fowler associates the Victorian representation of war with distance above all because it lacks an expression of the hatred of war that he has just discovered himself.

The Quiet American was first filmed in 1958 (USA, dir. Joseph L. Mankiewicz), when Indochina was still a conflict area in the news; the film then toned down the novel's anti-American sentiment. The 2002 adaptation (USA, dir. Phillip Noyce) was more faithful to the novel and produced at a time when the portrayal of a war correspondent's ethical dilemma had become topical again in the wake of the Yugoslavian wars. The second adaptation of Greene's novel is thus part of a whole new surge of fictional representations of war reporters that includes, as Chapter 5 will show, a number of British examples. Between Greene's novel and the 1990s, however, the fictional portrayal of war correspondents was dominated by the Vietnam War and films about that conflict, most of which are of American origin.

Vietnam and Beyond. Correspondents in War and Anti-War Films of the 1980s

The correspondents of the Vietnam War added new facets to the lore about the profession, and they helped to create an ambivalent image of the war reporter as both war addict and war critic. Western reporters in Vietnam were able to operate without restrictions by the US military, hitching rides with military units, even in helicopters, to wherever they chose to go. This gained them a reputation of dare-devil investigators and later gave rise to the myth that their unrestrained reporting had turned public opinion against the war and lost the United States the war at home. The most famous Vietnam reporters were American, including David Halberstam, Neil Sheehan, Sydney Schanberg and Michael Herr, whose *Dispatches* (1977), written in the subjective and dynamic mode of the so-called New Journalism, became a cult book among journalists that shaped the writing and the image of later reporters. The following passage is typical of Herr's breathless style and frequent use of the second person, which also draws the reader into the narrated experience. Furthermore it exemplifies the (American) Vietnam correspondent's empathy with the soldiers and a view of the war as a mad and terrible but, at the same time, fascinating and almost addictive experience. Indeed, as presented in *Dispatches*, the Vietnam reporter is as infatuated with war and its violence as some of the real and fictional Victorian correspondents discussed above (albeit with a distinct lack of patriotic commitment):

»Whichever way it went, you were covering the war, your choice of story told it all and in Vietnam an infatuation like that with violence wouldn't go unrequited for very long, it would come and put its wild mouth all over you.
›Quakin' and Shakin'‹, they called it, great balls of fire, Contact. [...] Amazing, unbelievable, guys who'd played a lot of hard sports said they'd never felt anything like it, the sudden drop and rocket rush of the hit, the reserves of adrenalin you could make available to yourself, pumping it up and putting it out until you were lost floating in it, not afraid, almost open to clear orgasmic death-by-drowning in it, actually relaxed. Unless of course you'd shit your pants or were screaming or praying or giving anything at all to the hundred-channel panic that blew word salad all around you and sometimes clean through you. Maybe you couldn't love the war and hate it inside the same instant, but sometimes those feelings alternated so rapidly that they spun together in a strobic wheel rolling all the way up until you were literally High On War, like it said on all the helmet covers. Coming off a jag like that could really make a mess out of you« (Herr 1978, 63).

British reporters in Vietnam tended to be more marginal figures than their American colleagues who were, after all, covering a war of their own country and the plight of their own soldiers. As Phillip Knightley (2004, 420) observes, »the British press seemed reluctant to get deeply involved«, and »British magazines relied for their Vietnam coverage mostly on freelance journalists and photographers, who visited Vietnam for short periods.« Some of the British reporters in Vietnam also commented on their special ideological position in this American war. Max Hastings, for instance, writes in his memoirs:

»I was never a Vietnam radical, committed to the victory of the communists. I was merely one of many Europeans who recoiled from the poisonous, crass, irredeemably materialist anti-culture America had imported to that marvellous society. People like me found ourselves in uneasy political no man's land, despairing of Washington's unwinnable war, yet convinced that the Vietnamese deserved better than a life under Hanoi's commissars« (Hastings 2000, 90f.).

Like Hastings, Michael Nicholson also reported from Vietnam and Cambodia for British television,[15] but the best-known British correspondent of this war was James Cameron, especially when he was among the first journalists permitted to enter North Vietnam in 1965.[16] Cameron's

---

15 See Nicholson (1991, Chapter 6).
16 Cameron wrote about this experience in his book *Witness* (1966).

human commitment to the Vietnamese population has already been pointed out (pp. 33-34). The Australian journalist John Pilger wrote features for various British newspapers and magazines, being primarily associated to the London *Daily News*. His *The Last Day* (1975) covers the American retreat at the end of the war hour by hour and in a style inspired, like Michael Herr's, by the New Journalism. The Scottish newspaper reporter John Burrowes looked back to his experiences in Vietnam in a similarly expressive and subjective style, emphasising the male bonding between soldiers and reporters in which he also took part. But while many of his colleagues immersed themselves fully in the war experience, Burrowes claims that he tried to keep his distance and remain an observer – also of his colleague's ›cool‹ display amid the havoc of war:

»In the war that was everywhere and nowhere, nowhere and everywhere, there was a lot of action around Saigon, end-of-the-road point of the incredible Ho Chi Minh trail, which made it possible for those journalists of the Saigon brigade who wanted to cover more than the Follies [the military's official press conference] to do a Hemingway and grab a taxi telling the driver, ›Follow that war.‹ They could ride out in a big Citroen, see a whole battle, return for the five o'clock statistics and still be in time for cocktails, their story having been filed and already read at foreign desks in a variety of Fleet Street offices« (Burrowes 1982, 27f.).

Vietnam has been considered the first real television war since it was the first time a war reached a television *mass* audience. Knightley claims that this mediation of the war had effects for its perception by the public, in particular their sense of the war's ›reality‹. But the place of television in everyday life also affected the perception and behaviour of soldiers and correspondents who developed a tendency to perceive the war through cinematic frames and to perform a role in front of cameras:

»For many Americans in Vietnam, there emerged a strange side to the war that became directly related to television – the fact that the war seemed so unreal that sometimes it became almost possible to believe that everything was taking place on some giant Hollywood set [...]. GIs – and even correspondents – brought up on Second World War movies shown on television, used to seeing Errol Flynn sweeping to victory through the jungles of Burma or Brian Donleavy giving the Japanese hell in the Coral Sea, tended to relate their experiences in Vietnam to the Hollywood version of America at war. Michael Herr, making a dash [...] from one position at Hué to another, caught himself saying to a Marine a line from a hundred Hollywood war films: ›We're going to cut out now. Will you cover us?‹ One should not be surprised, therefore, to find that GIs sometimes behaved, in the presence of television cameras, as if they were making *Dispatch from Da Nang*. [...]

So it is not difficult to understand how, when seen on a small screen, in the enveloping and cosy atmosphere of the household, sometime between the afternoon soap-box drama and the late-night war movie, the television version of the war in Vietnam could appear as just another drama, in which the hero is the correspondent and everything will come out all right at the end« (Knightley 2004, 454).

In this light, it is hardly surprising that most fictional representations of Vietnam reporters are found in film, notably the genre of war film, but here the correspondent is not always the hero, and his portrayal is often ambiguous and strongly dependent on a film's general ideological stance. The early Vietnam film *The Green Berets* (USA 1968, dir. Ray Kellogg and John Wayne) is anti-communist, patriotic and propagandist. It was made to counter scepticism in the US as to the necessity and legitimacy of American intervention in Vietnam, and it was intended by its makers – in particular John Wayne – to be a tribute to the men fighting in Vietnam. This explains why the film focuses almost exclusively on military-media relations and employs its war correspondent figure to depict a conversion, or even re-education. At the beginning of the plot, George Beckworth (played by David Janssen) represents war-critical voices in late-1960s America. Challenged by Colonel Kirby (played by John Wayne) to go to Vietnam himself in order to find out what the war is really about, Beckworth experiences a fierce North-Vietnamese attack on a US Special Forces camp and is afterwards convinced of the justification of fighting the communists. He affiliates with his country's soldiers and even crosses the line between correspondent and combatant. As Stephen Badsey writes in his analysis:

»At the end of the battle sequence, Beckworth carries a carbine rather than his typewriter, and has abandoned both his journalistic detachment and his newspaper prejudices. ›If I say what I feel I may be out of a job‹, he tells Kirby, who replies ›we'll always give you one.‹ Beckworth says that he can do Kirby more good with his typewriter. At the film's end Beckworth, wearing uniform and with a military kit-bag to balance his typewriter, returns to ›where the war is‹ to continue reporting« (Badsey 2002, 247).

In the film's pro-military frame, Beckworth thus changes from a ›bad‹, that is, anti-military journalist to a ›good‹ war reporter who feels and demonstrates his solidarity with the soldiers.[17]

---

17 The pattern is repeated in a later pro-military Vietnam film, *We Were Soldiers* (USA 2002, dir. Randall Wallace), where a correspondent also takes a gun voluntarily and fights with the soldiers who find themselves in a desperate situation during the Battle of la Drang.

The Green Berets shares an assumption with later films about the Vietnam War that war reporters cannot be impartial. However, Vietnam films of the 1980s, produced from some distance to the war itself and usually with anti-war tendencies, developed this assumption under different ideological premises. Accordingly, the character of the war correspondent is employed as a medium to depict war's futility and cruelty. Furthermore, correspondents in these later films also tend to reflect the ethical implications of their own engagement in the war, including the issue of detached versus attached journalism that was already at the core of Greene's *The Quiet American*. This mode of representation is in accord with Phillip Knightley's observation that covering Vietnam stands out in the history of war reporting »for it was there that correspondents began seriously to question the ethics of their business« (Knightley 2004, 448). Two of the most famous of the 1980s anti-war films about Vietnam are British (co-)productions: *The Killing Fields* (1984, dir. Roland Joffé) and *Full Metal Jacket* (1987, dir. Stanley Kubrick). The latter stands in particularly poignant contrast to *The Green Berets* since military-media relations are also at the core of its story.

Full Metal Jacket is based on a novel, Gustav Hasford's *The Short-Timers* (1979). It was co-written by Michael Herr, who also modelled a few characters on the soldiers he had got to know in Vietnam while reporting for *Esquire* magazine and later described in *Dispatches*.[18] The film has not only become a classic of (anti-)war film – cited, for instance, in *Jarhead* (see pp. 134-135) – but also an iconic point of reference for war correspondents, as in Chris Ayres's *War Reporting for Cowards* (see pp. 66-67). The main character of *Full Metal Jacket*, Private (later Sergeant) ›Joker‹, is a drafted soldier working as a marine combat reporter for the military newspaper *Stars and Stripes.* For him, military and journalistic habitus, military and journalistic field, become entangled and lead to a double perspective through which Joker is privileged to perceive the madness and absurdities of the war with great acuteness and personal involvement. Acting as both combatant and reporter, Joker is a character torn between different role expectations as well as his personal attitude towards the war. At heart a pacifist (wearing a peace button on his uniform) he is obliged not only to fight but also to cover the war affirmatively in order to counteract its negative coverage in the civilian media. The film underlines Joker's double status by showing him interviewing other soldiers *and* as an object of media attention himself, for example when he is filmed by a civilian camera team after having been

---

18 When working on the narration for Francis Ford Coppola's *Apocalypse Now* (released in its first version in 1979), Herr had also drawn on *Dispatches*.

involved in an attack. Stephen Badsey emphasises the meta-dimension of these scenes:

»The brief appearance in the film of a television camera crew during the Battle of Hué is for comic purposes, highlighting the difference between the ›emotional truth‹ of combat and whatever can be caught on documentary film. Kubrick underscores the point by introducing the camera team with a long sideways tracking (or crabbing) shot – showing them filming the marines with a long sideways tracking shot. The director's camera duplicates the action of the supposed combat documentary camera« (Badsey 2002, 249).

While the civilian journalists have the choice to leave the battlefield (and to report the war critically), the film makes it clear that Joker, as part of the military, does not have this option: Like his comrades in arms, he cannot escape the war of which he is forced to be a participant, and he cannot write as an impartial or even critical correspondent. An early scene in the *Stars and Stripes* newsroom shows how the soldier-reporters are instructed precisely what to cover and in what manner. Joker may be able to act subversively to a certain extent, even wearing his peace button, but his writing is subjected to military control. Indeed, as an individual soldier Joker has greater freedom to express his opinion and humanity than as a journalist. Significantly, since the autonomy of his actions as a *military* reporter is highly restricted in the first place, Joker makes his most decisive ethical decision as a combatant rather than as a reporter: Acting within the military field, he can commit an act of mercy towards the enemy, when, with a group of fellow soldiers, he comes across a lethally injured North Vietnamese woman who asks to be killed quickly rather than to be left dying in agony. In a reversion of the audience's likely role expectations, Joker is humanly committed as a warrior, not as a journalist.

The Killing Fields, by contrast, depicts reporters practicing a journalism of commitment. The film is based on the memoirs of a *New York Times* reporter, Sydney Schanberg's *The Death and Life of Dith Pran* (1980). Schanberg was in Cambodia, a secondary theatre of the war in Vietnam, from 1973 and witnessed the population's suffering in the war between the country's US-supported national army and the communist Khmer Rouge. Schanberg stayed in Cambodia with other Western journalists when Phnom Penh was surrendered to the Khmer Rouge in 1975. The film focuses on the friendship between Schanberg (played by Sam Waterston) and his Cambodian colleague and interpreter Dith Pran (played by Haing S. Ngor). The two men see themselves as committed reporters aiming to expose the war's atrocities and the United States' responsibility for the plight of the Cambodian people. When Westerners are evacuated from Cambodia, Schanberg manages to get papers for Pran's family, but Pran decides to stay behind and help to cover the communist take-over. Pran even manages to save his American and British colleagues when they are taken captive by the Khmer Rouge and face immediate execution. In turn he needs their assistance when the Khmer Rouge force all remaining Westerners to evacuate and demand that Cambodian citizens in their company be delivered into their hands. His colleagues try to provide Pran with a British passport but the attempt fails. In the course of Pol Pot's ›year zero‹ campaign against undesirable citizens, Pran is imprisoned in a forced-labour camp and only survives because he manages to pose as an uneducated peasant. After an ordeal of several years during which he witnesses and experiences the Khmer Rouge's crimes against their own people, Pran manages to escape and reach a Red Cross camp on the border of Thailand in 1979.

His decision to continue his professional work has almost cost him his life, and this turns him into the film's hero – not the action-hero type of war correspondent we have encountered before, but the journalist risking to become a martyr to his profession in the name of truth and the human commitment he sees as part of his professional ethos. While Pran is, in this manner, almost canonised, Schanberg is shown conducting futile attempts to rescue his friend through international aid organisations and through making his fate public. In a scene set in New York, Schanberg receives the Journalist of the Year award and takes the opportunity to accuse the US government of a lack of concern for the Cambodian people when they interfered in Cambodia, that is, he uses his status as a prominent journalist to make a political statement and thus also expresses his engagement. However, juxtaposing Pran's suffering in Cambodia with Schanberg's career in New York, the film also exposes the First World correspondent's privilege over the local Third World journalist. Schanberg and his Western colleagues also lead a dangerous existence, but their passports and press cards help to evacuate them in time, while their local contacts, from whom they have profited, remain behind. But despite this note of critique, the most lasting impression derived from *The Killing Fields* is the image of the war correspondent determined to expose crimes against humanity and the irresponsibility of interventionist politics. With this humanitarian and political concern, *The Killing Fields* takes care not to sensationalise the war reporter; neither Pran nor Schanberg, as embodied by their respective actors, bear any resemblance to the maverick type but come across as quiet and considerate men afraid for their own lives but still committed to political and humanitarian ideals.

This is a general note in 1980s war films. *The Year of Living Dangerously* (AUS/USA 1982, dir. Peter Weir)[19] is set in 1965 and in Indonesia, where President Sukarno faced growing discontent in the population and political resistance. This situation is witnessed by the main character, the young Australian foreign correspondent Guy Hamilton (played by Mel Gibson), who works for the Australian Broadcasting Service. At the beginning of his career, Hamilton is after big stories but at first has problems getting any information at all. Even his more experienced colleagues have to piece their news together from a variety of sources that include the government, the communist party (PKI), the conservative Muslim military and various embassies. In the course of the plot Guy learns that his profession is about more than just good stories and demands serious ethical choices. Guy's mentor in this educational process is his Chinese-Australian photographer Billy Kwan (played by Linda Hunt) who has lived in Jakarta for a long time. Once a sympathiser of Sukarno, he is now disillusioned with the regime, seeing how the Indonesian people still live in misery. Kwan takes action and protests against Sukarno; he is killed when he hangs a sign from a hotel window that reads »Sukarno feed your people.« After his friend has thus died for his political conviction, Guy also learns that he cannot avoid involvement in the chaotic political situation. Instead of getting his big story he suffers bodily harm himself and only barely escapes from the country at the last moment.

A similar element of a war reporter's political and ethical awakening is the subject of *Under Fire* (USA 1982, dir. Roger Spottiswode). This film, which is based on experiences of actual journalists, is set in Nicaragua in 1979 and criticises the United States' covert involvement in the country's civil war between Sandinista revolutionaries and the Contra military government. Russell Price is a tough and cynical American war photographer who, after Vietnam, has turned up in every theatre of war in the developing world. He is introduced in a scene in Africa, where he comes across a mercenary whom he has met regularly in many other conflicts over the years. The loose comradeship between the two men suggests that the correspondent capitalises on war just like the mercenary soldier and is thus a morally ambiguous character. But in Nicaragua Price matures from a war addict to a journalist with political and humane awareness, and this process includes his conversion from impartial to attached correspondent to such an extent that Price even compromises the objectivity of the photographic record on which his career has always

---

19 The film is based on a novel of the same title (1978) by Australian writer Christopher Koch, who also worked on the screenplay.

relied before. A catalyst in this development of his professional and personal self-image is Price's relationship with his colleague Claire, who leaves her husband and fellow reporter Alex Grazier for Price.

The issue of photographic objectivity and hence the photograph's special status in war reporting is foregrounded in the film by a specific use of intercuts: Several times the film shows how Price shoots a picture, and then immediately the shot picture itself, in black and white. The viewer is thus startled out of the film's narrative for a moment and sees, on a meta-level, to what extent the respective photo matches the scene actually photographed. Even where the match is close, the image always loses the colour of the original scene and freezes only a specific moment. By this juxtaposition the film emphasises that even an authentic image presents just a selection and is open to interpretation. This prepares the viewer for the moment in which Price fakes a photograph in order to support a group of Sandinistas with whom he and Claire have established a relationship and with whose political aims they have come to sympathise. The revolutionaries have lost their leader in a fight but want their enemy – and the enemy's American supporters – to believe that the man is still alive since this will delay another delivery of military aid from the United States. After some hesitation, Price agrees to take a photograph on which the dead man looks alive and which therefore has the desired effect. The journalistic observer has become an active and willing participant of the conflict and a direct player in the political field. But Price is also involved in the political play against his will when some of his photos of guerilleros are stolen by the secret service and the men and women are identified and executed. A Contra militia also kills Alex Grazier. Price's photo of this act of murder gets him into immediate danger, but he manages to escape and his picture is shown on television, with major consequences for the further course of the civil war. The film thus asserts the power of the media, but does not celebrate the war correspondent unambiguously. Reporters are shown to be courageous and committed, some even becoming martyrs of their profession, but the film also shows them acting selfishly and exploiting foreign wars for the sake of their own ego and their careers. When the picture of Alex's murder is shown on television, a Nicaraguan woman remarks cynically that this image of a dead American journalist will finally outrage the Americans – something the reports about dead Nicaraguans apparently did not achieve. A dead journalist in this case seems to be of greater use than the living ones.

Oliver Stone's *Salvador* (USA 1986), loosely adapted from the »true story« of American journalist Richard Boyle, goes ideologically in the same direction as *Under Fire*. The film is set in the early 1980s when the

Nicaraguan revolution swept over to El Salvador. Its main character Boyle (played by James Woods) is a former television reporter of the Pacific News Service who has lost his job and his wife; Boyle drowns his sense of failure in alcohol and drugs. In order to make some money with reporting from the place where his career began and to join up with his former lover Maria, Boyle decides to go to El Salvador, where he is immediately confronted with the chaos and danger of the war. He meets old colleagues and revives his friendship with John Cassady (played by John Savage), a *Newsweek* photographer whose dream it is to take a ›Robert Capa‹ photo, that is, a picture revealing the truth about war because the photographer dared to get close enough to his object. Lacking a camera team and equipment, Boyle also begins to photograph the war and its atrocities. At first he does not care on which side of the conflict these atrocities take place, understanding himself merely as an uninvolved witness. Increasingly, however, and also through reconnecting with Maria, Boyle sympathises with the revolutionaries and thus gets into opposition to his own country's political aims. In the American embassy, he openly accuses a CIA representative of disregarding human rights.

In a predictable episode, Boyle's colleague Cassady is fatally injured while taking his Capa photo, which proves the Americans' interference in El Salvador. Boyle promises his dying colleague that he will take the film to the US. This gets him into trouble, but although he is wounded himself, Boyle manages to return to the States with Cassady's photographs and Maria, who is, however, refused entry to the US because immigration authorities do not accept her as a refugee. Despite this setback, the film's final titles reveal that Boyle does not return to his former routine of drink and drugs but spends the next months looking for Maria and getting Cassady's story published. His experience in El Salvador has effected a change for the better in him, professionally and personally.

The war-critical films of the 1980s sketched in his section portray correspondents as investigators and as journalists whose political and ethical awareness is raised through their experiences so that they are forced into reaction and even outright political action. All reporters are shown to take risks and some, especially Price in *Under Fire*, bear traces of men addicted to the excitement of armed conflict. Belonging to the Vietnam generation, they have a strong understanding of themselves as individual reporters acting with a high degree of autonomy. Even in the films about Vietnam, none of the reporters betray any patriotic affiliations; on the contrary, they are highly critical of the manner in which their country interferes in wars of the developing world. The reporters are portrayed as complex, torn characters with some dubious traits, but they are drawn positively where they become committed to the humane cause and protest against a war's cruelty and injustice instead of being mere ›objective‹ observers.

In the films discussed, British correspondents appear as marginal characters (for instance in *The Killing Fields*), if they appear at all – after all, most of the wars in question were overt and covert wars of the United States. However, in 1982, the British also fought a war of their own in the South Atlantic. Chapter 2 has cited excerpts from correspondents' reminiscences of the Falklands War, relating, above all, to its strict censorship and the nature of military-media relations which struck many reporters as a relapse into routines that seemed distinctly out-of-date – especially to those who had experienced the freedom of covering the war in Vietnam. Robert Fox, a BBC radio reporter in the Falklands campaign, remembers the epigonal quality of the Falklands experience in his memoirs:

»Reporting the war was a strangely difficult experience. It was an enclosed, remote and relatively brief episode, with far less scope for vicarious experience of it by those at home than in the television campaigns in the Middle East and Vietnam. The way we moved in the fields, mostly on our feet, gave it an oddly old-fashioned quality. Much of the language of the troops was the same as in the trenches of the Western Front and the land campaigns of the Second World War [...]. The hacks who had covered other, bigger, noisier wars seemed infected by the brilliance of Michael Herr's *Dispatches*, the cult work of New Journalism on the Vietnam War. But this was war on a more liliputian scale, and there were no PXes, telexes or Intercontinental Hotels, only the Upland Goose and a succession of ›bivvies‹ and ›bashers‹ across the island. It was at once an intimate and remote experience. Intimate because we lived so close to the soldiers and shared their thoughts and worries with them. [...] It was remote because it was so old-fashioned; some of the officers spoke in the gentlemanly way that their predecessors might in the Desert War or the Battle of Britain« (Fox 1982, 312f.).

As a conflict of limited national interest, the Falklands War yielded a limited number of correspondents' memoirs because they gave these journalists an opportunity to write about everything they had been restricted to report while the war was still going on, and to complain about the control measures to which they had been exposed. There are no significant fictional representations of the Falklands correspondents, however, which indicates that public interest in their performance was limited and that this performance also had no impact on existing perceptions of the war correspondent. Max Hastings had his scoop of being the first man into Port Stanley (see p. 37), but there were no other memorable journalistic exploits. There was also no occasion in the Falklands for the committed journalism that was evolving as a dominant perceptual frame in the course of the 1980s, so that the correspondents of this conflict, just like the short war in general, soon vanished from cultural representation and cultural memory.

A Century of Changing Images

This chapter has traced some major changes which the image of the war correspondent underwent in representations from the First World War to the 1980s. Literary representation indicates to what extent the Golden Age image inherited from the 19th century had been shattered until 1918, due to working conditions that kept journalists on a short leash and under strict military and political control. Journalists themselves felt they had to write against this bad image, and some, such as Philip Gibbs and Ellis Ashmead-Bartlett, developed a new critical habitus of working against the officially sanctioned view of war and/or expressing their compassion for war's victims. They thus prefigured a pattern that became significant in the second half of the 20th century. In-between, however, the Second World War first reconsolidated the correspondents' image and established war reporters, in their own and others' perception, as valued players in the field of war and important interpreters of the soldiers' experiences for the people at home – a complete reversal of the image correspondents had acquired during the First World War. In close contact with the soldiers, the correspondents of the Second World War not merely observed its events but often became participants in its actions, which helped to re-generate a notion of the correspondent as a war hero in his own right. The war in Vietnam, largely covered by ›unilaterals‹, also gave correspondents the opportunity to ›do a Hemingway‹ and exhilarate in the dangers of martial action; but anti-war films about Vietnam, most of which were produced in the 1980s, disseminated other facets of the correspondent's image: They show reporters as independent and critical individuals, personally engaged and often shaken into ethical awareness in relation to war itself and their own role as its mediators. The same pattern is found in 1980s films set in other war scenarios, located in the developing world and thus also raising issues of Western intervention and the reporting of such intervention in Western media.

By the end of the 1980s, then, fictional representations of a largely war-critical nature had helped to construct a dominant role perception of the autonomous war reporter who questions the reasons for wars, speaks up for their victims and refuses to be manipulated by politics and the military. This positive image of war journalism provides an important foil for the cultural perception and representation of correspondents in the 1990s, a decade when public awareness of correspondents and their portrayal in novels and films soared to a new height, for various reasons and under quite different conditions. While the civil wars in former Yugoslavia encouraged the habitus of the critical and ›attached‹ journalist, it was severely challenged by new modes of information warfare in the Gulf.

CHAPTER 5: 1990s TO PRESENT.
THE MEDIA IN WAR FROM GULF TO GULF

»No other war [...] has been fought so much in
public, under the eye of the camera. At least the
Gulf campaign was waged mainly in the desert,
and reported under conditions of military
censorship. In Bosnia there was no desert except
that created by the conflicting armies, especially
the Serbs; and no censorship either, for it
occurred anarchically in the decade of the dish,
that ubiquitous concave disc that uplinks all our
tragedies and connects us to them. It was this
peculiarly twentieth-century combination, of the
means of mass destruction with the means of
mass communication, that brought the war's
daily horrors into the living rooms of the world«
(Martin Bell 1995, 137).

New Cultural Awareness of
War Correspondents

The new surge of cultural interest in war correspondents in the 1990s can
be attributed to a number of reasons. First of all, the nineties were the
decade when real-time television transmissions from remote war zones
became possible and 24-hour news channels began to call for a continual
supply from their correspondents. It was also the decade when the military recognised the necessity of information warfare and, accordingly,
new modes of military-media relations. As a new type of ›video war‹, the
Gulf War of 1991 captured the public's attention and created general
interest in how wars are communicated. In Phillip Knightley's analysis,
the Gulf War »marked an important turning point in the history of war
correspondents«, not only as »a war in which the military succeeded in
changing people's perceptions of what battle was really like [...], but one

in which the way the war was communicated was as important as the conduct of the war itself« (Knightley 2004, 500). One could argue that the remote images with which television audiences were ›bombarded‹ during this war caused a special demand for interpretation by correspondents within the actual theatre of war. CNN's live reports from enemy territory in Baghdad certainly served such demand (and they were also a classic scoop). On the allied side, pooled correspondents provided views from the front and interviews with soldiers, while their non-pooled colleagues publicly lamented the military's control over information and images that clashed with their ideal of autonomous journalism.[1]

While coverage of the war in the Gulf thus strongly emphasised military-media relations and aspects of mediation as such, the civil wars in former Yugoslavia drew the public's attention to another facet of contemporary war journalism: engagement for a harassed civilian population which most correspondents felt to be ill-served by the United Nations and NATO presence established for their protection. As mentioned in Chapter 2, the Yugoslavian wars initiated a debate about a ›journalism of attachment‹ that was conducted in the media themselves and spread to the general public. With its focus on the ethics of war and war journalism as well as many prominent reporters who openly expressed their humanitarian engagement, the conflicts in ex-Yugoslavia attracted the attention of more literary writers and filmmakers than any of the preceding wars. Before turning to the Yugoslavian wars, this chapter will first address the Gulf War and the controversial (self-)representations that resulted from this conflict. It will finally return to the Persian Gulf, the war on terror and its implications for war reporting and the representation of war correspondents.

---

1   On the difficulties of reporting the 1991 Gulf War see several contributions in Walsh (1995). See also Smith (1992), Thomson (1992), Baroody (1998) and Taylor (1998). The reporting of the Gulf War was a major topic in British newspapers (both broadsheets and tabloids) and magazines. During the war and in subsequent months they all (from *The Economist* and *The Times* to *The Sun*) published articles in which correspondents described their war experiences and reflected on the conditions of war reporting in the contemporary media.

Pooled and Fooled? Representing Reporters of the First Gulf War

Until operation ›Iraqi Freedom‹ in 2003, the 1991 war in the Gulf was »the most widely and most swiftly reported war in history. Journalists from all over the world jostled with each other to follow the events as they occurred and beamed them by satellite to waiting multitudes whose hunger for news was insatiable« (Hudson/Stanier 1999, 209). The world-wide audience for each night of the conflict consisted of up to 600 million people (ibid., 224). British correspondents selected into the allied forces' pooling system experienced a proximity to the military that had its pros and cons (see pp. 51-52). Others preferred to work independently (or unilaterally), reporting the war from enemy territory, without military protection and risking to be criticised as unpatriotic at home (see pp. 52-53). Several reporters' memoirs appeared right after the war, taking advantage of its topicality and the reporters' own celebrity status of the moment. Fictional representations of Gulf War correspondents, however, only emerged with a certain delay. Indeed, the most significant ones, all American productions, did not appear until the ›war on terror‹, declared after 9/11, had rekindled interest in the Persian Gulf region as a theatre of potential and finally actual war. With respect to the construction of a cultural image, it seems significant that only one of these productions retrospectively presents Gulf War reporters in positive terms and that these journalists were *non*-pooled correspondents reporting from Baghdad.

The television film *Live from Baghdad* (USA 2002, dir. Mick Jackson) was produced by the American HBO network, but with an eye on global distribution. Its cast includes international stars such as Michael Keaton and Helena Bonham Carter. In fictionalised form, the film narrates the rise of CNN during the Iraqi invasion of Kuwait and CNN's legendary live reporting from Baghdad during the early phase of the American attacks, which complemented the military's long-distance images with authentic eyewitness reports. *Live from Baghdad* focuses on the team around local producer Robert Wiener (on whose book of the same title the film is based), and much of its drama is provided not by the war but the journalistic field itself. The film celebrates Wiener and especially his reporters Peter Arnett, John Holliman und Bernard Shaw, who fought an exhausting war of their own to inform the public and to triumph over CNN's competitors. At the end of the plot, the reporters have overcome all difficulties they had to face and all rivalry among themselves, and thus have been able to write a chapter in the history of (war) journalism.

Live from Baghdad is a celebration of autonomous journalism. By contrast, pooled reporters in the Gulf had no chance to become the object of celebration or even heroisation. Like the ground troops, they hardly encountered any fighting at all. Above all, they were subjected to military control and thus eluded the dominant role perception that identified ›good‹ reporters as critical and independent. In two major feature films about the Gulf War, *Three Kings* and *Jarhead*, war correspondents are marginal figures portrayed either negatively or as completely insignificant. They are also part of a television team and fit into a pattern that Stephen Badsey has identified as a new stereotype in recent Hollywood war film: »[T]he new ›infotainment‹ style of instant television news of the 1980s rapidly produced a stock Hollywood character of the television reporter as a comic and contemptible figure. [...] By the 1990s this portrayal of the television reporter [...] as a comic intruder into the world of the fighting man was well established« (Badsey 2002, 254).

Three Kings (USA 1999, dir. David O. Russell) is set in the aftermath of the Gulf War and shows its three military protagonists looking for the gold treasure Saddam had stolen from Kuwait. Eventually, however, they take on a nobler role when they rescue a group of Iraqis who have rebelled against Saddam and are desperate to cross the border into Kuwait. A cable news reporter, Adriana Cruz (played by Nora Dunn in a manner that recalls CNN celebrity Christiane Amanpour, who had worked as a pooled reporter in this war), is a tough woman determined to get her story at all cost. She pesters the three heroes for information but ironically becomes their dea ex machina when she helps them to get the refugees out of Iraq and to escape punishment themselves. Her motivation is not a humanitarian one but the chance, once more, to get a good story. And her interference is successful since the military is highly sensitive to the power of television. As a general says, this is »a media war«, and it must not be turned into »another Vietnam« through hostile reporting.

Jarhead (USA 2005), a film by British director Sam Mendes, is more bitter in its satire of both the military and the media, in the manner of Kubrick's *Full Metal Jacket*, which Mendes cites in several scenes. *Jarhead* is based on the memoirs of ex-marine Antony Swofford, whose unit was deeply frustrated when they entered the war fully trained and highly motivated but hardly saw any action because the war was fought with long-distance weapons. Like *Three Kings*, Swofford's book and the *Jarhead* film satirise a media war in which journalists are courted and utilised at the same time. It is in this respect that the film's references to *Full Metal Jacket* are particularly telling. As a member of the military, Joker in Kubrick's film has to obey military orders, also in his reporting.

Nevertheless, his behaviour is subversive and he speaks up wherever he can. The reporters in *Jarhead*, by contrast, are presented as a flock of sheep under full control of their military minders. A television team led by a female correspondent is taken to Swofford's unit in order to interview the marines who have before been shown practising all the answers they are expected to deliver. The soldiers themselves identify this as »un-American« censorship, but the reporters do not even seem to notice how the men have been prepared, and they also follow all the prescribed rules for their own behaviour. When the marines are ordered to stage a game of football for the reporters, in the glaring heat and in full gear, they react anarchically and perform a »field fuck« instead, but the television crew permit themselves to be quickly removed before they can grasp the significance of the incident. These reporters, the film suggests, are no adequate witnesses; they are ineffective, marginal figures quite distant from any ideals associated with their profession.

The utterly negative image conveyed in these two films differs from the self-representation of Gulf War reporters. As Chapter 2 has shown, reporters' memoirs also discuss the Gulf War as a new kind of media war and do so in a manner that is often critical. But neither John Simpson (who covered the war from Baghdad) nor Kate Adie (who was pooled with the troops) seem to be worried that their performance in the Gulf War could have harmed their public image. This discrepancy between autobiographical and fictional representation might be explained by the fact that for most war correspondents, the Gulf War was only a brief episode soon to be followed and ›overwritten‹ by the Yugoslavian wars and their entirely different conditions of and challenges for reporting, which also had significant consequences for the reporters' self- and public perception. Humanitarian issues were at the fore of what the media conveyed from this zone of war, and the media players had the satisfaction of achieving something in the political field:

»The catalyst which finally compelled the world to react was the combined force of the world's press and television. Probably never before had the influence of the media been more powerfully felt by the governments of the world than in the ensuing months and years of the war in Bosnia. During the spring and summer of 1992, the world's television screens were filled with scenes of death and destruction in Bosnia« (Hudson/Stanier 1999, 278).

Individually, correspondents contributed to this success by reporting in a personalised mode and openly expressing their own political and humanitarian commitment.

Reporting the Civil Wars in Former Yugoslavia

In retrospect, journalists in Bosnia have been stylised as participants in the war more dedicated to the ›peace-keeping‹ and humanitarian mission than the United Nations troops detached for this purpose:

»The war in Bosnia has been reported to the world through all its vicissitudes by a team of brave and committed journalists who have spent longer and endured in many cases far greater danger than the soldiers who have tried to keep the peace. They have told the truth as they have seen it, but, as we know with the benefit of hindsight, it was so often only a part of the truth. The pictures of destruction and mutilation have put pressure on the leaders of the world to act, often unwisely and in haste. [...] Yet without those same pictures, there is little doubt that few if any of the attempts would have been made at all« (Hudson/Stanier 1999, 299).[2]

This view of humanly committed war journalists is shared by many correspondents of the Bosnian war. Martin Bell remembers how he was emotionally involved and often overwhelmed:

»For all of us who came to it from the outside, the Bosnian conflict has been not just another foreign war, but a shocking and defining experience, which has changed our way of doing things and seeing things. It was my eleventh, in a catalogue running from Vietnam to the Gulf, and it was quite unlike all the others. It had this impact on us because of its brutality and ferocity, because of its merciless targeting of civilian populations, because of a level of risk and danger that none of us had expected, and perhaps also because of its closeness to home. None of us had been prepared to see a war on such a scale in our continent and in our time« (Bell 1995, 135).

While Bell covered Bosnia for television, his colleague Janine di Giovanni reported for *The Times*. Her account of two years in Bosnia (1992-94), most of them spent during the siege of Sarajevo, mentions the dangers she experienced herself under sniper fire. Its main emphasis, however, is on the suffering of the civilians, with whom she established friendships and whom she wanted urgently to assist:

---

2   For Kosovo, the role of the media tends to be assessed more critically than for Bosnia: »With very few exceptions, Western journalists uncritically framed the conflict in these terms: Nato was trying to help. This volume aims to challenge the received wisdom, subjecting both the war, and the media coverage it received, to critical scrutiny« (Hammond/Herman 2000, 1).

»Something happened inside all of us who reported the war in Sarajevo on a long-term, consistent basis, because Sarajevo was an emotional story. Despite the endless diplomatic dithering, the broken ceasefires, the days and weeks spent waiting for air strikes, and the belief that hope was slowly filtering out of the place as the West refused to act. It was difficult to be just an observer, unable to make or affect policy, facing friends and families in Sarajevo who constantly asked for help. The only way to channel the anger and, at times, the bitterness was to report what was happening inside the city and hope that someone was reading it« (di Giovanni, 1994, 2f.).

More than other conflicts, the war in Bosnia provoked the kind of journalism which Martin Bell has characterised as »attached« and which aims to interfere in the political field:

»Two things had changed between the old journalism and the new. One was that we were no longer bystanders but players, and not all the time marginal players, in the conduct of armed conflict. The war of words and clash of arms ran parallel to each other and interacted. [...]
The other change was that, over the years, and not by design but by evolution, we had humanized the reporting of warfare. When I started in Vietnam and Israel in 1967, I had studied the practice of others and supposed it was about strategies, military formations and weapons systems. When I finished, in Bosnia in 1996, it was about people – the people who wage war and the people who suffer from war, who are often the same people« (Bell 2004, 163f.).

This ›humanising‹ of war reporting fitted into the already established cultural perception of the critical correspondent as a positive icon of the profession, and it gave rise not only to many memoirs, but also an increased appearance of Bosnia reporters in novels and fiction films.[3]

Welcome to Sarajevo (UK 1997, dir. Michael Winterbottom) is based on Michael Nicholson's *Natasha's Story*, the account of his support of an orphanage in Sarajevo and the evacuation of some of its children; Natasha, one of the orphans, was later adopted by Nicholson. In the film, the Nicholson character is called Michael Henderson and the girl he

---

3   They were also the subject of Marcel Ophüls's four-hour documentary film *The Troubles We've Seen* (F/GER/UK 1994). Here, reporters who had covered Bosnia and especially the siege of Sarajevo, talk about the perils of their job and the adrenalin kicks it gives them, their camaraderie and competition, the influence of television on politics, and their moral responsibility. But Ophüls also intersperses the journalists' usually positive self-presentations with ironic citations from feature films that relativise the interviews and suggest the extent to which the journalists were also part of the media business.

saves, Elmira. Henderson is at first a detached observer, filming atrocities without apparent emotional involvement. However, he becomes increasingly haunted by what he sees, especially after he has begun to report about the orphanage whose dead children have to be buried in its own garden. The director of the orphanage speaks into Henderson's camera: »Everyone must know we are dying. Tell them that we are dying.« While Henderson does try to tell at least the British public, politicians of various Western states and the United Nations remain inactive. Images from the children's graves in Sarajevo are cross-cut, among others, with Prime Minister John Major's statement in Parliament that injured Bosnian children should be treated »on the spot« in Yugoslavia rather than being taken abroad. UN representatives likewise claim that an evacuation of children from Bosnia would mean ›collaboration‹ with the Serbs and their policy of ›ethnic cleansing‹, since it would remove ›unwanted‹ citizens from Bosnia.

When showing attacks and politicians, the film uses stock footage from ITN, the BBC, CBC and other channels, and many scenes of the reporters in action are shot with a hand-held camera. This documentary effect underlines the film's political intent and helps to establish Henderson and his colleagues as protagonists who fight political and military inefficiency by making them public and appealing to their audience's own humanitarian concerns. Henderson enters the political field most demonstratively when he reports in front of a plane that was sent to evacuate some of the war's victims but will leave Yugoslavia empty because of the international community's tardiness in intervening. His personal solution is to take action on a smaller but also more effective scale and to help evacuate the orphans himself.

However, the film does not praise journalistic intervention in an entirely uncritical light because it shows that humanitarian engagement can also serve the media and their representatives themselves. At the beginning of the film, one sees correspondents filming civilian casualties. These are members of a wedding party attacked on their way to church. One of the reporters, the American Flynn, bravely carries an injured woman, the bride's mother, into the church. Since this heroic performance makes him a media celebrity, the scene suggests, according to one critic, the selfish side of journalistic interference:

»Flynn offers a commentary on his action, affirming that the display of this event on television in the United States will bring home the plight of Sarajevo to Americans.
Flynn remarks that this will be achieved both by showing the shots of his courage and by the fact that he is, for his American audience, more famous and important than the siege and its anonymous victims. [...] The question posed by

the film is to what degree is he exercising self-aggrandizement here, as opposed to wanting to ›help‹« (Camino 2005, 117f.).

Flynn's pride in his performance is a foil to Henderson's more noble and selfless intervention, and Henderson thus emerges as a hero, not in the sense of spectacular action heroism, but in the modern conception of a defender of basic human rights. The film also suggests, however, that on a more personal level Henderson's active engagement for the war's victims helps him to preserve his psychological health. Other films about correspondents in Bosnia put special emphasis on the trauma experienced by journalists exposed to human suffering. Indeed, more than any other conflict, the wars in former Yugoslavia seem to have inspired representations of the psychological vulnerability of war correspondents.

Before the Rain (1994, dir. Milcho Manchevski) is a Macedonian episodic film co-produced by Britain and France. It is partly set in Britain, and the film thus indicates that the war in former Yugoslavia has consequences for the whole of Europe. Nobody in Europe remains unconcerned by what seems ›just‹ a local civil war. In a drastic scene, the enmity between two Yugoslavian exiles in London leads to a massacre in a restaurant, killing many innocent people. The film's main concern, however, is the trauma of its male protagonist, the Macedonian war photographer Alexander who works for a British photo agency. Returning from Bosnia to London, Alexander gives up his job, claiming that he has become too involved and even killed a person. Alexander returns to Macedonia in order to find peace of mind, but this part of Yugoslavia is now also haunted by ethnic conflict, and Alexander is drawn into the course of events again. Saving a young Albanian woman from his fellow Macedonians, he is killed by one of his own people. Before this conclusion, Alexander has revealed what has happened to him in Bosnia: After a careless remark that he has not taken a ›sensational‹ picture yet, the member of a Serbian militia decides to ›help‹ the photographer and shoots a prisoner on the spot. Alexander, who photographs this killing automatically, feels complicit in the act of murder: »I took sides. My camera killed a human being.« Taking sides once more, this time deliberately when he helps the young Albanian woman, is Alexander's redemption for his traumatic guilt, but it also leads to his own death.

Beautiful People (UK 1999, dir. Jasmin Dizdar), another episodic film, also shows that the war in Bosnia had repercussions in Britain. One of its episodes centres on the BBC television reporter Jerry Higgins. In Bosnia, Higgins has witnessed the amputation of a leg in a field hospital in Srebrenica. He seems to be more disturbed by this incident than his own injury when he is shot in the leg by a sniper. Higgins is taken back

139

to Britain (with a lot of media attention for having been shot),[4] where it becomes obvious that he suffers from post-traumatic stress disorder. First he refuses to hand over his tape of the amputation, and then he suffers a complete breakdown and demands that his own injured leg must be amputated. A psychologist diagnoses ›Bosnia syndrome‹, the urge to identify with victims and see the world through their eyes – an exaggerated manifestation of the attitude many journalists developed in Bosnia. The episode ends on a lighter satirical note, however, when a guru tries to heal Higgins by hypnosis and then demands a fee so high that it seems to shock Higgins out of his trauma and back into British everyday life.

While the satire of *Beautiful People* is tempered with humour, a Slovenian film about Bosnia offers a bitterly sarcastic view of the war and its mediation. *No Man's Land* (2001, dir. Danis Tanović), co-produced with British money, makes the media a central object of its critique and for this purpose introduces the character of a British television journalist. In contrast to most other portrayals of correspondents in Bosnia, this journalist is an unsympathetic character since her humanitarian engagement is revealed to be a mere fashionable pose. The film is set in Bosnia in 1993, where three men, two Bosnians and a Serb, are trapped in a trench in no man's land. One of the Bosnians, Cera, is lying on a mine where he has been put by the Serb, who believed him to be dead, to demonstrate how this special kind of mine is made to explode – not when a weight is put on it, but when its pressure is removed again. Since the man on the mine is still alive, outside help is required and offered by a French UN unit who are then, however, ordered by their command to stay neutral and not get involved. Their radio communication is overheard by a team of Global News Channel whose reporter, Jane Livingstone, is keen on an exclusive story. Enacting the attached correspondent outraged by the UN's inactivity and threatening with the media's power to influence public opinion, Livingstone intimidates the colonel in command, another Briton: »I am preparing a news report which will go off in about half an hour, and it will be fascinating to monitor the response of millions of viewers who watch the show.« This report is sent indeed, with additional archive material on the UN's previous failure in Bosnia, and things are getting started. More UN soldiers arrive at the trench, officially ordered to help, as well as more reporters in pursuit of a story. Freed from the trench, the Serb and the mobile Bosnian start attacking each other again, with the result that the Bosnian kills the Serb and is then shot himself by a soldier. Before that shocking incident, the Bosnian

---

4   This may have been inspired by the experiences of Martin Bell, whose coming under fire in Bosnia was a similar media event (see p. 27).

has attacked the journalists, comparing them to vultures feeding on the misery of others. He is confirmed by Livingstone's first words to her cameraman after the shootings: »Did you get it?«

With biting irony, the film then reveals, however, that the media do not ›get‹ everything, in particular the most scandalous and hence ›biggest‹ part of the story: Since not even a German specialist is able to defuse the high-tech mine, the UN soldiers cannot save Cera, the man on the mine, but, for the media's sake, stage a cover-up and rescue a substitute instead. Cera is simply left to his fate – another act of UN inefficiency that the media miss because they have permitted themselves to be fooled by the military's rescue show. The UN may be unable to fulfil their humanitarian mission, but they have mastered the principles of Information Operations (see pp. 50-51), and successfully managed the journalists who believe that they have the military in their hands. Livingstone's demonstration of media power has achieved nothing, leaving two men dead and a third one certain to die. The committed journalism practiced in ex-Yugoslavia could not have been parodied more scathingly. Arguably, the films' temporal distance to events in Bosnia encouraged the satirical view of the war reporters in *Beautiful People* and *No Man's Land*. Despite such critique, however, the attached reporter has remained an influential template for the portrayal of war correspondents in former Yugoslavia. In 2003, two complex novels appeared with correspondents as central characters, Pat Barker's *Double Vision* and Michael Ignatieff's *Charlie Johnson's War*, and in both novels experiences in former Yugoslavia trigger the journalists' personal breakdowns.[5]

In Barker's novel, the war correspondent is part of a more general investigation of the ethics – or non-ethics – of a merely observing attitude towards life. The ethical problem of viewing human suffering is one of the essential points in Susan Sontag's meditation about *Regarding the Pain of Others* (2003), a book she wrote in reaction to a media culture in which images of atrocities proliferate. In today's »culture of spectatorship« (Sontag 2003, 105), the confrontation with the suffering of other human beings is impossible to avoid and calls for some kind of reaction, even though people may be uncertain as to what reaction is appropriate: »Photographs of an atrocity may give rise to opposing responses. A call for peace. A cry for revenge. Or simply the bemused awareness, continually restocked by photographic information, that terrible things happen«

---

5   My discussion of the two novels is based on an earlier article (Korte 2006b). In a plotline of Sarah May's novel *The Internationals*, which was also published in 2003, a hardboiled photojournalist discovers his conscience in a refugee camp in Macedonia during the NATO bombing of Serbia in 1999.

(ibid., 13).[6] Sontag's book is one of the sources which Pat Barker acknowledges in *Double Vision* (2003).

Barker joins a familiar contemporary critique where her novel points to the predominance of the image in news representation and the fact that this flood of images threatens to numb the audience's moral sensibility. Her correspondent character, Stephen Sharkey, remembers the video game images from the 1991 Gulf War, »the first war to appear on TV screens as a kind of *son et lumière* display« and wonders about the ethical consequences of such images: »What happens to public opinion in democracies – traditionally reluctant to wage war – when the human cost of battle is invisible?« (Barker 2003, 241). In Sharkey's eye, the television images from the war in Kosovo also failed to convey anything humanly essential because they too left human loss and pain invisible:

»None of this had been visible at the time. Not even to the pilots who dropped the bombs, still less to the audience watching Pentagon briefings on television in their living rooms. On the screen set up in the briefing room, and on the television screens, puffs of brown smoke appeared underneath the cross-hairs of the precision sights. Doubly screened from reality, the audience watched, yawned, scratched and finally switched channels. Who could blame them? War had gone back to being sepia tinted. Sanitized. Nothing as vulgar as blood was ever allowed to appear. And all the while, under the little spurts of brown dust, this. A child torn to pieces. Human bodies baked like dog turds in the sun« (ibid., 131).

In contrast to the viewers of sanitised images, Stephen Sharkey has seen things close-up, and he has eventually been broken by what he has experienced in the course of his career. Sharkey has recently lost his photographer friend, Ben Frobisher, in Afghanistan, but it is an earlier incident in Bosnia through which he has been traumatised in the first place, and it is this incident to which his memory goes back again and again while he tries to heal himself by writing a book about »[t]he way wars are represented« (ibid., 57) back home in England. In Sarajevo, he and Ben had ventured into a building and found the dead body of a young woman raped before she was killed. To Sharkey, this episode has an epiphanic quality:

»In a corner of the landing, away from the danger of flying glass, a girl huddled on a mattress. [...] Eyes wide open, skirt bunched up around her waist, her splayed thighs enclosing a blackness of blood and pain.

---

6   On the ethics of press photographs of human suffering and death see also
    Taylor (1998).

Stephen fell on his knees beside her and pulled down her skirt. A voice in his head said, Don't touch anything. This is a crime scene. And then he thought, Bugger it. The whole fucking city is a crime scene. He wanted to close the terrible eyes, but couldn't bring himself to touch her face« (ibid., 52f.).

Stephen is shocked and deeply touched by the close-up sight of this dead body, whose face in particular makes a powerful ethical demand on him. The physical quality of this moment of revelation recalls the importance of ›visage‹ and ›contact‹ in the philosophy of Emmanuel Lévinas. To Lévinas, it is through the naked face that the other demands an ethical response,[7] and touching the other's skin is an elementary manifestation of ethical behaviour: »Le contact où j'approche le prochain n'est pas manifestation ni savoir, mais l'événement éthique de la communication que toute transmission de messages suppose, qui instaure l'universalité où mots et propositions vont s'énoncer« (Lévinas 1982a, 236). Even though Sharkey cannot bring himself to close the woman's eyes in the actual situation itself, the element of touch is later literalised, as physical contact, in his nightmares:

»Stephen lay cramped and wakeful inside his sleeping bag, thinking about the girl, and the way her eyes had looked up at him, seeing nothing. Her head was beside his on the pillow, and when he rolled over on to his stomach, trying to get away from her, he found her body underneath him, as dry and insatiable as sand« (Barker 2003, 55).

As expressed in his dream, Stephen's psycho-physical memory indicates how his whole being has been affected by the traumatising encounter and his accumulated experience of war in general: his intellect, emotions, conscience as well as his body. As far as Barker's novel is concerned, it is through this wholly human engagement that Stephen's attitude towards war and its representation resembles that of the artist.

In order to develop this analogy, Barker creates two artist figures as foils for Stephen Sharkey: Kate Frobisher, the photographer's widow, is a sculptor; Peter Wingrave is a young man who has just written his first set of short stories. Of these two, Kate is Stephen's positive foil. Like the war correspondent, she has to overcome a trauma, that of her husband's violent death, and a physical injury to boot. Kate heals herself through sculpting a giant figure of the resurrected Christ for the local Cathedral. Considering the importance of touch in the novel – both in its literal and

---

7   See Lévinas (1982b, 196): »L'épiphanie de l'absolument autre, est visage où l'Autre m'interpelle et me signifie un ordre de par sa nudité, de par son dénûment.«

transferred meanings – it is significant that Kate works with her hands and creates a Christ whose expression is as much physical as spiritual. By contrast, Peter Wingrave, Stephen's negative foil, stands for an approach to life that is distanced and primarily visual. He is a voyeur who lacks the capacity to empathise with other people (he has even committed murder when still a young child[8]) and merely observes and mimics them – an attitude of dis-engagement that is also reflected in the stories he writes and gives Stephen to read. The male characters of these stories are violent stalkers, and Stephen is put off by the fact that the stories – like their author – have no discernible »moral centre« and ethical commitment:

»Again the emphasis on female helplessness, the detailed observation that always implied empathy, and yet, somehow, mysteriously failed to deliver it. The stories kept slipping into sympathy with the predatory behaviour they attempted to analyse. There was no moral centre. That was Stephen's final verdict, and it was this ambiguity in the narrator's attitude to predator and prey, rather than the actual events, that made the stories so unsettling« (ibid., 164).

Lacking a moral centre, displaying a morally ambiguous attitude and not sympathising with those who deserve compassion, is a severe human and artistic deficit as far as Stephen's – and indirectly Barker's – judgment goes. This is particularly obvious in the conversations that Stephen and Kate have about Goya, whose images of atrocities and human suffering they both admire. In her reference to Goya, Barker is inspired by Sontag's *Regarding the Pain of Others* and her discussion of Goya's famous etchings of scenes from the Napoleonic wars, *Los Desastres de la Guerra*. Sontag looks at these etchings in terms of their moral impact on the viewer which is achieved, apart from the pictures themselves, by Goya's captions:

»The account of war's cruelties is fashioned as an assault on the sensibility of the viewer. The expressive phrases in script below each image comment on the provocation. While the image, like every image, is an invitation to look, the caption, more often than not, insists on the difficulty of doing just that. A voice, presumably the artist's, badgers the viewer« (Sontag 2003, 45).

Barker uses captions from *The Disasters of War* for her novel's epigraph: »*No se puede mirar*. One cannot look at this. *Yo lo vi*. I saw it. *Esto es lo verdadero*. This is the truth.« The captions are also discussed by her

---

8   Another character in the novel who suffers from incapacity to feel with others is Stephen Sharkey's young nephew, who has Asperger's syndrome.

characters. Goya, to both Kate and Stephen, represents something essentially human, he has a »compassionate eye« (Barker 2003, 153), and even though he shows atrocities, his representations can inspire hope because they convey the artist's sympathetic view (ibid., 152). Goya's art, in contrast to Peter Wingrave's stories, does have a moral centre and a clear, moral point of view.

This point of view – or attachment as defined by Martin Bell – is also the mark of good war reporting in Barker's novel. Such reporting witnesses the pain caused by war in order to »giv[e] people the raw material to make moral judgements« (ibid., 227). Even war *photography* can achieve this moral effect when the human subject who takes the picture is perceptible – as in the case of Ben Frobisher's best pictures (which Stephen therefore intends to use for his book).[9] Frobisher has always looked for images that would have an emotional impact on the viewer, and he has died his own violent death while taking precisely such a picture. Stephen is particularly struck by two photographs that are flawed as news photography but, in this very ›deficit‹, disturb the viewer. In these two pictures of an execution – which might just have taken place because he was there to record it – the photographer has included himself, not only through his point of view, but with his own body as a visible marker of the human perspective and his own possible complicity in the killing:

»A man on his knees staring up at the men who are preparing to kill him. But Ben had included his own shadow in the shot, reaching out against the dusty road. The shadow says I'm here. I'm holding a camera and that fact will determine what happens next. In the next shot the man lies dead in the road, and the shadow of the photographer, the shadow of a man with a deformed head, has moved closer.

This wasn't the first execution recorded on film, nor even the first to be staged specifically for the camera, but normally the photographer's presence and its

---

9   This is also the central theme of a feature-length documentary about one of the leading war photographers of our time, the American James Nachtwey. In *War Photographer* (CH 2001, dir. Christian Frei), Nachtwey is shown working in various scenarios of war, always intent that his pictures capture the emotions of the distressed people he ›shoots‹ with his camera, and that they express his own compassion. In this context, see also Susan Sontag's statement about photography's special blend of objectivity and subjectivity: »Their credentials of objectivity were inbuilt. Yet they always had, necessarily, a point of view. They were a record of the real – incontrovertible, as no verbal account, however impartial, could be – since a machine was doing the recording. And they bore witness to the real – since a person had been there to take them« (Sontag 2003, 26).

impact on events is not acknowledged. Here Ben had exploded the convention« (ibid., 123).[10]

Ben has created artistic images that indicate the man behind the pictures and physically demonstrate the war reporter's inevitable engagement in what he reports.

Looking back from Barker's novel to Kipling's *The Light That Failed*, which also established an analogy between war correspondence and art, one finds a basic similarity and an essential difference. Both novels portray war correspondents as being engaged in war mentally and physically. Barker's reporters do not fight, but as participant observers they are just as vulnerable as the Victorian correspondent. The novels differ in their correspondents' moral perception: As far as war is concerned, Dick Heldar seems to lack a moral centre; what makes him a successful war artist is the immediacy with which his illustrations capture the experience of war, not his ethical position. In Barker's conception, by contrast, which participates in another cultural perception of war and war representation, a moral attitude makes all the difference – in both art and the reporting of war.

The traumatised correspondent in Barker's novel eventually manages to recuperate, writing his book and also falling in love with a young woman whose live body manages to overwrite his traumatic memory of the dead woman's body in Bosnia. Michael Ignatieff's novel *Charlie Johnson in the Flames* portrays a war reporter beyond the chance of healing. In his academic and journalistic work, Ignatieff, who is Carr Professor of the Practice of Human Rights at Harvard University, is concerned with the dynamics of ethnic conflicts, interventionist warfare in the name of human rights, and the mediation of such wars. He knows many of the war zones he discusses from personal experience. In his study *The Warrior's Honor* (1998), Ignatieff looks at the relationship between the television representation of ethnic conflicts in the 1990s and the emergence of a ›global conscience‹ that found expression in a universalist ethics and, ultimately, in military intervention. The multiple connections between a culture of spectatorship, increased human-rights awareness and intervention are crystallised in Ignatieff's fictional correspondent Charlie Johnson, an American television correspondent working for a London channel.

---

10 In this context, see also Sontag's comment on a famous photograph of an execution in the Vietnam War: »[General Loan] would not have carried out the summary execution [of a Vietcong] there had they not been available to witness it« (Sontag 2003, 59). See also the photographer's guilt as depicted in *Before the Rain* (p. 139).

Charlie Johnson is an experienced journalist whose career began in Vietnam and whom the novel introduces in a scene set in Kosovo. In the opening paragraphs, Charlie finds himself at the side of a severely burnt woman in the middle of a scene that might be taken directly from a war film (specifically one about Vietnam, in which helicopter scenes are a stock element):

»When Charlie saw the helicopter, he was sure everything was going to be all right. It settled down in the stubble-bare, garbage-strewn field by the edge of the refugee tents, and it came down so close he had to shield her face with his hands from the cloud of dust and refuse thrown up by the blades. It made Charlie feel young again, like Danang in '71, to see the pair of medics in the open door unsnap their belts, sling out the stretcher and break into a low crouching run beneath the rotors« (Ignatieff 2003, 1).

After this ›filmic‹ beginning, reference to war mediation through pictures remains a prominent theme. It plays a particular role in Charlie's relationship to his Polish cameraman, Jacek, with whom he has worked through the major conflicts of the 1990s: »Slovenia, summer 1991; Novska and Pakrac, October 1991; Sarajevo, Christmas 1992; Mostar, summer 1993; and on and on: Mogadishu, Luanda and Huambo, Kabul, all the assignments lined up in his mind like so many rows of tape« (ibid., 43). Until the incident with which the novel begins, Jacek's pictures have always framed and contained the war for Charlie, helping him to keep the distance of a mere observer of cruelties that remain strangely unreal:

»They were holidays from hell every one of them, and Jacek seemed to survive them by keeping everything contained within the black frame of his viewfinder. It was often all Jacek would say about a bad situation: ›Look‹, he would say, having framed up, and then he would gesture at the machine, and Charlie would look through into the digital world and think: Yes, it looks like something when Jacek frames it up. I can deal with this. They'd seen the world together, though they'd seen it too close to know what it really meant. Sometimes they both felt like spectators at a terrible and violent play. Sure, they wanted to go on stage and stop it. But these plays couldn't be stopped. The worst thing was that their experience got blurred, lost definition, one bad play shading into the next« (ibid., 43).

By prioritising an attitude of spectatorship, Charlie and Jacek stay within the habitus of ›objective‹ reporting. Reviewing his career, Charlie diagnoses that he has never been really ›touched‹ by what he has seen, an attitude that has also tinged his life generally: »he had been left almost completely untouched by his life« (ibid., 76). In Kosovo, however, Charlie experiences a moment of epiphany (comparable to that in Barker's novel) when a war victim's pain becomes so manifest that he feels obliged to ›go on stage‹ at last and intervene. For the first time in his life, Charlie truly inter*acts* with the ›characters‹ he is professionally expected only to observe.

Charlie's habituation is disturbed by the incident that has taken him to the helicopter landing place. For the sake of a »good story« (ibid., 12) he and Jacek have ventured into territory occupied by Serbs to prove that Muslim guerrilla fighters are still active in the area. They have to hide in a Muslim family's house for a while and later witness from a safe distance how this house and its occupants are blown up by a Serb commando. A young woman tries to escape but a Serbian officer deliberately sets her on fire. The burning woman runs towards the place where Charlie and Jacek are hiding, which causes Charlie to give up his observation post, run out of cover and extinguish the flames on the woman's body with his own hands. Through this active engagement, which leaves Charlie injured himself, he experiences a baptism of fire in a literal as well as a metaphorical sense: Although he has been in so many war zones before, this is the first time he has permitted himself to experience war outside the secure framing of Jacek's camera, and Charlie realises immediately that he will never be able to resume his old habit because he has at last been touched – a sensation that is also literal as he feels the woman in his arms and the flames on his skin. To him, this touch feels like an anointment, a ritual touch that initiates him into a different mode of war experience: »As if he, Charlie Johnson, had been chosen by her embrace and anointed like her with the flames. [...] They were so tightly entwined that he could not see her face, but he could hear her moaning next to his ear« (ibid., 6). As in Barker's novel, the physical quality of Charlie's moment of revelation recalls the importance of ›visage‹ and ›contact‹ in the philosophy of Lévinas. However, the new way of experiencing war to which Charlie Johnson is initiated, through emotion and conscience as well as observation, ›burns‹ him for his profession:

»As for Charlie, he knew he was finished. For thirty years he had been fucked around by rogues and chancers and drugged-up hoods at checkpoints from Kabul to Kigali, but none of them had ever laid a glove on him, not really. He had heard the bullets whine over his head but in all that time he had never believed any of them were meant for him. He had seen the flames and always believed they would not touch him. Until that afternoon. When he pulled his hands away to see that they were covered with the carbonised remnants of her flesh and his own. Afterwards, waiting for the helicopter, he had sat in the dark, shaking from head to foot, so fully given over to fear that there seemed nothing left of him but terror. Yes, he was finished« (ibid., 7f.).

The Muslim woman later dies in an American field hospital, but the traumatised Charlie cannot forget her. In his memories and dreams, he relives the incident again and again and, significantly, a haptic rather than visual dimension prevails in this recollection:

»He woke the next morning to the bright stab of late morning sun, knowing he had dreamed of the woman on fire. Nothing definite in the way of an image, just the physical sense of her holding on to him, a strange feeling, full of desire, at her pressing her body against his and the flame leaping between them. With the difference that none of it had hurt, and as they fell together, he had felt her breasts against his chest. It was strange to be lying on a bed so far away wanting someone and wishing he could whisper her name« (ibid., 50).

Emphasis on touch – even in a disturbingly erotic form – indicates how the experience in Kosovo has finally made the war *real* for Charlie and turned it into something to which he must relate and react.

The novel depicts various stages of Charlie's reaction, from initial trauma to a final act of deep moral indignation and retaliation. Charlie believes that only another war reporter can understand him and, a man also physically ill by now, he seeks refuge at Jacek's home in Poland, where he is nursed by the cameraman and his wife. When Charlie eventually arrives back home in London, he completely loses his grip on his former life. He separates from his wife and falls out with his editor when the latter forbids him to return to Yugoslavia and find the man who set the woman on fire. This, however, is what Charlie feels he must do, as if to make up for the non-engagement he had formerly cultivated in his career.

At the risk of his own life, Charlie locates the Serbian officer and actually meets him for an interview. At first, Charlie believes that he does not seek to avenge the woman but merely wants to be given some reason for her suffering. He also wants the killer to feel culpable for what he has done and experience the same ethical awakening that he has experienced himself:

»A reckoning. That was what he wanted. Not vengeance, just a reckoning. So that the Colonel would understand what it really means to snuff someone out. So that Charlie would understand. So that the distinctions, the clarity, that life requires would be restored. Something like that. And maybe more. He wanted the man to feel fear, wanted him to know what being burned would feel like. That was it. A laying on of hands. The flame of recognition and shame would jump the gap between one soul and another. Something like that. One way or the other, a kind of religious occasion, a righteous moment« (ibid., 113).

However, the Colonel refuses to be encompassed by Charlie's humanitarian ethics. His own ethics is that of a warrior in an ethnic war in which universal human rights are subordinated to the rights of a specific community. Apart from his resistance to Charlie's values, the Colonel upsets the correspondent even more by pointing out to him that he, as a journalist, is also responsible for the woman's death. If he had not been present and taken shelter in the Muslim house, this house and its inhabitants might not have been destroyed. Outraged by the Serb's callousness and intimation of his own complicity in the woman's violent death, Charlie intends to kill the man with his hands, in an ultimate act of intervention: »Charlie rose with a roar in his throat and lunged across the dark space, catching the Colonel's neck with the force of both hands« (ibid., 143). However, before he can accomplish his deed, he is himself thrown from the balcony and dies.

With his final act, Charlie asserts his new-found conviction that regarding the pain of others should have consequences. Nevertheless, the novel is ambiguous in its evaluation of Charlie's intervention. His indignation and resulting engagement may be understandable and perhaps even commendable in terms of the humanitarian ethics to which Charlie now subscribes, but his death is also futile. Charlie has jumped on stage but not been able to stop the terrible play. When his friend and colleague Etta brings his body home, she diagnoses a naive idealism as a driving force for his deed, an inability to accept that bad things will always happen: »Charlie, she said, was an innocent because he never lost his surprise at this fact about the world. He should not have been surprised« (ibid., 148). Furthermore, the means to which Charlie eventually resorts – becoming a killer himself – are also at least questionable. The same issue of how far a correspondent should go when his conscience is awakened is the subject of a recent Hollywood film also set in former Yugoslavia. Like *Beautiful People* and *No Man's Land*, this film has a satirical approach; at the same time however, it uses the templates of the attached and traumatised correspondent and even revives the correspondent as an action hero.

The Hunting Party (USA 2007, dir. Richard Shepard) fictionalises a real-life adventure of three American correspondents (Scott Anderson, John Fall and Sebastian Junger) in Bosnia in the summer of 2000. Anderson's reportage about the bizarre events, »What I Did on My Summer Vacation«, was published in the October 2000 issue of *Esquire* and is written as a mock school essay. At the beginning, the reader is told in a tone of cool understatement that the journalists' adventure was »strange business« and »a complicated story, but I suspect that's usually the case when a group of friends on vacation are mistaken for a CIA hit team and cause the launching of a transnational black-ops mission to hunt down a notorious war criminal« (Anderson 2000, n.p.). The criminal in question was Radovan Karadžić.

»It was planned as a reunion of sorts: five journalist colleagues [two Belgian reporters apart from the Americans] meeting up in their old Balkan stomping grounds, a couple of days knocking around Sarajevo, then heading down to the Adriatic coast for some fun. [...]
For some time, the conversation was given over to catching up on personal news, the recounting of old war stories, but it eventually turned to the last great story to be had in the Balkans: the hunt for fugitive war criminals. In the four and a half years since the war in Bosnia had ended, only forty-eight of the ninety-four men indicted for war crimes by the International Criminal Tribunal in The Hague had been captured, and among those still at large were the two principal architects of the Bosnian genocide, Dr. Radovan Karadzic and General Ratko Mladic« (ibid.).

Since they know from a newspaper that Karadžić is hiding in Čelebići, a village in the Republika Srpska, a Serbian enclave in Bosnia near the border with Montenegro (and since they have also drunk a lot of Slibovic), the men develop a new plan for their vacation: »Somehow we would penetrate [Karadžić's] ring of bodyguards, haul him to justice, split the bounty money. We'd give new meaning to the term ›advocacy journalism‹« (ibid.).

The American correspondents are mistaken for a CIA hit squad by the Ukrainian UN official Boris, who gets them into contact with Dragan, a secret Serbian policeman willing to betray Karadžić. They pursue their plan until stopped by an American lieutenant colonel who delivers a serious warning that they should no longer interfere and tells them that the CIA will use their contacts themselves in order to capture Karadžić. Anderson's account casts serious doubt on this intention:

»In the four months since that last meeting, the lieutenant colonel has not called, and Radovan Karadzic remains at large. This silence and inaction has led some of us who were on that fateful vacation to wonder if perhaps our take on the Dark Side's [the CIA's] mission was precisely wrong: that rather than use Boris and Dragan to apprehend Karadzic, they had been dispatched to close down a channel that just might achieve that and disrupt the Bosnian ›peace‹« (ibid.).

Although the tone of Anderson's article is ironic and humorous, it is also committed to an ethical cause when it attacks NATO's and the United Nation's inefficient pursuit of war criminals:

»For years, NATO governments and the UN had been proclaiming that true peace could never come to Bosnia until fugitive war criminals like Karadzic were caught. At the same time, most had done absolutely nothing to bring that about, fearful of the unrest that might ensue and give the lie to the charade of peace and nation-rebuilding they had created« (ibid.).

The Hunting Party takes up all these elements from Anderson's original story, but extends the plot in a dramatic manner and provides a more satisfactory ending for a Hollywood film. It also shapes the character of its main protagonist, the aptly named Simon Hunt (played by Richard Gere) to match prevailing popular notions of the war correspondent. Hunt incorporates elements of the typical Bosnia reporter haunted by the human rights violations he has witnessed, and of the courageous investigative journalist. The film is narrated by Hunt's former cameraman Duck (played by Terence Howard), who initially provides Hunt's background: Until Bosnia, Hunt was an award-winning reporter for the American national networks, a war junkie with the philosophy that only danger makes you aware that you are really alive. However, Hunt's career came to a sudden end in 1994 when, cracked up by the atrocities of the Bosnian war, he attacked UN inefficiency and let down his pants (literally) during a live broadcast. Fired by his network, Hunt remained in his job for some time, freelancing for small channels, but then disappeared. In the meantime, Duck has become chief cameraman for his network's celebrity anchorman, and the cosy job has alienated him from ›true‹ war reporting.

The two friends meet again in 2000 when Duck and his team cover the official reconciliation celebrations in Sarajevo. Hunt tells Duck that he urgently needs a cameraman because he has come across a potential scoop: He has found out where Radoslav Bogdanovič, ›the Fox‹, is hiding, a Serbian war criminal (who closely resembles Karadžić), and plans to get an exclusive interview with him. Duck is willing to go along, and the two seasoned journalists are joined by a novice, Benjamin (played by Jesse Eisenberg), who has a Harvard degree and is the son of the network's vice president. The team thus has an interesting constellation: Hunt, who has never lost the instinct of a good war reporter, Duck, who has to re-discover his passion for the job, and Benjamin, who has to develop this passion in the first place. By the end of their adventure, all three will know what war reporting is all about.

As in Anderson's article, the trio are assisted by Boris, who mistakes the reporters for CIA agents and gets them into contact with the former girlfriend of one of the Fox's guards. More openly than the article, how-ever, the film shows that the CIA are protecting the Fox in return for his promise to give up his influence in Bosnia. This is classic material for investigative reporting, but a flashback reveals that Hunt also has a per-sonal reason for hunting the Fox. Like Charlie Johnson in Ignatieff's novel, he wants revenge because the Fox was responsible for the death of Hunt's Bosnian lover and their unborn child, who were killed in a Serbian attack on their village. Personal, professional and political motives intersect and involve the correspondents in the war both as professionals and private individuals.

Eventually, the three hunters are hunted themselves and trapped by the Fox. They are about to be murdered by one of his henchmen when real CIA agents intervene and save the journalists but also let the Fox es-cape. The CIA then try to deport the three unwanted investigators, who manage to escape, however, and capture the Fox while the latter, a pas-sionate hunter himself, is hunting a fox. The correspondents drop him in a Bosnian village whose Muslim population will know what to do with him. This is a solution of the ethical dilemma of revenge more suitable to a mainstream feature film than Charlie Johnson's attempted murder of the war criminal in Ignatieff's novel. In *The Hunting Party*, the journal-ists merely trace their prey and leave punishment to the victims of ethnic cleansing. The journalists are thus established as unblemished heroes, more effective and more moral than the UN and, above all, the represen-tatives of their own country. Their triumph stands unquestioned at the end, even though the film otherwise tends to ironise heroic poses: When the derelict Hunt turns up in Duck's hotel room in Sarajevo at the begin-ning of the plot, we see him watching a Chuck Norris action film, sug-gesting that this is a kind of he-manship from which the journalists are meant to be distanced. In their own way, however, Hunt and his friends do take action and fight for the good, and as a reward, all three discover or rediscover the true ethos of their profession.

All novels and films discussed in this section show that the scenario of former Yugoslavia, and Bosnia in particular, encourages representa-tions of one type of war correspondent in particular: the reporter aware of the moral challenge the profession brings with it, and willing to engage for a humanitarian cause and against the crimes of war. In the Bosnian context, the unsympathetic and ambitious reporter in *No Man's Land* is an exception rather than the rule. As the next section will show, the scenario of the war on terror yields a more varied image of war cor-respondents in which some older templates are revived as well.

153

Representing Correspondents
in the War on Terror

The positive image of the critical correspondent also occurs in the context of the war on terror, but in general representations of war reporters are more ambivalent here, and sometimes downright negative. There seem to be two reasons for this representational tendency. On the one hand, it appears that widespread doubt about the legitimacy of the war on terror also encouraged a more critical attitude towards the men and women who covered it for the media, often in close proximity to the military and sometimes in a distinctly patriotic voice.[11] On the other hand, the surge of patriotism in the US after 9/11 encouraged a positive representation of the military, at least in popular film and television, that revived notions of the good versus bad war correspondent from the soldier's point of view. Productions set in Iraq use the topical type of the embedded reporter. As was shown above (pp. 54-58), embedded reporters such as Chris Ayres and Oliver Poole reflect in their memoirs about the consequences their close relationship with soldiers had for their self-perception as autonomous and critical journalists. The following popular productions, by contrast, adopt a military perspective and are less subtle than journalists in their self-representations.

In older pro-military war films, such as *The Story of G.I. Joe* or *The Green Berets*, the ›good‹ correspondent is, or learns to be, on the side of the fighting men, while a ›bad‹ reporter is critical of the war and the military and/or only interested in them as material for a good story or picture. The long-lived American television series *J.A.G.* (1995-2005, 227 episodes) centres on a group of military lawyers and was developed and produced with support by the US Navy. It kept up with America's overt and covert wars and, from 2001, included settings in Afghanistan and Iraq. There is a general tendency in *J.A.G.* to portray correspondents with little sympathy, as a necessary evil in the information war. They characteristically appear as reporters and cameramen of ZNN, a thinly disguised fictionalisation of CNN. Episode 222, »Death at the Mosque« (originally aired on 1 April 2005), took the pattern of good versus bad reporters to the war in Iraq. The episode is set in Karbala, where a ZNN team led by reporter Brad Holliman[12] has filmed a marine killing an Iraqi civilian in a mosque. Their footage seems to prove that the soldier shot

---

11 For a similar tendency, see the portrayal of pooled reporters in war-critical films about the first Gulf War (pp. 134-135).

12 The reporter's name seems very close to the real CNN correspondent of the first Gulf War, John Holliman.

an unarmed man begging for his life, while the soldier claims that he acted in self-defence, believing that the Iraqi was a suicide attacker. The tape is important evidence in the marine's military trial, where Holliman also appears as a witness for the prosecution. This establishes him early on as an antagonist of the military – despite his apparent good relationship with the marines – and this antagonism is confirmed when the further course of the action reveals that the reporter is more interested in a good story than the honour and even the lives of his country's soldiers. The J.A.G. defence lawyer can prove his client's innocence when he demonstrates that the dead Iraqi did indeed have access to explosives and that the reporter's evidence against the soldier was too superficial. In a coda, Holliman's carelessness and recklessness is proved once more when he uses strong lights when filming a night operation and thus endangers the life of the whole unit. This incident finally loses him the soldiers' respect.

A similar representation of an embedded reporter is found in a rather bizarre TV horror movie. In *Manticore* (dir. Tripp Reed, 2005), produced for the American SciFi channel, a reckless female television reporter is on her own search for weapons of mass destruction in occupied Iraq. Ashley Pears, correspondent for GNN, is officially embedded with a unit of Marines but moves about independently, always hunting for news. Right from its start, the film alludes to Iraq as the site of a television war by means of pictures taken with a hand-held camera that imitate the look of the war for a television audience. While this is an attempt to create authenticity, Ashley Pears is a crude caricature of the investigative war correspondent, greedy for stories and images which her intimidated cameraman has to shoot for her. And she is highly conscious of her image: Before Ashley does a piece to camera in a desert village, she smears dirt on her face and chest in an attempt to give herself a tough appearance.

Instead of discovering modern arms of mass destruction, however, Ashley hits on the Manticore, a fabulous beast from Persian mythology (with the head of a man, the body of a lion, and the tail of a scorpion), who has been revived by a terrorist leader. While the TV crew hide in a desert village, an army squad is sent to their rescue since in an age of new military-media relations, the military cannot afford to be held responsible for dead or missing journalists. When the journalists are found, there is immediate dislike between Ashley and the soldiers. Their relationship deteriorates further when Ashley asks her cameraman to film the body bag of a soldier killed by the monster. The soldiers protest, and a cliché-ridden dialogue develops between Ashley and their commanding officer: »Did you ever hear of the First Amendment?« – »Did you ever hear of common decency?« Lacking that decency and after she has dis-

obeyed orders once more, the reporter is killed by the monster which ex-
cretes a deadly slime on her before she is torn apart. Supporting the soldiers' unsympathetic view of the reporter, the film presents her death –
and the particular manner of that death – as an act of poetic justice.

A more ambitious American television film portrays correspondents
in the war on terror with greater differentiation but also resorts to a mix
of familiar types. *War Stories* (USA 2003, dir. Robert Singer) was produced after the war in Afghanistan but still before the war in Iraq. It is
critical of American military involvement in the Middle East and uses its
war reporter characters to voice that critique in a manner familiar from
1980s war-critical films about Vietnam and South America. *War Stories*
is set in Uzbekistan and the conflict between the Uzbek government and
what is left of the militant Islamic Movement of Uzbekistan (IMU),
which is backed by Al-Qaeda and remnants of the Taliban. The Uzbek
military is supported by US air power. While this intervention is presented in a critical light, the film also motivates the United States' fight
on terrorism: One of its main characters, the young photographer Nora
Stone, has lost her sister in the 9/11 attack on the World Trade Center.

Nora Stone is the first of four war reporters introduced in the film's
opening sequences. She has been traumatised by her sister's violent death
and ducks whenever she hears a bang. This does not recommend her for
her job as war photographer, and she finds it hard to be accepted by her
more experienced colleagues in Uzbekistan. These include Ian Rhys, a
macho television reporter, and Gayle Phelan, who also works for television. She is another representative of the tough female correspondent, an
ambitious, cynical woman who does not mind sleeping with her colleagues if this will get her a story. The male protagonist and focus of
sympathy is Ben Dansmore (played by Jeff Goldblum), who works for a
newspaper. Like Stephen Sharkey in Pat Barker's novel, Dansmore is
mourning a photographer friend who, emulating Robert Capa even in his
moment of death, has stepped on a landmine. Nora has been sent to re-
place this Pulitzer Prize-winning photographer, and as might be expected, Dansmore is unwilling to accept her at first. The loss of his friend
has turned Dansmore from a daredevil reporter into a more pensive man
who ponders the purpose of his profession and is thus able to become an
ideal mentor for Nora. After she has been initiated properly into war
journalism and proved her mettle, Nora and Dansmore even manage to
become professional »partners« – the final word actually spoken in the
film.

Nora's initiation involves the issue of objective vs. attached journalism. Ben Dansmore tells her that war correspondents should never be
partial: »That isn't how this works. Good guys, bad guys. We're journal-

ists.« Nora needs this lesson because she lacks emotional distance towards the horrors of war, and these horrors make her take sides. When she and Dansmore are abducted from a journalists' convoy by the IMU in order to interview one of the movement's leaders, Nora reproaches him: »Why did you kill my sister?« After their return from the interview she agrees to help the Uzbek secret service to find the leader's hide-out, while Dansmore strictly refuses to cooperate and betray a source. Neither of them knows, however, that they have already *been* utilised and manipulated several times: They have only been granted the interview with the IMU leader because they published a piece of anti-American reporting earlier, revealing, based on Nora's photographs, that American planes intentionally bombarded a refugee camp. This ›discovery‹, however, was staged by the Uzbek and American secret services in order to make the reporters appear anti-American. Nora's belief in the objectivity of her camera (»It captures clear, unambiguous truth«) is shattered, but the experienced Dansmore, who has cautioned Nora that absolute truth is never possible (»There's no such thing as truth. That's why they call them stories«), has been doubly fooled. His recorder, another ›objective‹ technical device, was bugged before the interview and has already led the secret services to the Islamists' hide-out while Dansmore is still refusing to betray his source. Dansmore is outraged by this instrumentalisation, not least because several of his colleagues were killed by the IMU immediately after his and Nora's abduction – »collateral damage«, as a CIA agent tells Dansmore to his face. The film presents this killing in a long and brutal sequence, dramatising the fact that increasingly journalists in contemporary war zones are not perceived as neutral observers any more and become victims of their profession. That Nora and Dansmore are manipulated confirms this perception. However, *War Stories* does not end on this bleak note. Despite all conflicts and difficulties, the film has a positive ending that restores belief in the possibility of ›good‹ critical journalism (and thus resembles the conclusion of *The Hunting Party*). As already mentioned, Ben and a more professional Nora become partners, and their partnership will be devoted to the quest for ›truth‹ despite all difficulties which governments and the military will lay in their way. With a touch of investigative heroism they are determined to reveal the CIA's doings in Uzbekistan, even if this will put their lives at risk.

War Stories suggests that the image of the war correspondent after 9/11 has become multifaceted, and that the image oscillates between positive and negative perceptions. The complexity of the contemporary image also acknowledges that the number of female war correspondents has increased significantly in recent decades. This has helped to deconstruct some gender stereotypes associated with the profession, but it has also created new ones.

War Correspondents and Gender Performance

Wars were reported by women as early as the 19th century; during the Spanish Civil War, the Second World War and the war in Vietnam, some female correspondents and photographers even became well-known.[13] Martha Gellhorn in particular has been a model for many younger female war reporters. In public perception, however, war corresponding is still usually associated with men and a display of masculinity, and women reporters have long been perceived to ›stand out‹ in the men's world of war and its mediation. In fact, their access to the battlefield was often barred by representatives of the military on the grounds that women simply did not belong in the field of war.[14] Since the late 20th century, however, female reporters have become more visible thanks to television.[15] CNN's Christiane Amanpour has been an international celebrity since the 1990s, and the BBC's Kate Adie at least a national one:

»Nowadays women are as likely to report on wars as men are, and some – Maggie O'Kane, Marie Colvin, Janine di Giovanni, Orla Guerin among others – do so with real distinction. The Hackette in the Flakette Jackette, as the satirical magazine *Private Eye* calls them, has become as familiar as the Hack at scenes of grief and trouble. But Kate Adie set the standard, and is admired accordingly« (Simpson 2002, 279).

It has been claimed that women are more ›sensitive‹ and ›emotional‹ reporters than men and have had a considerable influence on the emer-

---

13 See, among others, Wagner (1989) on female correspondents in the Second World War, and Elwood-Akers (1988) on correspondents in Vietnam. The image of women war reporters has not always been positive, however. See, for instance, the negative portrayal of Alice Schalek in *The Last Days of Mankind* (p. 98n2).

14 See, for instance, Elwood-Akers (1988, 4).

15 During the Gulf War, *The Times* had a double page-article by Libby Purves on female war reporters in its ›Life and Times‹ section: »Brave Fronts, Front Women and Front Lines« (21 January 1991, 14f.). On her experiences as a female embed in Iraq, see Skiba (2005).

gence of human-interest reporting towards the end of the 20th century.[16] Such rather intuitive claims still call for verification,[17] however, and there is indication that they have to be contested. Female correspondents may occasionally display their femininity in a playful manner,[18] but they usually claim that their work does not differ significantly from that of men, and that they wish to be perceived in the same manner as their male colleagues. Women also report from the battle zone, and, as we have seen, stories with a human-interest approach are written by men as well as women.[19] Fictional representations, however, tend to stereotype female correspondents, and often in an unfavourable light.

---

16 See, for instance, a statement in Hohenberg (1995, 313) about correspondents in former Yugoslavia: »The correspondents, particularly the women who often seemed more sensitive than the men, have done their part by calling the world's attention to the crimes confirmed in the UN report.«

17 Research on the gendering of war reporting is still in its early stages and contradictory in its preliminary results. Apart from the thesis of a special sensitivity of female correspondents, it discusses the sexism of male colleagues and the military, or the special danger for women reporters to become victims of sexual assault. See, among others, *Feminist Media Studies* (2005) and Williams (1994) on women as war photographers.

18 See, for instance, Kate Adie's ironic depiction of her hunt for a wearable uniform during the Gulf War in 1991: »The only woman in the two-dozen-strong press team with the British army in the Gulf, I was facing a table heaped with Uniforms, Size Various. Female antennae waving, I shoved past the bespectacled RAF clerk who thought himself capable of holding up bits of clothing and ›guessing‹ my size and burrowed through the mound of clothes on his table, years of experience at the sales putting me well ahead of my colleagues. Armed with a monstrous heap of ›desert combats‹ [...] I tried on a dozen bits and pieces. The RAF looked on bemused, completely unable to grasp that if a woman is going to have to go into the desert and live with a front-line unit of two thousand men, several hundred miles from a bathroom and a hairdresser, never mind the shops, she is at least going to get a uniform that fits« (Adie 2002, 371f.).

19 Also see Elwood-Akers (1988, 2) on reporters in Vietnam: »In fact, a comparison of Vietnam War accounts written by men and women reporters indicates that there was little difference between the sexes insofar as the topics of their reporting was concerned. Women wrote the so-called ›human interest‹ stories which have traditionally been expected of the woman reporter, but male reporters in Vietnam wrote ›human interest‹ stories as well. Both male and female reporters analyzed the effects of the war on South Vietnamese society. And both male and female reporters covered combat.«

One can name the caricatured, over-ambitious correspondent in *Manticore* here, or Gayle Phelan in *War Stories*, who uses sex to gain an advantage over her male colleagues[20] and is contrasted with the positive Nora Stone. She too, however, is subjected to gender clichés: She is at first too emotional to qualify as a competent war photographer and requires the guidance of an experienced male colleague. After Nora has overcome her excessive emotionality, however, her gender ceases to matter. Ben Dansmore eventually accepts her as a partner because she proved her competence and became fully professional – an honorary male, so to speak.[21] There is one consequence of her sex that cannot be ›undone‹, however: Nora is threatened with rape by the Islamists, and not even Dansmore can help her in this situation.

The sexual vulnerability of the female war correspondent is at the core of a recent crime novel by Minette Walters, *The Devil's Feather* (2005). In other respects, however, this novel challenges rather than confirms current stereotypes about female (war) reporters. Its protagonist Connie Burns has worked for Reuters in many war zones. While covering the civil war in Sierra Leone, she comes across a serial killer. She suspects a Scottish mercenary who takes advantage of the chaos of war to realise his sadistic fantasies about women, but the man is not arrested. In Iraq in 2004, their paths cross again, and Connie is determined to end his deadly game. The man, however, kidnaps Connie and subjects her to sexual torture. Deeply humiliated, Connie is unable to communicate her experience. Like the correspondents in Pat Barker's and Michael Ignatieff's novels, she suffers from post-traumatic stress disorder, but in this case as a consequence of something done to her own and not another person's body. Like Barker's Sharkey, Connie returns to England in order to heal. Here her tormentor finds her again, but with the assistance of another woman, Connie is able to set him a trap and kill the killer.

---

20 In this context, see Knightley (2004, 506) on the opinion of some male war reporters that female colleagues use »their sexual allure to gain an advantage with the army.«

21 In this context, see also Camino (2005, 120) on *Welcome to Sarajevo* and this film's stereotypical representation of women war journalists. The character Jane, Henderson's producer, is accepted in the community of correspondents because she has adopted the habitus of »the boys.« Otherwise, according to Camino, the film marks »the exclusion of women from the discourses and practices of war, from war journalism, and from the books and films dealing with them« (ibid., 124). On the negative portrayal of female war correspondents in film, for instance in *Three Kings*, see also Badsey (2002, 56).

Walters's novel explicitly addresses »the dangers women face when the moral and ethical bases of society are shattered by war« (Walters 2005, 20). But *The Devil's Feather* does not only present women as victims; it also shows that wars can cause women (just like men) to violate the norms of human decency. Walters makes specific reference to the case of the American soldier Lynndie England, whose abuse of male prisoners in Abu Ghraib, according to the novel's main character, increased the danger for other Western women in Iraq, including correspondents:

»There was no venturing out on the streets of Iraq alone at that time, not if we valued our lives and freedom. With an al-Qaeda bounty on every Western head – and women being targeted as potential ›sex slaves‹ after Lyndie [sic] England's part in the prisoner abuse – press accreditation was no protection. Baghdad had been dubbed the most dangerous city in the world and, rightly or wrongly, women journalists saw rapists round every corner« (ibid., 12f.).

And Walters's correspondent herself behaves in an ethically dubious manner. Since the novel is written in the first person, Connie as the narrator of her own story is able to disguise the extent to which her ethical standards have been compromised by her experience of violence. It becomes obvious nevertheless that her revenge on her torturer is questionable in moral terms, and that Connie is both victim and perpetrator. Violence observed and endured has turned this reporter into a person who now acts violently herself, like Charlie Johnson in Ignatieff's novel. Although Connie escapes punishment, the doubtfulness of her behaviour is emphasised at the end of the novel when one of Connie's friends, a policeman, cites Nietzsche: »Do you know Friedrich Nietzsche's quote about being corrupted by evil? I have it pinned to a board above my desk. Simplified, it says: ›When you fight with monsters take care not to become one yourself‹« (ibid., 357). *The Devil's Feather* presents a female war correspondent who is as multifaceted as the troubled male reporters in Ignatieff's and Barker's novels. Walters's character undermines all stereotypical views of female war correspondents outlined above, and she is also part of a contemporary tendency, at least in more demanding forms of representation, to represent war correspondents as complex figures in today's media world: not only as heroes, scoop-hunters or committed advocates of human rights, but as mediators of war deeply involved in their practice not only as professionals but also as individuals confronted with bodily harm, psychological trauma and ethical dilemma.

A New Golden Age?

The period since 1990 has generated the highest number of fictional representations of all periods reviewed in this book and, in terms of quantity, might be referred to as a new Golden Age of the war correspondent's (self-)representation. With Barker's and Ignatieff's novels, it has also generated two of the aesthetically and intellectually most rewarding representations so far, which have therefore received particular attention. The recent wave of literary and cinematic interest in war correspondents is, in part, a response to the heightened visibility of and interest in war correspondents in contemporary culture. It reveals, above all, that the image of war correspondents today is heterogeneous and ambivalent, although it also still incorporates perceptual patterns that have accumulated since the 19th century. This variety is caused, among others, by the divergent conditions under which correspondents worked in the wars discussed, from the first Gulf War through the civil wars in former Yugoslavia to the second war in the Gulf. Journalists worked independently or pooled and embedded in military units; they were on the side of the wars' victims as well as on the side of the attackers. The most unambiguously positive image in the late 20th and early 21st centuries is the critical investigative reporter who puts his or her life at risk for the truth and the human cause. Negative portrayals of war reporters show them as war addicts or reckless pursuers of scoops. Films and novels present journalists aware of their power in today's media societies, but also as players directed by a military that has learnt to wage war at the media front. War correspondents in contemporary fiction are de-mythologised and, at the same time, continue the profession's mythical story.

Chapter 6: Conclusion.
Drawing Some Threads Together

> »*What had I done?* Leaving the front lines of
> Iraq after nine days seemed like failure by any
> measure. I thought of all the reporters who'd
> lasted months, or years, in arguably worse
> places: Bosnia, Rwanda, Chechnya, even
> Baghdad under the 1991 bombing campaign. [...]
> Historically, my nine-day career as a war
> correspondent became even more meaningless.
> Ernie Pyle reported from the battlefronts of
> World War II, on and off, for nearly five years,
> until his death. And Winston Churchill, at the
> age of twenty-two, lasted six weeks in
> Afghanistan's Swat Valley with Sir Bindon
> Blood and his troops« (Chris Ayres 2005, 268f.).

War correspondence is a branch of journalism with a high profile in modern societies. It has a distinct cultural impact and a cultural history that reflects changing attitudes towards war and the purposes of its mediation. In the so-called Golden Age, the war correspondent was seen and saw himself in close affiliation with the military. British correspondents covering the activities of British troops participated in a generally affirmative attitude towards war and, in particular, the wars of their own nation. As close to the frontline as they could be, and sometimes taking part in the fighting themselves, war reporters of the 19th century were often perceived as heroes and cultivated a heroic image in their self-presentations, setting an influential and sometimes intimidating example for the generations that followed in their footsteps. The favourable image of war correspondents suffered a considerable setback during the First World War; among others, literary representation helped to disseminate a negative perception of correspondents who had allegedly succumbed to military control and failed not only the common soldier but also their readers. Some correspondents, notably Philip Gibbs and Ellis Ashmead-Bartlett, thus felt provoked to provide counter-representations and to fashion themselves as journalists with a critical attitude towards the politicians and staff officers who had administered the war. This type of the independent and investigative war reporter came to dominate cultural perception in the late 20th century, but it is not the only image circulating in contemporary society. The Second World War revived the notion of the brave war reporter at the side of his country's soldiers and acting as their interpreter. Later wars in which reporters were pooled or embedded with soldiers, notably the wars in the Persian Gulf, also reactivated this image. It now clashes, however, with the image of war correspondents as highly autonomous journalists that was cultivated in Vietnam and received particular impetus during the coverage of the wars in former Yugoslavia. The latter scenario also promoted the war reporter with a humanitarian commitment as a positive template of contemporary perceptions.

This book has attempted a cultural reading of war correspondents based on various modes of their cultural representation. It has been grounded in the assumption commonly made in cultural studies that identities are essentially constructed – and reconstructed – through acts of representation by self and others. For war correspondents, representations are found in great numbers and in a variety of forms, both fictional and non-fictional. As soon as the profession of the war correspondent was created in the mid-19th century, its protagonists entered the cultural imaginary and became the subject, among others, of memoirs and fictional depiction. Such representations configure and foreground certain aspects of war correspondents and their behaviour. They indicate the cultural significance associated with the profession at a specific time and interfere in the further negotiation of this significance. Representations of war correspondents can thus be regarded as part of a cultural circuit: They engage with existing conceptions and have their own repercussions on the understanding of war correspondents; through depicting frames for behaviour, they can also affect correspondents' actual performances, which, in turn, may give rise to new representations (see p. 15). Representations of war correspondents indicate changes and continuities within the profession and its image and they are thus also of interest in historical perspective.

Public interest in journalists and their practice was part of a general reflection of the media society as early as the 19th century. Within journalism, however, war correspondents have always been perceived as ›special‹ since they practice a spectacular form of reporting with an aura of adventure but also a special social and ethical responsibility. War correspondence has generated myths and icons that shape not only the public's perception of the profession, but also that of its members. War correspondents gain their cultural significance as »essential contributors to the public understanding« of war (Tumber/Webster 2006, 166); they not only report the events of wars, but depict them in terms of their culture's prevailing frames of interpretation. Above all, they cover wars as eyewitnesses for the public – or rather as wholly human witnesses involved with all faculties of mind and body. It has been argued above that the necessity for this human element in the mediation of war has even increased in times when wars are fought with long-distance weapons and are presented in ›sanitised‹, remote images. In today's media world, audiences flooded with images and news bites from wars all over the globe and on a daily basis seem to be in particular need of a personal interpreter. The military have also recognised the special importance of this personal mediation and made correspondents a target, and at the same time an instrument, in new forms of information war:

»Information war, for those people inhabiting advanced parts of the globe, is chiefly about mediated experiences. [...] When conflict breaks out, even before it starts, there is an enormous upsurge of information from, about and beyond the war zone. Frontline correspondents play a central, but not solo, role in the presentation of what is often spectacle – vivid pictures of explosions, aerial images, cities lit up at night by tracer fire – to audiences around the world whose actual experience of war is far removed from combat« (ibid., 172).

Last but not least, war news also sells, and the media have thus always been willing to invest in war coverage and grant it a prominent place in newspapers, radio reportage, cinema newsreels and, of course, television news. Since the days of William Russell in the Crimean War, journalists covering ›popular‹ wars have stood a good chance to gain celebrity. This tendency has been intensified by television and its recent inclination to serve the infotainment industry, but within the scope of earlier media and occasions for performance, the profession has generated and cultivated ›stardom‹ from its very beginnings. War correspondents' memoirs appeared and sold in impressive numbers in the 19th century and were produced after each of the later conflicts that attracted public attention, with new peaks after the ›media wars‹ of the late 20th and early 21st centuries. Literature and film have depicted correspondents in modes appealing to middle- and lowbrow tastes and thus helped to shape a popular impression of the war correspondent and his – and increasingly her – most typical forms of demeanour.

The habitus manifested in this demeanour is often displayed with a distinct ›performative‹ element. War correspondents show a marked inclination to play up to existing role conceptions: They ›dress up‹ in mock uniforms and real flak jackets, adorn themselves with equipment from water bottle to revolver and from sketchbook to videophone, pose for dramatic photographs and duck theatrically in front of running cameras. This performativity highlights the extent to which the professional behaviour of war reporters is governed by role images and rules of the game. The element of theatricality is often observed in correspondents' memoirs, and it emerges with particular poignancy when it is caricatured in literature and film. (Self-)representations of war correspondents depict their professional ideals and aims as well as parameters of the field in which the ›act‹: structures and infrastructures of media systems and markets; developments in media technology and their consequences; the journalist's relation to politics and the military with its various practices of media control. Changes in each of these areas have consequences for the practice of correspondents, but there are also constants such as the journalist's need to hunt for scoops. Beyond the professional habitus and field, an individual journalist's performance is determined by the circumstances of the specific war which he or she reports, and of course features of his or her personality and personal intentions.

Although they are forms of self-writing, the memoirs of war correspondents are marked by a strong focus on the professional side of their lives. They accentuate incidents and reflections the authors have selected as significant for their self-interpretation as journalists and as interesting for other people's conceptions of the war reporter's role. Memoirs reveal how much correspondents are aware of their own and their colleagues' dispositions, and they indicate that, apart from observing each other as competitors, war journalists are keen consumers of their colleagues' books as well as the novels and films in which war correspondents are portrayed, including ›classics‹ such as Evelyn Waugh's *Scoop*, Graham Greene's *The Quiet American* and Stanley Kubrick's *Full Metal Jacket*. Chris Ayres's *War Reporting for Cowards* is exemplary in this respect, although it stands out from the mass of correspondents' memoirs through its pronounced mock-heroic stance.

The fictional representation of war correspondents has unfolded in a wide range of modes. Distinctly popular representations in literature and film use war correspondents as figures with an aura of adventure, romance and heroism but also professional recklessness, and they tend to emphasise positive and negative stereotypes. Thanks to their pronounced habitus, war correspondents are also a frequent subject of satirical representation, most famously perhaps in Waugh's *Scoop*, but also earlier in Sir Arthur Conan Doyle's »The Three Correspondents«, and later in films like *Beautiful People* or *No Man's Land*. Typical role behaviour is also foregrounded in a frequently employed plot pattern that shows how a novice to his or her profession is initiated by seasoned colleagues, as in Doyle's story or in recent films like *War Stories* and *The Hunting Party*.

The most intriguing fictional representations portray the war correspondent as a psychologically complex and/or dynamic character. Film as a performative mode of representation emphasises the correspondent's actions and habitus. Literary narrative, with its possibility of internal focalisation, lets readers participate in the fictional correspondent's perceptions, thoughts and feelings. We find this already in Rudyard Kipling's *The Light That Failed*, one of the earliest novels about a war correspondent, which, like most extended narratives about war correspondents, weaves the protagonist's professional experience into a plot that also shows the character in private dimensions of his life. In a number of novels and films discussed above, correspondents undergo a development from detachment to commitment or have an epiphanic experience that suddenly changes their attitude towards the reporting of war. Fowler in Greene's *The Quiet American* seems prototypical in this respect, awakening from a position of deliberate distance to a state of being deeply engaged in the Indochina War on a professional, a political and a very private level. The war photographer in *Under Fire* undergoes a similar development, as do the main characters in Pat Barker's *Double Vision* and Michael Ignatieff's *Charlie Johnson in the Flames*.

At a time when war is most prominently reported on television, the visual image has gained a special significance in negotiating the war reporter's ethical responsibility and dilemma. The photographic apparatus as such records an image ›objectively‹ and thus suggests itself as a metaphor for an ›objective‹ stance of reporting. Most novels and films with photographer characters then proceed to show, however, that there is always a human being behind the camera who determines the picture's point of view and hence its message. This is what Stephen Sharkey finds out in Barker's novel. In *Under Fire*, the reporter who discovers his commitment to one side in the Nicaraguan war even compromises his medium's documentary potential when he fakes a photograph and thus makes a political statement. In *War Stories*, the journalists are fooled themselves because the incident which their camera records has been staged by the secret service. In such examples the notion of impartial reporting is thoroughly undermined, responding to the debate about objective vs. committed or attached reporting that has been conducted within the profession itself, especially in the wake of Bosnia. Indeed, the conflicts in former Yugoslavia have initiated a particularly active phase of the war correspondent's representation in novels and films. Although *No Man's Land* features a highly unsympathetic caricature of a television reporter, the dominant type of correspondent in the Yugoslavian scenario is the reporter with a high ethical sensitivity and humanitarian commitment, exemplified in the character of Henderson in *Welcome to Sarajevo* and echoed in Barker's and Ignatieff's characters as well as Simon Hunt in *The Hunting Party*. The Bosnia correspondent specifically is also often portrayed as deeply traumatised by what he has witnessed. *The Hunting Party* makes an attempt to combine this template with the notion of the correspondent as hero, but the more conspicuous tendency is to portray the Bosnia correspondent as a human being sensitive to, and challenged by, the devastation of war. This tendency was anticipated in anti-war films of the 1980s, such as *The Killing Fields*, where correspondents in Cambodia take high risks to expose the consequences of American interventionism and the atrocities committed by the Khmer Rouge regime, but are also shown as human beings in fear of torture and death.

In the Vietnam War, correspondents acted with a high degree of autonomy in relation to the military. *Full Metal Jacket*, a classic of anti-war cinema, depicts how even a soldier-correspondent to a military newspaper retains a subversive attitude towards the institution in which he is obliged to serve. This pattern of the independent war journalist was challenged by new ways of managing military-media relations. As their memoirs reveal, pooled reporters in the 1991 Gulf War and embeds in Iraq in 2003 were disconcerted by their close relationship with the soldiers, and in fictional representation, especially in war and anti-war films, pooled and embedded reporters are rarely portrayed as positive figures. In pro-military productions they come across as antagonists of the soldiers or as a cumbersome plague, and in war-critical films such as *Jarhead*, they appear as insignificant figures manipulated by the military – a mode of representation known from literature about the First World War. *War Stories*, which is set in the war on terror but before Iraq, ends with an evocation of the positive image of the investigative reporter, but for most of its duration shows journalists who are not autonomous players but the plaything of secret services and terrorist organisations.

The ambivalent representation of war correspondents in the present appears to correspond to a sense of crisis of the profession observed in recent times, for instance in Greg McLaughlin's study:

»The rapid changes in both military and media technologies, the development of sophisticated military public relations, the cult of celebrity journalism: these have all contributed to a crisis in the role and function of the war reporter in the 1990s; these all put into question the ability or willingness of the journalist to be imaginative, to say something meaningful about the nature of modern warfare« (McLaughlin 2002, 4).

By keeping different images of war correspondents and ideas about their purpose active in the cultural imaginary, (self-)representations of war correspondents may provide orientation in this time of crisis and bring two central functions of war correspondents to the fore: First, they articulate their respective culture's attitudes towards war and, in the best case, help their audiences to come to an understanding of the war(s) they are covering. They also raise important questions as to the ethics of war and specific kinds of war. Second, war correspondents are actors in the limelight of mediatised societies. They reflect and display if and how the media act responsibly and how the dissemination of information and knowledge about contemporary society is subjected to political and economic forces of regulation. War journalism focuses pressing questions in today's societies: Whether what we see, hear and read is ›reliable‹ or not, or with which ethical attitude we can face the images of atrocities and disasters that accumulate in our media. The urgency of such issues suggests the prognosis that war correspondents will continue to occupy the cultural imaginary and be the subject of memoirs, literature and film.[1]

1   This book has grown out of a project funded by the German Research Council (DFG). The Freiburg Institute for Advanced Studies (FRIAS) allowed me the time to complete the book. I should like to thank Dr Stefanie Lethbridge and Dr Jochen Petzold for being critical readers of the manuscript, and Sandra Schaur and Georg Zipp for their careful editing.

Bibliography

Primary Sources

Correspondents' Memoirs and Collected Reports

Adie, Kate. *The Kindness of Strangers: The Autobiography*. London: Headline, 2002.

Anderson, Scott. »What I Did on My Summer Vacation.« *Esquire* 134.4 (Oct. 2000). 3 Dec. 2007 <http://www.esquire.com/features/ESQ1000-EQ12224_57.F>.

Ashmead-Bartlett, Ellis. *Port Arthur: The Siege and Capitulation*. 2nd ed. Edinburgh: Blackwood, 1906.

Ashmead-Bartlett, Ellis. *The Uncensored Dardanelles*. London: Hutchinson, 1928.

Ayres, Chris. *War Reporting for Cowards: Between Iraq and a Hard Place*. London: Murray, 2005.

Beck, Sara, and Malcolm Downing, eds. *The Battle for Iraq: BBC News Correspondents on the War against Saddam and a New World Agenda*. London: BBC, 2003.

Bell, Martin. *In Harm's Way*. London: Hamish Hamilton, 1995.

Bell, Martin. *Through Gates of Fire: A Journey into World Disorder*. 2003. London: Phoenix, 2004.

Bellamy, Christopher. *Expert Witness: A Defence Correspondent's Gulf War 1990-91*. London: Brassey's, 1993.

Burrowes, John. *Frontline Report: A Journalist's Notebook*. Edinburgh: Mainstream, 1982.

Busvine, Richard. *Gullible Travels*. London: Constable, 1945.

Cameron, James. *Witness*. London: Gollancz, 1966.

Cameron, James. *Point of Departure: Experiment in Biography*. London: Barker, 1967.

Capell, Richard. *Simiomata: A Greek Note Book 1944-1945*. London: MacDonald, 1946.

Churchill, Winston S. *Frontiers and Wars: His Four Early Books Covering His Life as Soldier and War Correspondent*. London: Eyre and Spottiswoode, 1962 [includes *The River War* (1899), pp. 131-357 and *London to Ladysmith* (1900), pp. 359-474].

Churchill, Winston S. *Young Winston's Wars: The Original Despatches of Winston S. Churchill, War Correspondent 1897-1900*. Ed. Frederick Woods. London: Cooper, 1972.

Doyle, Arthur Conan. *A Visit to Three Fronts: Glimpses of the British, Italian and French Lines*. London: Hodder and Stoughton, 1916.

Deedes, W.F. *At War with Waugh: The Real Story of* Scoop. 2003. London: Pan, 2004.

Dickson, William K.-L. *The Biograph in Battle: Its Story in the South African War Related with Personal Experiences*. London: Unwin, 1901.

di Giovanni, Janine. *The Quick and the Dead: Under Siege in Sarajevo*. London: Phoenix, 1994.

Dimbleby, Richard. *The Frontiers Are Green*. London: Hodder and Stoughton, 1943.

Fenton, James. *All the Wrong Places: Adrift in the Politics of Asia*. 1988. Harmondsworth: Penguin, 1990.

Forbes, Archibald. *My Experience of the War between France and Germany*. 2 vols. Leipzig: Tauchnitz, 1871.

Forbes, Archibald. »My Campaign in Pall Mall.« *Barracks, Bivouacs and Battles*. By Forbes. London: Macmillan, 1891. 307-28.

Forbes, Archibald. *Memories and Studies of War and Peace*. London: Cassell, 1895.

Fox, Robert. *Eyewitness Falklands: A Personal Account of the Falklands Campaign*. London: Methuen, 1982.

Gander, Leonard Marsland. *Long Road to Leros*. London: MacDonald, 1945.

Gibbs, Philip. *The Soul of the War*. London: Heinemann, 1915.

Gibbs, Philip. *Realities of War*. London: Heinemann, 1920 [published in the United States as *Now It Can Be Told*. New York: Harper, 1920].

Gibbs, Philip. *The Pageant of the Years: An Autobiography*. London: Heinemann, 1946.

Glossop, Reginald. *Sunshine and Battle-Smoke: Reminiscences of a War Correspondent*. London: Brown, 1907.

Hales, A.G. »The Life of a War Correspondent.« *Pall Mall Magazine* 23.94 (Feb. 1901): 204-11.

Hanighen, Frank C., ed. *Nothing but Danger: Thrilling Adventures of Ten Newspaper Correspondents in the Spanish War*. London: Harrap, 1940.

Hastings, Max. *Going to the Wars*. London: Macmillan, 2000.

Hastings, Max, and Simon Jenkins. *The Battle for the Falklands*. London: Joseph, 1983.

Hawkins, Desmond, and Donald Boyd. *War Report: A Record of Dispatches Broadcast by the BBC's War Correspondents with the Allied Expeditionary Force, 6 June 1944-5 May 1945*. London: Oxford UP, 1946.

Herr, Michael. *Dispatches*. 1977. New York: Avon, 1978.

Hodson, James Lansdale. *Gentlemen of Dunkirk: Being Leaves from a War Correspondent's Diary*. London: Withy Grove, 1940.

Hodson, James Lansdale. *Through the Dark Night*. London: Gollancz, 1941.

Hodson, James Lansdale. *War in the Sun.* London: Gollancz, 1942.

Johnston, Denis William. *Dionysia: An Account of the Author's Experiences as a BBC War Correspondent, 1942-45.* Ts. British Library, 1949.

Knight, E.F. *Reminiscences: The Wanderings of a Yachtsman and War Correspondent.* London: Hutchinson, 1923.

Lewis, Jon E., ed. *The Mammoth Book of War Correspondents.* New York: Carroll and Graf, 2001.

Loyd, Antony. *Another Bloody Love Letter.* London: Headline, 2007.

Lynch, George. *The Impressions of a War Correspondent.* London: Newnes, 1903.

Malins, Geoffrey H. *How I Filmed the War.* 1920. London: Imperial War Museum, 1993.

[Maurice, Sir John F.]. *The Ashantee War: A Popular Narrative by the* Daily News *Special Correspondent.* London: King, 1874.

McCullagh, Francis. *In Franco's Spain: Being the Experiences of an Irish War-Correspondent during the Great Civil War Which Began in 1936.* London: Burns Oates and Washbourne, 1937.

Moorcraft, Paul L. *What the Hell Am I Doing Here: Travels with an Occasional War Correspondent.* London: Brassey's, 1995.

Moorcraft, Paul L. *Guns and Poses: Travels with an Occasional War Correspondent.* Swallows Dell: Millstream, 2001.

Moorehead, Alan. *African Trilogy: Comprising Mediterranean Front, A Year of Battle, The End in Africa.* 1944. London: Hamish Hamilton, 1965.

Nevinson, Henry W. *Changes and Chances.* London: Nisbet, 1923.

Nevinson, Henry W. *More Changes, More Chances.* London: Nisbet, 1925.

Nicholson, Michael. *A Measure of Danger: Memoirs of a British War Correspondent.* London: HarperCollins, 1991.

Nicholson, Michael. *Natasha's Story.* London: Macmillan, 1993.

Orwell, George. *Orwell in Spain: The Full Text of* Homage to Catalonia *with Associated Articles, Reviews and Letters from* The Complete Works of George Orwell. Ed. Peter Davison. Harmondsworth: Penguin, 2001.

Pax, Salam. *The Baghdad Blog.* London: Atlantic, 2003.

Pilger, John. *The Last Day.* New York: Vintage, 1975.

Poole, Oliver. *Black Knights: On the Bloody Road to Baghdad.* London: HarperCollins, 2003.

Price, Julius M. *On the Path of Adventure.* London: Lane-Bodley Head, 1919.

Prior, Melton. *Campaigns of a War Correspondent.* London: Arnold, 1912.

Scudamore, Frank. *A Sheaf of Memoirs.* London: Unwin, 1925.

Simpson, John. *News from No Man's Land: Reporting the World.* London: Macmillan, 2002.

Simpson, John. *The Wars against Saddam: Taking the Hard Road to Baghdad.* London: Macmillan, 2003.

Skiba, Katherine M. *Sister in the Band of Brothers: Embedded with the 101st Airborne in Iraq.* Lawrence, KS: UP of Kansas, 2005.

Snow, Jon. *Shooting History: A Personal Journey.* London: HarperCollins, 2004.

Steevens, G.W. *With Kitchener to Khartum.* New York: Dodd, Mead, 1899.

Steevens, G.W. *From Capetown to Ladysmith: An Unfinished Record of the South African War.* Ed. Vernon Blackburn. Leipzig: Tauchnitz, 1900.

Villiers, Frederic. *Port Arthur: Three Months with the Besiegers: A Diurnal of Occurrents.* London: Longman's, 1905.

Villiers, Frederick. *Villiers: His Five Decades of Adventure.* 2 vols. London: Hutchinson, 1921.

Waugh, Evelyn. *Waugh in Abyssinia.* 1936. London: Methuen, 1984.

Fiction about War Correspondents

Barker, Pat. *Double Vision.* London: Hamish Hamilton, 2003.

Boyd, William. *Any Human Heart.* London: Hamish Hamilton, 2002.

Bradford, Barbara Taylor. *A Secret Affair.* London: HarperCollins, 1996.

Coleridge, Patrick. *Rut.* 2006. *Authors OnLine.* 3 Dec. 2007 <http://www.authorsonline.co.uk/viewbook.php?bid=163>.

Cooper, A[lfred] B[enjamin]. *Frank Flower: The Boy War Correspondent.* London: Pearson, 1913.

Doyle, Arthur Conan. »The Three Correspondents.« *The Conan Doyle Stories.* By Doyle. London: Murray, 1929. 188-212.

Falconer, Colin. *Dangerous.* London: Coronet, 1996.

Foden, Giles. *Ladysmith.* London: Faber, 1999.

Gant, James. *Zero-O-One.* London: Horwitz, 1957.

Greene, Graham. *The Quiet American.* 1955. London: Vintage, 2001.

Herbert, A.P. *The Secret Battle.* 1919. Oxford: Oxford UP, 1982.

Hilton, James. *Knight without Armour.* 1933. London: Macmillan, 1949.

Ignatieff, Michael. *Charlie Johnson in the Flames.* London: Chatto and Windus, 2003.

Kipling, Rudyard. *The Light That Failed.* 1891. London: Macmillan, 1964.

Mann, Jessica. *The Survivor's Revenge.* London: Constable, 1998.

May, Sarah. *The Internationals.* London: Chatto and Windus, 2003.

Perry, Anne. *No Graves as Yet.* London: Headline, 2003.

Perry, Anne. *We Shall Not Sleep.* London: Headline, 2007.

Rayner, Claire. *Flanders*. The Poppy Chronicles II. 1988. Thirsk: House of Stratus, 2001.

Temple, Peter. *In the Evil Day*. London: Bantam, 2002.

Tickell, Willow. *Cooling Off*. London: Sceptre, 1997.

Tomlinson, H.M. *All Our Yesterdays*. London: Heinemann, 1930.

Walters, Minette. *The Devil's Feather*. Basingstoke: Macmillan, 2005.

Waugh, Evelyn. *Scoop*. 1938. London: Chapman and Hall, 1964.

Wodehouse, P.G. *The Swoop! Or, How Clarence Saved England, A Tale of the Great Invasion*. London: Rivers, 1909.

Other Literature

Blunden, Edmund. *Undertones of War*. Rev. ed. London: Cobden-Sanderson, 1935.

Carson, Ciaran. »The War Correspondent.« *Times Literary Supplement* 29 Dec. 2000: 8-9.

Hamilton, Helen. »Certain Newspaper Correspondents at the Front.« *Napoo! A Book of War Bêtes-Noires*. By Hamilton. Oxford: Blackwell, 1918. 63.

Kipling, Rudyard. »A Matter of Fact.« *Many Inventions*. By Kipling. London: Macmillan, 1949. 163-81.

Kraus, Karl. *The Last Days of Mankind: A Tragedy in Five Acts*. Abr. and ed. Frederick Ungar. New York: Ungar, 1974.

Montague, C.E. *Disenchantment*. 1922. London: Chatto and Windus, 1928.

Sassoon, Siegfried. *Memoirs of an Infantry Officer*. London: Faber, 1930.

Swofford, Antony. *Jarhead*. London: Scribner, 2003.

Wells, H.G. »The Land Ironclads.« *The Complete Short Stories of H.G. Wells*. 1927. London: Benn, 1966. 115-38.

Film and Television Productions

The Angry Hills, USA 1959, dir. Robert Aldrich.

Beautiful People, UK 1999, dir. Jasmin Dizdar.

Before the Rain, Macedonia 1994, dir. Milcho Manchevski.

Full Metal Jacket, UK 1987, dir. Stanley Kubrick.

The Green Berets, USA 1968, dir. Ray Kellogg and John Wayne.

The Hunting Party, USA 2007, dir. Richard Shepard.

J.A.G. (USA 1995-2005), Episode 222: »Death at the Mosque« (2005).

Jarhead, USA 2005, dir. Sam Mendes.

The Killing Fields, UK 1984, dir. Roland Joffé.

The Light That Failed, USA 1939, dir. William A. Wellman.

Live from Baghdad, USA 2002, dir. Mick Jackson.

The Lost World (CAN 1999-2002), Episode 54: »Brothers in Arms« (2002).

Manticore, USA 2005, dir. Tripp Reed.
No Man's Land, Slovenia 2001, dir. Danis Tanović.
Objective, Burma! USA 1945, dir. Raoul Walsh.
The Quiet American, USA 1958, dir. Joseph L. Mankiewicz.
The Quiet American, USA 2002, dir. Phillip Noyce.
Salvador, USA 1986, dir. Oliver Stone.
The Story of G.I. Joe, USA 1945, dir. William A. Wellman.
Three Kings, USA 1999, dir. David O. Russell.
The Trench, UK 1999, dir. William Boyd.
The Troubles We've Seen, F/GER/UK 1994, dir. Marcel Ophüls.
Under Fire, USA 1982, dir. Roger Spottiswode.
The War Correspondent, USA 1913, dir. Robert G. Vignola.
War Correspondent, USA 1932, dir. Paul Sloane [aka *Soldiers of Fortune*].
War Photographer, CH 2001, dir. Christian Frei.
War Stories, USA 2003, dir. Robert Singer.
We Were Soldiers, USA 2002, dir. Randall Wallace.
Welcome to Sarajevo, UK 1997, dir. Michael Winterbottom.
The Year of Living Dangerously, AUS/USA 1982, dir. Peter Weir.

Secondary Sources

Abrams, M.H. *A Glossary of Literary Terms*. Fort Worth, TX: Harcourt Brace, 1993.
Allan, Stuart, and Barbie Zelizer, eds. *Reporting War: Journalism in Wartime*. London: Routledge, 2004.
Badsey, Stephen. »The Depiction of War Reporters in Hollywood Feature Films from the Vietnam War to the Present.« *Film History* 14 (2002): 243-60.
Baroody, Judith Rain. *Media Access and the Military: The Case of the Gulf War*. Lanham: UP of America, 1998.
Baudrillard, Jean. *La Guerre du Golfe n'a pas eu lieu*. Paris: Galilée, 1991.
Bell, Martin. »The Truth Is Our Currency.« *Press/Politics* 3.1 (1998): 102-109.
Bottomore, Stephen. »Frederic Villiers: War Correspondent.« *Sight and Sound* 49 (1980): 250-5.
Bottomore, Stephen. »The Biograph in Battle.« *The First World War and British Military History*. Ed. Karel Dibbets and Bert Hogenkamp. Amsterdam: Amsterdam UP, 1995. 28-35.
Bourdieu, Pierre, *Outline of a Theory of Practice*. Cambridge: Cambridge UP, 1977. Trans. of *Esquisse d'une théorie de la pratique, précédé de trois études d'ethnologie kabyle*. Geneva: Droz, 1972.

Bourdieu, Pierre. *In Other Words.* Cambridge: Polity Press, 1990a. Trans. of *Choses dites.* Paris: Minuit, 1987.

Bourdieu, Pierre. *The Logic of Practice.* Cambridge: Polity Press, 1990b. Trans. of *Le sens pratique.* Paris: Minuit, 1980.

Bourdieu, Pierre. *The Field of Cultural Production: Essays on Art and Literature.* Ed. Randal Johnson. Cambridge: Polity, 1993.

Bourdieu, Pierre. *Sur la télévision. Suivi de L'emprise du journalisme.* Paris: Liber, 1996.

Bruner, Jerome. »The Autobiographical Process.« *The Culture of Autobiography: Constructions of Self-Representation.* Ed. Robert Folkenflik. Stanford, CA: Stanford UP, 1993. 38-56.

Bullard, Frederick Lauriston. *Famous War Correspondents.* 1914. New York: Beekman, 1974.

Camino, Mercedes Maroto. »›The war is so young‹: Masculinity and War Correspondence in *Welcome to Sarajevo* and *Territorio Comanche.*« *Studies in European Cinema* 2.2 (2005): 115-24.

Christie, Clive. The Quiet American *and the* Ugly American*: Western Literary Perspectives on Indo-China in a Decade of Transition 1950-1960.* Occasional Paper 10. Canterbury: U of Kent Centre of South-East Asian Studies, 1989.

Collier, Richard. *The Warcos: The War Correspondents of World War Two.* London: Weidenfeld and Nicolson, 1989.

Connelly, Mark, and David Welch, eds. *War and the Media: Reportage and Propaganda, 1900-2003.* London: Tauris, 2005.

Coustillas, Pierre. »*The Light That Failed* or Artistic Bohemia as Self-Revelation.« *English Literature in Transition (1880-1920)* 29.2 (1986): 127-39.

Daniel, Ute. »Bücher vom Kriegsschauplatz: Kriegsberichterstattung als Genre des 19. und frühen 20. Jahrhunderts.« *Geschichte für Leser: Populäre Geschichtsschreibung in Deutschland im 20. Jahrhundert.* Ed. Wolfgang Hardtwig and Erhard Schütz. Stuttgart: Steiner, 2005. 93-121.

Daniel, Ute, ed. *Augenzeugen: Kriegsberichterstattung vom 18. zum 21. Jahrhundert.* Göttingen: Vandenhoeck und Ruprecht, 2006a.

Daniel, Ute. »Einleitung.« *Augenzeugen: Kriegsberichterstattung vom 18. zum 21. Jahrhundert.* Ed. by Daniel. Göttingen: Vandenhoeck und Ruprecht, 2006b. 7-22.

Daniel, Ute. »Der Krimkrieg 1853-1856 und die Entstehungskontexte medialer Kriegsberichterstattung.« *Augenzeugen: Kriegsberichterstattung vom 18. zum 21. Jahrhundert.* Ed. by Daniel. Göttingen: Vandenhoeck und Ruprecht, 2006c. 40-67.

du Gay, Paul, et al. *Doing Cultural Studies: The Story of the Sony Walkman*. Milton Keynes: Open U, 1997.

Elwood-Akers, Virginia. *Women War Correspondents in the Vietnam War, 1961-1975*. Metuchen, NJ: Scarecrow, 1988.

Engesser, Evelyn: *Journalismus in Fiktion und Wirklichkeit: Ein Vergleich des Journalistenbildes in literarischen Bestsellern mit Befunden der empirischen Kommunikationsforschung*. Köln: von Halem, 2005.

Evans, Harold. *War Stories: Reporting in the Time of Conflict from the Crimea to Iraq*. Boston: Bunker Hill, 2003.

Farrar, Martin J. *News from the Front: War Correspondents on the Western Front 1914-18*. Phoenix Mill: Sutton, 1998.

Feminist Media Studies 5.3 (2005) [thematic issue on female war correspondents].

Furneaux, Rupert. *The First War Correspondent: William Howard Russell of* The Times. London: Cassell, 1944.

Furneaux, Rupert. *News of War: Stories and Adventures of the Great War Correspondents*. London: Parrish, 1964.

Good, Howard. *Acquainted with the Night: The Image of Journalists in American Fiction, 1890-1930*. Metuchen, NJ: Scarecrow, 1986.

Hallin, Daniel C. *The ›Uncensored War‹: The Media and Vietnam*. New York: Oxford UP, 1986.

Hammond, Philip, and Edward S. Herman, eds. *Degraded Capability: The Media and the Kosovo Crisis*. London: Pluto, 2000.

Hankinson, Alan. *Man of Wars: William Howard Russell of* The Times. London: Heinemann, 1982.

Harris, Robert. *Gotcha! The Media, the Government and the Falklands Crisis*. London: Faber, 1983.

Hohenberg, John. *Foreign Correspondence: The Great Reporters and Their Times*. 2nd ed. Syracuse, NY: Syracuse UP, 1995.

Hudson, Miles, and John Stanier. *War and the Media: A Random Searchlight*. Rev. paperback ed. Phoenix Mill: Sutton, 1999.

Hume, Mick. *Whose War Is It Anyway? The Dangers of the Journalism of Attachment*. London: BM InformInc, 1997.

Ignatieff, Michael. *The Warrior's Honor: Ethnic War and the Modern Conscience*. London: Chatto and Windus, 1998.

Ignatieff, Michael. *Virtual War: Kosovo and Beyond*. London: Chatto and Windus, 2000.

Jacobi, Jutta. *Journalisten im literarischen Text: Studien zum Werk von Karl Kraus, Egon Erwin Kisch und Franz Werfel*. Frankfurt am Main: Lang, 1989.

Jenkins, Richard. *Pierre Bourdieu*. Rev. ed. London: Routledge, 2002.

Kamalipour, Yaliya R., and Nancy Snow, eds. *War, Media, and Propaganda: A Global Perspective*. Lanham, MD: Rowman and Littlefield, 2004.

Katovsky, Bill, and Timothy Carlson, eds. *Embedded: The Media at War in Iraq*. Guilford, CT: Lyons, 2003.

Knightley, Phillip. *The First Casualty: The War Correspondent as Hero and Myth-Maker from the Crimea to Iraq*. Baltimore, MD: Johns Hopkins UP, 2004.

Korte, Barbara. »Being Engaged: The War Correspondent in British Fiction.« *Anglia* 124 (2006a): 432-48.

Korte, Barbara. »Touched by the Pain of Others: War Correspondents in Contemporary Fiction. Michael Ignatieff, *Charlie Johnson in the Flames* and Pat Barker, *Double Vision*.« *English Studies* 88 (2006b): 183-94.

Korte, Barbara. »Dargestellte Kriegsdarsteller: Typisierungen des Kriegsreporters in Roman und Film des 21. Jahrhunderts.« *Kriegskorrespondenten: Deutungsinstanzen in der Mediengesellschaft*. Ed. Barbara Korte and Horst Tonn. Wiesbaden: VS Verlag, 2007. 197-214.

Lambert, Andrew, and Stephen Badsey, eds. *The Crimean War*. The War Correspondents. Phoenix Mill: Sutton, 1994.

Lévinas, Emmanuel. »Langage et proximité.« *En découvrant l'existence avec Husserl et Heidegger*. By Lévinas. Paris: Vrin, 1982a. 217-36.

Lévinas, Emmanuel. »La trace de l'autre.« *En découvrant l'existence avec Husserl et Heidegger*. By Lévinas. Paris: Vrin, 1982b. 187-202.

Loyn, David. *Frontline. The True Story of the British Mavericks Who Changed the Face of War Reporting*. London: Joseph, 2005.

Lutes, Jean Marie. *Front Page Girls: Women Journalists in American Culture and Fiction, 1880-1930*. Ithaca, NY: London: Cornell UP, 2006.

Mason, Jackson. *The Pictorial Press: Its Origins and Progress*. London: Hurst and Blackett, 1885.

McLaughlin, Greg. *The War Correspondent*. London: Pluto, 2002.

Mercer, Derrick, et al. *The Fog of War: The Media on the Battlefield*. London: Heinemann, 1987.

Miller, David, ed. *Tell Me Lies: Propaganda and Media Distortion in the Attack on Iraq*. London: Pluto, 2004.

Moorcraft, Paul, and Philip M. Taylor. *Shooting the Messenger: The Political Impact of War Reporting*. Washington, DC: Potomac, 2008.

Neuman, Johanna. *Lights, Camera, War: Is Media Technology Driving International Politics?* New York: St. Martin's, 1996.

Paul, Christopher, and James J. Kim. *Reporters on the Battlefield: The Embedded Press System in Historical Context*. Santa Monica, CA: Rand, 2004.

Pedelty, Mark. *War Stories: The Culture of Foreign Correspondents.* New York: Routledge, 1995.

Roth, Mitchel P. *Historical Dictionary of War Journalism.* Westport, CT: Greenwood, 1997.

Royle, Trevor. *War Report: The War Correpondent's View of Battle from the Crimea to the Falklands.* London: Grafton, 1987.

Schechner, Richard. *Performance Studies: An Introduction.* London: Routledge, 2002.

Seib, Philip. *The Global Journalist: News and Conscience in a World of Conflict.* Lanham, MD: Rowman and Littlefield, 2002.

Sibbald, Raymond, ed. *The Boer War.* The War Correspondents. Phoenix Mill: Sutton, 1993.

Smith, Hedrick, ed. *The Media and the Gulf War.* Washington, DC: Seven Locks, 1992.

Sontag, Susan. *Regarding the Pain of Others.* New York: Farrar, Straus and Giroux, 2003.

Spencer, Graham. *The Media and Peace: From Vietnam to the ›War on Terror‹.* Houndmills: Palgrave Macmillan, 2005.

Steinsieck, Andreas. »Old Boys-Netzwerke und formale Zensur: Die Ausweitung der Kriegsberichterstattung im Südafrikanischen Krieg (1899-1902) und die Folgen für das Verhältnis von Berichterstattern und Militär.« *Kriegskorrespondenten: Deutungsinstanzen in der Mediengesellschaft.* Ed. Barbara Korte and Horst Tonn. Wiesbaden: VS Verlag, 2007. 215-36.

Sylvester, Judith, and Suzanne Huffman, eds. *Reporting from the Front: The Media and the Military.* Lanham, MD: Rowman, 2005.

Taylor, John. *Body Horror: Photojournalism, Catastrophe and War.* Manchester: Manchester UP, 1998.

Taylor, Philip M. *War and the Media. Propaganda and Persuasion in the Gulf War.* Manchester: Manchester UP, 1998.

Thomson, Alex. *Smokescreen. The Media, the Censors, the Gulf.* Tunbridge Wells: Laburnham and Spellmount, 1992.

Tumber, Howard, and Jerry Palmer. *Media at War: The Iraq Crisis.* London: Sage, 2004.

Tumber, Howard, and Frank Webster. *Journalists Under Fire: Information War and Journalistic Practices.* London: Sage, 2006.

Vernon, Alex, ed. *Arms and the Self: War, the Military, and Autobiographical Writing.* Kent, OH: Kent State UP, 2005.

Virilio, Paul. *L'Ecran du désert.* Paris: Galilée, 1991.

Wagner, Lilya. *Women War Correspondents of World War II.* New York: Greenwood, 1989.

Walsh, Jeffrey, ed. *The Gulf War Did Not Happen: Politics, Culture and Warfare Post-Vietnam.* Aldershot: Arena, 1995.

Wilkinson, Glenn R. *Depictions and Images of War in Edwardian Newspapers, 1899-1914.* Houndmills: Palgrave Macmillan, 2003.

Wilkinson-Latham, Robert J. *From Our Special Correspondent: Victorian War Correspondents and Their Campaigns.* London: Hodder and Stoughton, 1979.

Willcox, David R. *Propaganda, the Press and Conflict: The Gulf War and Kosovo.* London: Routledge, 2005.

Williams, Val. *Warworks: Women, Photography and the Iconography of War.* London: Virago, 1994.

Willis, Jim. *The Human Journalist: Reporters, Perspectives, and Emotions.* Westport, CT: Praeger, 2003.

INDEX